817 LaCrescent

Three Boomer Broads
Remembering While We Still Can

Sara Slayton
Terry Visger
Lynn Wing

*To our Three Boomer Boys,
Brent, Ken, and Paul,
who put up with us
through thick and thin*

Contents

School..1
Home..13
Playing and Bruises....................................35
- *"Training Wheels"*

Holidays...59
- *"Things Were Different Then"*
- *"Two Things Meant Christmas"*

Pets..84
- *"Mom and Andy"*

Television..10
7 Cigarettes and Other Dangers...................125
- *"Not Always Like Donna Reed"*

Fashion..146
Cars..161
- *"My First Car"*
- *"Riding Around In Our Automobiles"*

Beauty...184
Sex...201
- *"First Date"*

The Green Thing..229
Turning Points...243
- *"The Kitchen Café"*
- *"Madison Girl"*
- *"Sam's Story"*

The Boomers Grow Up.............................283
- *"When the Clouds Gather"*
- *"Time It Was"*

Forward
by Paul Heckman

To have been born a Boomer – born and raised in the United States between the late forties through the early sixties – is to have witnessed several of the greatest cultural changes in the world.

For the first time, individuals in faraway places shared common experiences. From Hawaii to Chicago and the little suburbs of Madison, Wisconsin, radio, phones and television, newspapers and magazines became more accessible. Ideas of culture and different manners of living, marketing, advertising and prosperity spread a message that those of us in the U.S. were special.

Our mobility increased and we began to see where and how others lived. Cars, ships, and air travel gave us glimpses of unique cultural differences and some similarities.

The strength of our nation was found in our industry and increasing progress in agriculture. We set the standard for prosperity and innovation the world over.

Our consumerism, education, health, and politics led the way to a strong and healthy economy.

And among all these great changes, little children, for the most part, grew safely and happily. Racism continued, wars and rumors of wars were always present, but many of us didn't know. We were children. We had toys and well-stocked schools, and books. We were innocent boomers and the times reflected that for us.

I had the honor of adding a few lines and directing the four Boomer Broads shows at the Pump House Regional Arts

Center in La Crosse, Wisconsin, working with the authors and actors of this work you hold in your hands. They have compiled those common experiences many of us had in these essays, stories, and show transcripts, and they have presented them with the love and innocence of children and young adults who lived through those times.

Boomer Broads Recall 50s

Three storytellers gathered around Sara's kitchen table discussing ways to improve our performances. Beyond more stringent coaching, exploring new themes, or focusing on new audiences, we wondered what new approach we could take.

But over cups of hot tea we began instead to reminisce. Then, like Mickey Rooney and Judy Garland in the old movies, it came to us, "Let's do a show!" As I often tell my storytelling students, "Each of us is walking history." That was true of the three of us. We were of a certain, similar age -Baby Boomers- a group of people who had witnessed tremendous social change during the 1950s and 1960s. There was much to share about our early years.

But, how to begin? None of us were actors or had any experience with staging a performance of this type. But stories were our forte, so that was the natural starting point. That very night and for weeks afterward the tape recorder ran as stories about our youth came pouring out. These hours of tapes were laboriously transcribed into 100 pages of script from which we began to glean the stories and themes for our show. Slowly the format for the show began to emerge. Our childhood years would be divided into five year increments, some of our experiences would be shared in a scripted manner, the script would be supplemented with images and music from the time, and each of us would do a 'stand out' story. Exploring further, we hit upon the overarching theme of 'a loss of innocence'. We contacted a local art gallery with our idea and they were willing to give us stage and rehearsal space, the use of their 140 seat theater, and publicity. We contracted for a 40/60 split with the theater. They would take care of reservations and ticket sales and we would receive 60% of the ticket sales after expenses. This suited our needs. We had no idea how many people we would attract and were glad to not have to pay anything up front. The dates for the initial show were set. This first show was called *Three Boomer Broads: Remembering While We Still Can*. It was billed as 'the sights, sounds and stories of the 1950s and 1960s as told by three women who lived through them'.

A tech-savvy college student agreed to run the lights and sound for a small fee and my husband, who had years of stage experience, agreed to be our unpaid director. A local artist drew our caricatures for publicity purposes and then the painstaking process of developing a script and our stories began. It was agreed from the beginning that the director would have final say over the script, but the stories would be refined and coached by the three of us. The Boomers were all professional storytellers and we wanted creative control of our stories.

We met regularly over the next several months, picking through the transcripts looking for those memories that would be universal to our audience and which would suit our theme. Each of us also began developing our individual stories. During this time I spent hours collecting images and music from the time period and developing them into three short Power Point slide shows. A setting for the show also had to be determined. We tried to recreate the experience of sharing our memories from that first cold night. It was decided that the best setting would be three friends gathered around a kitchen table, looking at photo albums. From that, a basic set design was planned and a list of props was created.

Finally, a workable script emerged which could be shared with our director. We had several read-throughs during which our director slashed, refined, and generally improved our rough script in numerous ways. This was a fascinating experience for us as we watched pieces of the script change or be deleted entirely, and our director began to develop in us characters who would bring unique personalities to the show. The script went from 'nice recollections' to a tight and balanced piece. Then intense work began on our individual stories. Coaching sessions helped refine them into sharp, meaningful compositions. We found distinct ways to embrace our loss of innocence in early and middle childhood and during our teen years. The stories reflected the historic social transformations in which our own personal metamorphoses occurred. Lynn's story spoke about the loss of innocence of a child learning to ride a two wheel bike and striking her own balance in her world. Terry's story took the audience to her grandmother's Southern Illinois restaurant on the day that the first black man came in to be served. And my story recalled my teen years in Madison during the anti-war protests and the bombing of the Math building at the University there.

Our publicity also began during this time. We put together news releases, contacted local media services, were interviewed, and put hundreds of posters in local businesses. We also contacted everyone on our email and Facebook lists.

Routine rehearsals occurred in my home until the theater was available. During that last week we tweaked the script, blocked the action, revised the slide and music shows, and learned the show. One of our most interesting challenges was to find an exciting way to end the show. Throughout the performance the Boomers had been looking through old photos and projecting images from the past. This led to the thought that it might work to end with an image and song. That first script ended with us saying, "We have been looking at all these old pictures, let's take one of us today." We pretended to do so, stumbling a little with the technology of a digital camera, and then a picture of us (exactly as we were dressed and posed) was projected on the screen while Steppenwolf's song, *Born To Be Wild*, played underneath.

The show opened to standing room only crowds that first weekend. Obviously many fellow boomers were eager to watch their history come alive. Our director introduced the show emphasizing that what the audience was about to see was storytelling – dispelling the myth that storytelling is only for children and always follows a fairy tale format. What the audience members liked best was the very conversational tone of the show and that our reflections on significant events included humor and pathos. As we each stepped into the spotlight to tell our individual stories the listeners were at ease, but fascinated. Many patrons later remarked on how spellbinding and deeply meaningful the stories and recollections were.

The Boomer Broads were profoundly touched by the positive response to this new storytelling format. Although the learning curve was fairly steep for us as individuals, the show format helped us grow and become better at what we love most – telling stories.

Due to popular demand we restaged the same show a month later. A second show, "What Our Mothers Never Told Us" was written and produced in the spring of 2010. Plans for a Boomer Christmas show are now in the works.

Addendum: The Christmas show was titled, Over the Hill and Through the Woods and a fourth show, The 60s It's Not Just A Decade Anymore was developed and performed.

*this article first appeared in "Storytelling" magazine as Boomer Broads Recall 50s; September/October 2010 issue

How to Read This Book

You can read the chapters in any order. We placed them as we saw them evolve but you can start anywhere in your life that you want. Each chapter begins with the conversations Sara, Lynn, and Terry had while working on the plays. Some of this dialog appeared in the sketches and some ended up on the editor's floor…..and now in this book.

We all wrote original stories for the four plays so there are twelve of them. These stories appear in the chapters that fit them the best. And, since we are storytellers and filled with stories, there also are essays and our thoughts that where written specifically for this book. Our videographer, Sam, watched all the plays and was especially touched by Sara's story of Madison in the 60s. He sent us his experiences at that time and we loved his essay, so it is included in the *Turning Points* chapter.

Some of the photos are our own family photos. Others we found on the internet*. As we became immersed in our pasts and the fifties and sixties we couldn't resist adding the *Do You Remember These?* sections at the end of the chapters.

We hope you enjoy this book. But more than that, we hope it causes you to remember, reflect, and reminisce. Remember 'nostalgia isn't what it used to be'

Enjoy!

*all photos taken from the internet were licensed for commercial reprint with attribution

School Days

Na na na na na!

Dick's cooties....pass them on!

Sara's sister

The women are in a used book store when Terry picks up an old year book.

Terry: Have you gone to any class reunions lately? It's creepy hanging out with all those old people.
Lynn: Yes. Why is it at class reunions you feel younger than everyone looks?
Sara: But they're the only ones who remember what school was like in the 1960s.
Terry: We took our own lunches to school.

southsidepride.com

Sara: Yeah, we didn't eat hot lunch very often.
Terry: It was according to what was being served.
ALL: Spaghetti!!!
Lynn: The lunch lady would scoop it up with an ice cream scoop.
Terry: And I think milk was 2 or 3 cents a carton.
It was whole milk with no choices of chocolate milk or orange juice.
Sara: And we'd get a piece of white bread with every meal. It wasn't very healthy. Speaking of healthy, did you know that kids don't take showers after gym class now?

Terry: They don't have to change to other clothes either. We had to change into our gym clothes. We had red shorts and white blouses.
Lynn: We wore the same thing.
Terry: Did we go to the same school?
Lynn: You were in Chicago and I was in California.
Terry: Yeah, but did we go to the same school?
(Sara and Lynn exchange a knowing glance)
Lynn: Yes, Terry. We did.
Terry: Oh, Lynn. I'm sorry I don't remember you.
Lynn: That's okay. Don't even think about it. Remember, we had our names embroidered on the back of the blouses.
Terry: In red.
Lynn: And we had to wear a certain kind of socks and tennis shoes.
Terry: I don't remember the sock part but we had to have the uniforms cleaned and ironed every Monday. And you got graded on whether they were clean or not.
Lynn: Well, by the end of the week you'd open that locker and they'd say hello.
Terry: But still you got graded on it.
Sara: I wonder what the boys did. Our gym suits were just a one piece thing and they were a dark blue. There was only one store that sold them downtown. So you had to go buy them there and then take them to another store to have them embroidered.

pinterest.com

2

Terry: My mother did my embroidery. Everybody's mother did. And you could tell whose mother was good at it. Some people had these gorgeous things and then mine was sort of...well, she was good at lots of things but not embroidery.

Sara: And in those days gym shoes, which we called tennies, were the cheapest shoes you could buy.

Terry: Keds

Lynn: Or PF Flyers

Sara: They were the least expensive shoes you could buy, now they're the most expensive.

Lynn: And they had absolutely no support whatsoever. I remember I really wanted a pair that you just slipped on, no laces. You couldn't wear them for gym; you had to have laces for gym. Mom said they were boys' shoes. They only came in dark blue, red, or white and finally she let me have a pair. I wore those things to death until the rubber was just peeling away. I loved those shoes.

Terry: Those were also your play shoes. Because you had certain shoes you wore to school and then when you came home you changed from your school clothes to your play clothes and your play shoes.

Lynn: I always wanted to wear my PF Flyers as my school shoes, because some kids were allowed to, but not my mom. Oh no, you had your hard, leather shoes for school. When we were in elementary school, JFK came out with the physical fitness program.

Terry: What was it called?

Lynn: JFK physical fitness program

Terry: Oh yeah, in 1969.

wikimedia

Lynn: He was dead by then.
Terry: Fat lot of good exercise did him.
Lynn: We had to do all sorts of things for that, like pull ups.
Sara: The arm hang! I remember my little skinny arms just a-shakin' over that bar.
Lynn: Sit ups...
Sara: 50 yard dash – I was really good at that.
Lynn: And the biggy – the 600 yard run walk.
Terry: Name on your shoes.
Lynn: That's not a sport!
Terry: No, but it was on the list of things you had to do. I always got a star for my name on the shoes because I had good penmanship.
Lynn: Well, I have to give you that. Penmanship was very important and you had to be very precise.
Terry: We had to make big circles and then little circles and then lines. And then they'd give us paper.
Lynn: At school we had paper with red and blue lines. When my mom wrote a letter it was on plain paper. But she had a cheat sheet page with lines that she'd put under the plain sheet so she'd write straight.
Sara: We refilled pens. You didn't throw a pen away; you just took the inside out and put in a new inside. And it had that little spring. Or we'd use the barrel for spit wads. Or you had the little ink cartridge. We never threw the pen away. In high school we learned how to type but my typing class was all girls.
Terry: Not mine. I grew up in Wheaton, Illinois and John Belushi was in my typing class.
Sara and Lynn: The real John Belushi! No way!
Terry: Yes, way. We sat in the back typing GGG-HHH-JJJ-FF and screwed around. He was funny, weird, but funny. Loud, too. But the typing teacher didn't seem to notice.

Maybe she was deaf from all that dinging (Terry pretends she's typing and moving the carriage).
Lynn: The quick brown fox jumped over....the what? Where did we get the Z?
Terry: Xylophone
Sara: That's an x.
Lynn: Xanadu
Sara: That's an x too.
Terry: The quick brown fox jumped over the moon.
Sara: That's the cow.
Lynn: The quick brown fox jumped over the moon onto Buzz Aldrin.
Sara: There's your Z.
Lynn: My typing teacher would stand in front of the class with her arms crossed over her breasts saying, "Girls, you are not hitting those Z's!"
Sara: My Home Ec teacher was a woman named Mrs. M and she wore this orange make up; it was like a thick pancake. If she would have scratched her face you would have seen a white mark. It was a bit like Halloween.

Flickr.com

Terry: I bet you used *Butterick* patterns in Home Ec.
Sara: It was fun going to the fabric store.
Terry: They had those huge books; they were like wallpaper books.
Lynn: And you'd sit on those really tall, tall stools.
Terry: Our stores had slanted tables.
Sara: And the numbered drawers.
Terry: You'd pick patterns out and then you'd have your fingers crossed that they'd have the pattern in your size.
Sara: What did you make in home economics class?

Terry: We had to make skirts, with the waist band and gathered. Home ec class is where I got my first detention. Well, two. And I got them because I didn't put my bobbin away. You'd have 'your bobbin' that had 'your thread' on it. Everyone had their own bobbin. So when you were finished you had to take it out of the machine and place it in a special box so the machine would be ready for the kid in the next class. Two different times I left my bobbin in the machine so I got detention. I had to leave class and go up to the principal's office. I handed the detention slip to him and he said, "Oh, this is so ridiculous." But there I was in detention with all the hoods.
Lynn: Can't you just picture that?
"Whatcha' in for?"
Sara: "Smokin'. Whatch you in for?"
Lynn: "Ditchin' class. What she in for?"

manic pop thrilled

Terry: "I left my bobbin in the sewing machine."
Lynn: I have always been dyslexic when it comes to sewing. In fact my husband Brent won't even let me sew a button on a shirt for him. My mom made dresses, my sister sewed. But me, I go near a fabric store and break out in hives. I think my first shift was more of a 'shuff'.
Terry: We always had to wear dresses to school, did you? But at least we had swirling skirt contests.
Lynn: We'd play games in our dresses, baseball, dodge ball, tag. I always had skinned up knees because I didn't have pants to protect them from falls.
Sara: I remember hanging upside down on the monkey bars with my skirt over my face and my feet to the sky.

Terry: Did you know you could wear shorts under there? We wore shorts. I guess in Illinois we were smarter.
But we couldn't wear pants to school even in high school. Did you?
Sara: Yes, about half way through.
Terry: Well, we could only wear skirts. We were good girls. Did you have skirt checks?
Lynn: What do you mean?
Terry: You'd come to school and they would make you kneel down on the floor. You couldn't kneel like this (slumping), that was cheating. So you had to have your back up straight and they'd come by and check your skirt. If it didn't touch the floor, they sent you home to change.
Lynn: I wouldn't have had a problem; my skirts were never above the knee.
Sara: But we were smart, like all kids are. They had skirt check first thing in the morning. So when it was over we'd go to the bathroom and roll up our skirts. We'd have these big bulges around our waists, but our skirts were short.
Terry: Those bulges were getting you ready for middle age. Hey. Did you get checked for lice at school? With that purple light? This girl Becky had this really white hair and everyone wanted to be right behind her because when they put the light on her it make her hair purple. With my dark hair, it didn't change but with Becky's, well, she'd really be 'in' now with her purple hair.
Sara: Did you get polio vaccines?
Terry: Yes we all have our little scars.
(all three look for their scars. Sara and Lynn look at their arms but Terry looks at her butt)
Lynn: Wait, that's not polio. That was for small pox.
Terry: But we all got the polio shots, too. And then it was a liquid or something. Even my dad went. They gave out the liquid in the gym.

Lynn: They used sugar cubes soaked with this, I guess, a pink colored vaccine.
Sara: I tried to go back for seconds but they just glared at me.
When I think about it we did a lot in that gym. We had dances in there after football and basketball games. The boys would all on line up one side and the girls on the other. One boy, Tommy, bless his heart, was probably born with acne and had really thick glasses and he smelled a bit so nobody wanted to dance with him. He would start heading across the gym and the girls would part like the Red Sea. So he would just angle off and see if he could nab one. And if he asked me I never had the heart to turn him down.

jordynredwood

Lynn: Good.
Sara: Mom had taught me to be nice. I probably danced with Tommy more than any other girl in the world.
Terry: In junior high we just had dances with our own grade but in high school, it was the whole school, all four grades. So the upper classmen were there along with the freshmen.
Sara: I do remember my parents being a little concerned about boys like that, older boys, and especially the boys that we called greasers or hoods.
Lynn: Did your greasers wear the black velvet, pointy shoes?
Sara: I don't remember them being velvety but black leather, yes. And they would stand across the street from the high school and smoke. They were drinking at an

early age, plus they were sexually active earlier than most boys. They were just a different group, tough and sort of dark and mysterious.

Lynn: I wonder what ever happened to those guys.

Terry: They are some of those people that you don't recognize at your reunions. They don't look so tough anymore, now they just look old, like the rest of us.

You're a Boomer if you know what these are!

wikimedia *wikimedia* *iamremembering.com*

Answers at end of the of the chapter

Do you remember?

- The school Valentines party – we would all make 'mailboxes' and you had a card for each child in the class. Afterward the PTA moms would serve punch (from a glass punch bowl) and cookies.
- Halloween parties where we all wore our costumes (mostly homemade) and paraded through each classroom for treats like popcorn balls and candy apples.
- School Christmas programs when public schools would tell the Christmas story and sing religious songs.

PeterRukavina

- The card file in the library, the cards you signed to check out a book, and the date stamp.
- Sniffing the ditto worksheets
- Dick & Jane
- Little bank accounts

- Typewriters; retyping entire pages, carbon paper, special typewriter erasers, erasable paper (Mike Nesmith's mom invented *White Out*)

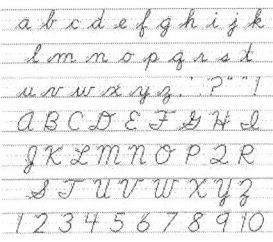

- Chalkboards, knocking the chalk dust out of erasers, the multiple line chalk maker.

wikimedia

- Prom, Homecoming, Sadie Hawkins Dance (when the girls asked the boys)
- Penmanship class, Penmanship paper with the blue lines and chunks of wood in it.
- Alphabet letters over the chalkboard
- Pull down maps
- The music teacher wheeling the piano into the classroom and the art teacher also coming to your classroom.

followpics.com

- Cement playgrounds with a merry-go-round, chain swings, the big metal slide and using the wax paper from your lunch to slick it up.
- Paste and paste-eaters
- Pencil sharpeners
- 16 mm film projectors, DuKane film strip projectors (beep)
- Lift up top desks

expattutor.com

   o Cleaning them during school time

11

- - Putting your heads on them to rest or if the class was in trouble
- Girl Scout and Boy Scout meetings after school
- Crossing Guards

hhs59.com

* Ditto machine, inside of hand crank pencil sharpener, Selectric Typewriter ball*

Home

My idea of housework is to sweep the room with a glance. Erma Bombeck

Sara, Lynn, and Terry are in Terry's attic sorting through trunks, boxes, and piles of 'treasures'. Terry is looking in a trunk with kitchen items. They have lemonade, pretzels, and peanuts as reinforcements.

Lynn's family

Terry: I have a theory about why we had fewer snacks back in the 50s. We couldn't get as much stuff in our refrigerators, they were smaller.
Lynn: The first refrigerator I remember only had that little tiny freezer.
Sara: And you had to defrost those things!
Lynn and Terry: Oh yeah.
Sara: You had to take all the food out and you'd run a fan and chip away at that stuff.

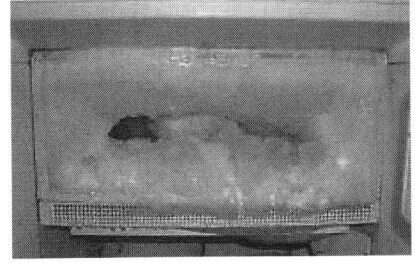

Flickr Dan4

Lynn: Or you'd boil water and set it in there to try to melt the frost.
Sara: Sometimes it would just become this little cave.

Lynn: And as it would defrost there was always the chance of discovering little treasures of something frozen in there, like peas or blueberries.
Terry: Or goldfish. My brother Bill told me to put our goldfish in the freezer and he said that I could thaw it out when I wanted to play with it. That way I wouldn't have to clean the bowl as much. He told me it would come back to life. And it did!
Lynn: Really?
Terry: We just put him in the metal ice cube tray in one of the little squares. I'm pretty sure he lived.
Lynn: The ice cube tray with the little levers? There was room for a fish?
Terry: He was a little long but we just had to bend him a bit. But he stayed there. Bill would also tell me to stick my tongue on the metal ice cube tray. I did it so many times. Bill would say, "Just try it once more." Whatever he told me to do, I did it.
Sara: Our appliances then were not what they are now. We just had a refrigerator, stove, oven, and a toaster. That was pretty much it.
Lynn: Now we have microwaves...
Terry: Blenders, coffee makers...
Lynn: Panini makers, tostado makers...
Sara: Food processors...
Lynn: IPads...
Terry: Cell phones and all the cords...
Sara: Laptops, charging stations...
Lynn, Sara and Terry: Progress!
Terry: You know what else has changed around the home - decorating. Plastic was huge back in the 50s. My mother covered everything in plastic to keep it nice for company. I think if I stood in one place for too long, she would have covered me.
Lynn: Oh and then the colors. All the porcelain in one of our bathrooms was pink – sink, tub, and toilet.
Sara: And then you'd get plaster things like a fish with bubbles.

And you'd put them on your bathroom wall. Sometimes it would be ballerinas or a swan.
Lynn: We had plaster starfish and seashells on the bathroom wall.
Terry: We had crabs.
Sara: Well, look at how much phones have changed in our lifetime. My aunt, in the little village of Wilton, had a phone where you told the operator who you wanted to call and she connected you.
Lynn: We went from dial phones on a stand, to wall phones, to princess phones.
Terry: We also had party lines.
Lynn: You had party lines?
Terry: When I came to La Crosse as an adult we still had party lines.
Lynn: I never had one.
Terry: You missed out because this is what you'd do. You'd sneak up on it – you had to be real quiet even before you got there. Then you'd lift up the receiver very quietly and you could listen to people's conversations. It was great fun!

Flickr marcfalardeau

Lynn: Did it ever occur to you that they were listening in on you?
Terry: No. Why would they want to do that?
Lynn: Sheer entertainment.
Sara: Do you remember your first telephone number? Mine was Alpine-62819.
Terry: Mine was Montrose- 1812.
Lynn: Mine was FA-48175
Terry: When we finally got a one line phone we thought we were at the height of technology. Yeah, we

took pictures with cameras and talked on the phone.
Lynn: We shared our music. And phone conversations were private.
Terry: It was great when we finally got a long cord so we could go into the closet and no one could hear you. We also always knew where the phone was. We weren't constantly looking for it and the battery never ran down. It didn't have a battery. And I only lost a call when the other person hung up.

Sara: Like you said, our phones didn't take pictures. We had cameras for that.

Terry: We'd always get up early on Christmas morning but we were not allowed to go out in the living room until my dad had the camera ready. He had a movie camera with a long rod of lights. It took forever for him to get it all set up and then we'd be blinded as we walked down

Flickr robscomputer

the hall. We never had surprised expressions. We couldn't see anything because of the lights.

Sara: All the still cameras had flash attachments that had a big reflector on them and you'd have to put the flash bulb in it every time.

Terry: And when you took the picture.
It would pop and then it blistered.

Sara: It would smell too.

Terry: I remember I had this Brownie camera that was a Christmas gift. It was my first camera. You had to be so careful because not only did you have to buy the film but then you had

to pay to develop it. And even if your picture didn't turn out you still paid. It was a big deal to take a picture.
Sara: And then there were slides.
Terry: Oh yeah!
Lynn: My grandpa loved his slide projector. And half of the time he'd load the slides upside down. Then he'd work to pry it out and put it right side up and then click to the next one which would be upside down. It'd take two hours to watch a minute and a half worth of slides.

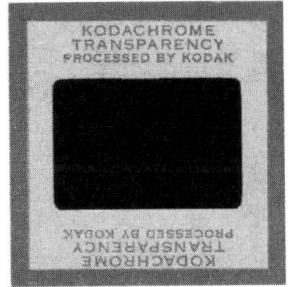

Flickr nesster

Terry: Why didn't he just turn the screen upside down?
Lynn: (ignoring Terry) Did you eat chips when you watched the slides?
Sara: In our house potato chips were for company. We never ate them except if there were guests in the house. Same with pop. Once in a while they'd let my sister and me split a bottle of pop.
Terry: You mean soda.
Sara: Pop
Terry: Soda
Sara: Pop
Lynn: We called it all coke.
Sara: All I know is that it was really company food. We had this thing when I was a kid that was a plastic straw that had a hollow ball about halfway up it. You'd put ice cream in that ball, put the straw in the pop bottle and you'd suck your pop right up through the ice cream ball – instant soda!

Flickr woody1778a

Terry: I really liked the two lipped sundaes at *Woolworth's*.
Lynn: You mean the sundaes in the tulip-shaped glass. Tulip

17

sundaes.
Terry: Mine never had any flowers in them.
Lynn: Never mind.
Terry: Remember when onion dip first came out?
Lynn: Oh yes, that that was for special occasions. You had bad breath for a week.
Terry: We'd often have that on Sunday nights—for supper. Sunday night was Mom's night off. And then when the box pizzas came out – *Chef Boyardee* – that was our Sunday night supper. Chef Boyardee, the San Francisco treat.
Lynn: You mean *Rice-a-Roni*.
Terry: Rice on pizza? Well, maybe you did that in California. But I was thinking the other day: What's with *Grape Nuts*? They aren't nuts and they aren't made out of grapes. Weird.
Lynn: There were three kinds of chips: plain, with ridges, and Bar-B-Que. Oh, and *Cheese Puffs*.
Terry: What about *Bugles*?
Sara: Yeah, we put them on our fingers.
Terry: We put them in our nose. *M&M's* too. But that wasn't until I was an adult. We did that with our kids.
Sara: Trying to be a good role model?
Lynn: Anyway, the big treat for us was popcorn made in a pan and drenched in melted butter.
Terry: Buttered popcorn was my favorite.
Sara: To eat or put up your nose?
Terry: Another favorite treat was

Flickr Gregg_Keonig

Twinkies. And they might have been gone forever! Did you know that they first started out with real cream in them-- not white, fluffy oil?
Sara: So that's why I heard that when they first came out people

would stick a straw in them and suck out the filling.
Terry: I just used my tongue.
Lynn: I remember going to a birthday party and they served us *Hostess Cupcakes*. It was the first time I ever tasted them.
Terry: That must have been a really fancy party. I was so cool and mature in Junior High school I'd sometimes buy *Hostess Snowballs* and peel off the outer layer, and I'd put it on my nose. I got lots of dates that way.
Lynn: You were so sophisticated!
Terry: We just liked processed food. Momma made *Shake and Bake* and I helped.
Lynn: I remember that commercial.
Terry: It was a commercial?
Lynn: We didn't talk much about 'healthy' foods. We just ate. I remember eating a lot of candy.
Sara: We had this wonderful candy store, Lizzy's, right across from our elementary school. As they say, "Location, location, location." She did a great business. I'd stop there almost every day to spend my allowance.
Lynn: I know I ate a lot more candy than I allowed my kids to eat. I'm not sure my folks thought it was harmful, except to our teeth.
Terry: My mom would send me on my bike to Mr. Meister's store to get bread or her cigarettes but I'd spend most of the time looking at his candy counter. I liked *Lik-M-Aid*.
Lynn: That powder stuff that you ate by licking your finger, sticking it in the package, and then licking off the powder that stuck? I loved that stuff. Then I'd pass the package around for my friends to have a lick.
Sara: Did you ever get those wax bottles with the sweet syrupy stuff inside? We'd look at how cute they were, then bite off the top and suck that sweet syrup down.
Terry: The wax stuff was so much fun! I liked the black mustache at Halloween but my favorite was those huge red lips.
Lynn: We'd wear them for a while and then gulp, down they'd go.

But sometimes I got a stomach ache from the wax.
Terry: You didn't have to swallow it, you know.
Sara: As for chewing, I loved *Black Jack* gum.
Lynn: For me it was *Juicy Fruit*.
Terry: *Teaberry*!
Sara: What about *Chunky Candy Bars*? "Big, big, big chunk *Chunky*. Open wide for *Chunky*!"
Terry: And they cost a nickel! All the candy bars cost a nickel except for the penny candy which cost a penny. We had this little popcorn shop in our downtown that was just as wide as a doorway. In the back of the shop was the candy. There were about a hundred jars of penny candy on shelves that went up to the ceiling. We had to squeeze past the little old lady who owned the place to get to the candy and then, the decisions. I could fill up the little white popcorn bag, it would cost about twelve cents and I'd have candy for all afternoon.
Sara: Did you get those different colored sugar dots on the long strip of paper? I think we got more paper than candy with those. Or candy cigarettes?
Terry: I loved the cigarettes; I could pretend to be grown up. I also loved the black licorice pipes but they cost more than a penny.
Lynn: Where did you get the money? Did your mom give it to you?
Sara: Like I said, I got an allowance every week.
Terry: I did too. I got a quarter every week for pulling dandelions, dusting, watching my brother, dumping the dishwasher.
Lynn: You 'dumped' the dishwasher?
Terry: Yes, what did you do?
Lynn: We emptied it.
Sara: I'm just shocked that you had a dishwasher. My sister and I did them by hand. We had a pressure cooker, though. Did you use pressure cookers?

Terry: That's a comfort sound in my house, that pff,pff,pff My mom always used one and then we got one for our wedding from Aunt Imy and Uncle Gov and we used it for years. Now the new ones don't make that noise and it was so hard for me to accept the new ones. I love that sound. We make all kinds of food in the pressure cooker. Some of my kids' favorite meals are made in the pressure cooker.
Sara: Meat is so much better and it cooks faster.
Lynn: Isn't it essentially like a crock-pot?
Terry: No, I do pork chops in the pressure cooker. After browning them you add potatoes and carrots, then you get it up to pressure and in 12 minutes it's all done. Yet it tastes like it has cooked for hours.
Sara: Pressure cooker food was always really good, although it scared me a little. I always thought it might blow up.
Terry: I think that only happens with pea soup. And who makes pea soup?

Flickr neotint

Sara: Me, maybe?
Lynn (Lynn picks up a lefse turner from the trunk she is sorting) What's with this? A huge letter opener?
Terry: This was my mother-in-law's. It's a lefse turner. She was Norwegian, but she took pills for it. I had never heard of lefse until I came to La Crosse, so watching her make it was ever so much fun. Different from anything I'd seen before. And of course the recipe was, "It should feel like this. You'll know." But I was never sure what THIS felt like.
Sara: My grandmother said the same thing about a pie crust.
Lynn: But somewhere along the line I figured it out. It's THIS - So now that's what I tell my kids.
Terry: So when are you going to tell me? (again Lynn ignores)

Sara: My grandfather had this family recipe for sauerkraut that he made in his garden. He had a stone crock that was buried in the ground, almost up to the lid. He'd cut the cabbage, put it in there and let it ferment. He'd go out every so often and skim off the crud on the top, the mold and stuff. That's how the sauerkraut was made and we loved it. One time I went out to the garden to sneak some and pinched my finger under the lid.
Lynn: My mom was a great cook but she didn't can or make sauerkraut in her garden!
Terry: Everyone always said my grandmother was a great cook, but, when I visited her, we always ate at her restaurant.
Sara: When we finally got a *McDonald's* in Madison, my dad would love to go there. He'd take everyone's order and drive there by himself. He had to go into the restaurant, there were no drive-ups, and then he'd bring it home for us to eat. The first *McDonald's* didn't have a space inside to eat. Once we got it home, we'd eat in front of the TV on the TV trays. I don't imagine it was very warm by the time we got it but no one seemed to care. And that's when the burgers were fifteen cents and the fries were twelve cents.
Terry: I loved eating at the lunch counters at *Woolworth's*. They had great fries too.
Lynn: We didn't go out to eat all that often. Mostly we ate homemade meals. Mom would start cooking in the afternoon and she always planned the meal around the meat she was cooking.
Sara: We had the four food groups and corn was considered a vegetable.
Lynn: Iceberg lettuce with Thousand Island dressing was the salad.
Terry: Iceberg is still Ken's favorite type of lettuce.
Lynn: He's a man of discerning taste.
Terry: He picked me, didn't he? We also had dessert every night. Usually Mom made something special but, if she didn't, then we'd at least have ice cream.

Sara: When my family went 'out' for dinner, it was very different from today. There was none of this mega stuff. We had 7 ounce *Cokes*, no buffets or chain restaurants except *McDonald's* or *Woolworth's*; each town had their own family owned restaurants.

Lynn: Everyone in my family had their favorite place to eat. Mine was going to Mexicali's and ordering a taco which was beef; they didn't have choices then, no chicken or fish.

Sara: I was an adult before I even heard of a taco! My family went for a fish fry every Friday night. Fish, cole slaw, potato salad, and white rolls. Your four food groups!

Lynn: Another place I loved served lamb chops with these little pink and blue ruffled panties on them. At least that is what I called them and I always ordered lamb so I could get the colored panties.

Terry: Lamb chops. You ate baby lambs? I would have thrown a fit if I'd been served baby lamb, with or without colored panties.

Sara: No, you wouldn't have. That would have been bad manners and manners were important at home and especially the few times we went out to eat.

Terry: You are right. I would have never been allowed to go out again if I'd thrown a fit anywhere.

Lynn: My parents would say, "If you don't use good manners, you can leave the table". They would never tolerate bad manners. We practiced our manners at home in case we ever did go out. Like I said, tablecloths and everything.

Sara and friend

Sara: I always set the table and it had to be just so. The napkin had to be folded, and the silverware was laid out in a specific way.

Lynn: Did you have to be excused from the table?
Sara and Terry: Yes
Sara: After we were excused we had to do the dishes.
Lynn: My brother was very talented at winding up that wet dishtowel and snapping me with it. I got pretty darn good at it too, just for survival.
Sara: Did you get a welt? My sister always gave me a welt.
Terry: My mom didn't interfere when I fought with my brothers. Bill would rub his pimply face on me and I'd scream. She never said anything; it was every man for himself. But there were a lot of other things she did tell me over and over again.
Sara: Oh yeah, like "Wait until your dad gets home."
Lynn: And the waiting was worse than any punishment.
Terry: "Don't worry, someday you'll grow."
Sara: Did she mean your height?
Terry: No, my boobs.
Lynn: "Nice girls do not beat up boys."
Terry: "Potatoes are done, people are finished."
Lynn & Sara: What?
Terry: Done is for things, people are finished.
Sara: "Wear clean underwear in case you're in an accident."
Lynn: "Never say never."
Terry: "Never trust a fart."
Lynn: You ought to needle point that on something.
Sara: "If you fall out of that tree and break your neck, you're not going to the store with me."
Terry: When she was angry at another driver, she'd say, "I'll give you the finger, mister!"
Sara & Lynn: What?
Terry: The finger (she demonstrates by shaking her pointer finger)
Lynn: "Don't hit" and then she'd give me a swat on my bottom.

Sara: Or "Keep crying and I'll give you something to cry about."
Lynn: "If you keep making that face, it will freeze that way."
Sara: Yes, when you crossed your eyes.
Terry: "A blister on your tongue is proof that you lied because the devil was sitting there."
Lynn: "If you're going to kill each other, do it outside. I just finished cleaning."
Sara: "If you're going upstairs take something with you."
Terry: "Put the dishes in the dishwasher so the house will be clean for the firemen in case we have a fire."
(Sara and Lynn just look at Terry)
Terry: Oh come on. Like your mother never said that.
Sara: NO!
Lynn: "You better pray that will come out of the carpet."
Terry: "I don't understand why Jews don't celebrate Christmas, they're Americans too."
Lynn: This explains a lot.
Sara: "One day you'll have kids and I hope they turn out just like you!"
Lynn: When I'd complain about my kids to mom, she'd say, "You deserve this."
Sara: "If I've told you once I've told you a thousand times, do not exaggerate!"
Terry: "Eat an orange instead."
Sara & Lynn: What?
Terry: When you have a sexual urge, "Eat an orange instead." Try it, Lynn. It works.

Broad Chatter
Living with Plastic
a memory from Terry

Plastic –the home decorating statement of the 50s. We had plastic on the floors, on our furniture, even in our flower vases! For about five years, my mom loved plastic.

My family moved to a brand new house in the mid 50s and I guess Mom wanted to keep it perfect. So the furniture in the den where the family hung out, was all plastic, oops, I mean vinyl (that was a more sophisticated term) AND TURQUOISE! We had a white vinyl couch, a brown vinyl recliner (I think that was the only color they came in) and two turquoise vinyl chairs that spun around. There was a pole lamp near the recliner and on the table between the two spinning chairs was a white lamp inlaid with fake turquoise. A woman who worked for my dad painted two 'paint by number' paintings of pointing dogs and they were the wall decoration. And people loved it! They thought my mom was great at decorating.

There was plastic in the living room too—this time it wasn't the actual furniture –just on it. We weren't allowed to sit in the living room; it was for company and holidays but she wanted to protect this new furniture anyway. So she put plastic covers, like clear sheets, on the couches and chairs. This was before central air conditioning. Have you ever sat on plastic in the middle of summer with shorts on? No wonder we never complained about not being able to sit in the living room. And most of the time when company came, she just left the plastic on the furniture. Everyone thought it was great; they probably had plastic in their houses too. No one thought anything of leaving it there.

The vases all had plastic flowers which were newly on the market. Prior to this my mom often went into fields and picked milkweed pods and other weeds which she would paint gold. This stopped when plastic flowers were available. Now our vases were filled with yellow plastic daffodils and pink and red roses. On the kitchen table we had a basket of plastic fruit. I would pick the plastic grapes off their plastic stems as I watched Mom make dinner. She didn't like this at all but they were easy to put back on so I really didn't listen when she told me to stop.

Mom protected the carpet with plastic too. Between the den and kitchen and the front door and kitchen she covered the carpet with plastic. These were strips of plastic runners about three feet wide with little teeth things on the bottom to keep them in place. Otherwise I guess we would have been slipping and sliding all over the room on them. The plastic on the living room furniture, the vinyl furniture in the den, and the plastic fruit and flowers only lasted about five years but those carpet protectors were there for years. Mom loved them!

And Another Thing….

In My Neighborhood
three memories

Terry: Kids, kids, kids! That is what I remember most about my neighborhood when I was growing up. There must have been a hundred of us. Almost every house teamed with kids. Oh, Uncle Ned (with the Smiley Head from Chicago's *Bozo Circus*), who lived at the end of the block, didn't have any kids and there was one family with an only child but most had three kids and some up to six.

We all played together so the age of our playmates went from five to thirteen. The older kids organized everything from what we were playing, to which team you were on, to when we would stop. We learned rules from them, how to take disappointment, and suffered the teasing that we thought would just make us tougher. And finally we were the olders and the power over everything became ours.

Our street didn't have curbs or sidewalks and was filled with potholes so our play extended to those relatively safe streets. We'd skate there after an ice storm, ride back and forth on our bikes as we followed the fogging truck, and ran across them without really looking as we played flashlight tag in the evenings. Everyone's yard was fair game. We played in all of them including the cemetery that was just a yard and a fence away.

A sewer creek was just a short bike ride away down a dirt road that we called the cow path. Besides the cemetery, that was the favorite away from home place to play. My mom was always cautioning us about drowning but never seemed worried about the creek where we would wade, build dams, become explorers, and get really dirty.

We seldom told our moms where we were going. We didn't have to since everyone's mom was a homemaker and would 'keep an eye' on us without us really knowing. And if we got into trouble, someone's mom was close enough by to either rescue us or punish us. Without consciously knowing it, I think we knew we were pretty safe.

As I walk or drive through the neighborhoods in my current town, I seldom see any children playing and my heart breaks. Those were the best times—freedom, safety, playing, and fun.

Sara: I grew up just outside of Madison, Wisconsin in a small community that was actually still quite rural. There were two farms still operating at the edge of our neighborhood and there was no public bus service into the city. The homes were very modest and the families who lived in them were mainly supported by men who worked in blue collar jobs. Every home was situated on a large lot and many people had gardens and fruit trees. Almost every home had a dog that lived outside and a detached garage. There were no sidewalks, but every lot had a ditch in the front yard that ran through culverts under the gravel driveways. We used to love to make boats out of pieces of wood and sail them down the ditches to see how far they would go. I recall having wet pants every spring as we played with those boats and tried to poke them out of the culverts when they got hung up on debris.

We played outside every day. There was a large empty lot next to my house which had all the sand from when they dug out the foundations for the homes. We called this pile of sand and rocks the 'Mountain' and it was surrounded by an acre of weeds. It was a perfect place for building forts, for playing war, and for climbing. In the winter it made for great sledding. There was also a small creek that ran along the back of the Mountain. There we collected frogs, snakes, salamanders, and turtles. We also played in everyone's back yards. Each home had a 'special' attraction: the Oscars had grapes, the Hutchinson's had lots of friendly dogs, the Scalisi's had a ball field, and we had good apple trees and a sandbox.

We made our own fun, often creating our own games and playthings. We made rope swings, tree houses, go-karts, and built snow jumps in the winter. We had wagon races and ball games. We played Statue, Mother May I, Red Light-Green Light, and Kick the Can. We drew hopscotch squares with a piece of gravel and played Jacks with a red rubber ball and metal jacks. We put on backyard fairs and shows.

Mine was a blessed childhood in which adults watched over us without interfering in our play, where we were allowed to experiment and invent our own games and toys, and we were physically active and close to all things natural.

Lynn: During my entire elementary school years, my family lived on Kaibab Avenue. It was the quintessential middle-America neighborhood lined by newly built cookie-cutter ramblers with two car garages and sprawling manicured yards

We children would freely roam the quiet streets playing our games unhindered by traffic. It seemed like the only time there was any hint of traffic was when our dads pulled out of their driveways at 7:30 in the morning and when they returned at 6:00 in the evenings.

It was a neighborhood teeming with families, making it a kid haven. We'd ride our bikes in packs, racing up and down the quiet street that for two full blocks was uninterrupted by cross streets. We seemed to naturally migrate to one another. When one of us strapped on roller skates, within minutes the squeal and clankity-clank of at least a dozen sets of metal wheels would be heard bumping over the sidewalk cracks.

Summer nights meant giant neighborhood-wide hide and seek games. Older kids would hide in amazingly clever spots which we younger kids never seemed to be able to find. Whenever I could keep up, I'd tag along with my older sister Pam. She had a gift for blending into the silhouettes of bushes and the shadows of fences, only to magically appear at 'home base' when the seeker's back was to her. Those times then I was able to grab hold of Pammy's coattails, she'd whisper instructions to me of when to run, when to duck and hold perfectly still, and when to race with all the speed my shorter legs could generate, while yelling at the top of my voice "free" as I tagged 'home'.

On at least one Saturday every March the sky above our houses was populated with dozens of paper kites with trailing tails made of pieces of torn sheets. The colorful kites stretched above the roof tops as far as the strings would allow. I'd max out the wad of string that I'd spent the year collecting and I'd call out "more string." This brought Dad to my side with a new spool that he'd securely tie to the unraveling old string, and my kite would soar farther than all the others. At least that's how I remember it.

Fourth of July was held at our house which had the best front yard seats for the fireworks show that was launched from the community college stadium two blocks away. The neighbors would first gather in our backyard where we'd host a potluck barbeque, after which we'd move to our front yard. Dad would crack open ripe watermelons that had been picked the day before from the fields of nearby growers, and we'd gorge ourselves on the sweet drippy melons. We children would dance about with our sparklers, writing our names with bold strokes in the air, each letter glowing for a fraction of a second before fading. Then the fireworks would begin and we'd lie on the cool grass watching the brilliant explosions directly overhead. It wasn't until we moved and were locked in a traffic jam leaving a fireworks show that I began to realize how perfect the Fourth had been on Kaibab Avenue.

I now know that all was not perfect in the neighborhood. Each house held its sorrows and disappointments. But as a kid I knew neighbors who cared about and watched out for one another. I knew that I was free to live safely and unencumbered.

You're A Boomer if you know what these are!

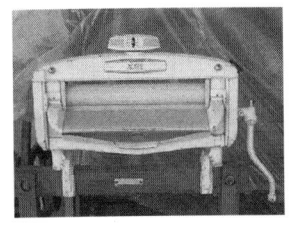

Flickr dvanzuijlekon

Flickr mikecog

Flickr Mad Mod Smith

Answers at the end of the chapter

Do You Remember?

- Peroxide on 'owies'
- Orange flavored *Aspirin*
- Heating up water for bath water – big families
- Metal wash tubs
- Pink Bathtubs
- Plastic tile
- *Mr. Bubbles*
- *Calgon* take me away
- *Air Wick*
- TV dinners
- Copper-colored appliances
- Detached, one car garages
- Shag carpet & rakes
- Doilies
- *Speedy Alka Seltzer*

Flickr 1950sunlimited

Flickr pds209

- *Formica*
- Naugahide
- Linoleum
- Storm windows you had to put up and take down
- Recipe boxes and handwritten cards with the woman's name on them
- Chenille bed spreads
- Hand crocheted afghans
- Telephone booths
- Telephone tables in the hallways
- Only one TV and one phone in the house
- *Tupperware* parties
- *Corningware*
- Melmac plastic dishes
- *Jewel Tea*

jshorpy.com

wringer from washing machine, fuse box, TV trays

Playing and Bruises

"Go outside and play" a quote from all our mothers

The women are still in Terry's attic and are now sorting through old magazines.

wikimediaTerp00

Lynn: I love looking at the ads in these old magazines. Not the cigarette ones, but the cars, appliances, and the toys.
Sara: Think about how toys have changed over the years. When we were young there were lots of building toys like *Erector* sets and *Tinker Toys* and *Lincoln Logs*.
Terry: You know I just read that if you pee on *Lincoln Logs* they turn color.
Lynn: Where do you come up with this stuff?
Terry: I read it somewhere. I don't know where; I read a lot. Or maybe it was from experience
Lynn: Speaking of peeing, I had a *Tiny Tears* doll.
Terry: I had a *Betsie Wetsie*!

Tinker Toys Circa 1920

Lynn: (ignoring Terry) There was a stopper on her back, and you'd take it out and fill her with water, then cork her back up. If you squeezed her just right, tears would come out of her eyes, or if you held her up she'd pee in her pants, or all over the Lincoln Logs.
Terry: So, you already knew about the color change thing!
Sara: My cousin Jim had this electronic football game. It was made out of metal with two teams of plastic players. We'd line them all up and plug that sucker in. It would start to vibrate; about half the guys fell over right away and the other half would bunch up in a corner and we'd unplug it and yell, 'First down!' He also had a lot of space age stuff. Robots, ray guns…

35

Terry: But the guns were different. I had a black holster with one gun for when I was a bad guy and a white holster with two guns for when I was a good guy. And then I had a lady's derringer; I guess that was for when I didn't know if I was bad or good. Brett Maverick had one too.
Of course, I had *Davy Crocket* underpants. I showed them to the *Good Humor* man and he liked them.
Sara: That's why he was in a good humor.
Lynn: I also remember when we got the first *Slip and Slide*. Dad didn't want it on the grass 'cause it would kill it. So he set it up on concrete. We'd run as fast as we could and then plop on that concrete. It just about killed us. When we came to a stop, we'd just lay there until we could breathe again, then we'd spring up and do it again.

Lynn

Sara: Speaking of springs, what about *Slinkies*. I loved them. But if they got twisted or even just a little kink in them, they weren't good anymore.
Terry: I read that some people are like *Slinkies*. They are not really good for anything; however, they still bring a smile to your face when you push them down a flight of stairs.
Lynn: *Silly Putty*! That was great, too. We used to put it on the funny papers and then stretch the faces out.
Sara: Oh, funny papers! Don't people call them 'comics' now?
Terry: *Hula Hoops* were the 'it' toy of the late 50s. They cost $1.98. I went into Chicago with my dad to demonstrate them at *Woolworth*

Flickr Kent Kanouse

stores. I sold a bunch of them. I even stood on a table one time as I demonstrated. One man watched me for a while and said, 'If she can do that, so can I." and he bought two!
Lynn: Can you still do it?
Terry: Of course. Easy pie, Daffy Duck.
Lynn: I was never very good at hula hoops, but I could skateboard. My first board was just a 2x4 with the front and back wheels of an old metal roller skate nailed to it. Others used 1x4 but I had the big guy. And it was amazing what I could do on that thing.
Terry: Hey, the skates with keys! You'd be going along and then suddenly it would come undone- screech; or it would stretch out- clank-a-clank-a-clank.
Lynn: Or they would lock up on you and you'd take a nose dive, a real face plant. Now that was fun.

pinterestBobbieBennet

Terry: If you had on tennis shoes, *Keds*, then your feet would hurt because you had to screw them on so tight. And then they were hard to get off. This could be a problem when you really had to go to the bathroom. I was skating at the neighbor's one time and I'd really tightened those skates. I had to go to the bathroom, but I didn't want to take the skates off. Of course I waited until the last minute. When I finally sat down to take the skates off—oops. I peed my pants! I left a wet spot on the step but my skates were still on so I kept skating and didn't go in until Mom finally called me for dinner. By then my pants were dry so she never noticed. The dog liked me though.
Lynn: Now that I think about it, we spent a lot of time playing outside, both at school and at home.

Sara: And the whole neighborhood was our play place. I don't remember there being any fences. We'd just run from one yard to the next.
Lynn: The suburbs, where we lived in California, had fences, but we managed to have secret entrances and passages from yard to yard.
Terry: We usually played in the cemetery. If you haven't played war or cowboys and Indians in a cemetery, you haven't lived. The best part was if the caretaker was there. He'd chase us and that made it really exciting. We also played a lot at the sewer creek. That's what we called it but I don't think it really had sewer water in it. It didn't smell and my Mom let us go and she was the one who said you could drown in a teacup. I've always had an unnatural fear of teacups. But we'd play near the sewer creek and in it and come home a real mess. No one seemed to worry about what we were doing as long as we were home on time.
Lynn: We played outside until the streetlights came on; that was our signal to go inside. But in the summer, all the neighborhood kids, about 5000 of us, would go out after dark and we'd play hide and seek.
Terry: We didn't need *Wii* when we were kids. We had us.
Sara: We thought we were unsupervised but when you look back on it, there were a whole lot more mothers who stayed at home and were watching us. I remember if I got in trouble at Debbie's house, her mother, Arvella, would scold me and send me home. And by the time I got home she would have called my mother and I'd get it again. But really it was when we were a little bit older, when we could ride bikes, that we really got our freedom.
Lynn: Ah...riding bikes.
Sara: Riding bikes and being free. Did you put playing cards on your bike to make that 'Brrrr' sound? I loved that!

Terry: It's funny that we had any cards left to play games. In the fall I loved riding my bike through the piles of leaves left by the curb before the neighbors burned them. People would rake up their leaves and put them in the street to burn. We'd go racing through them on our bikes and scatter them everywhere.
Lynn: I bet your neighbors loved you.
Terry: Of course. I was cute.
Sara: (ignoring Terry) Besides bikes, every family had a Red Flyer wagon.

Terry's brother Randy on left

Terry: I had a green one.
Sara: (turning to Lynn) We had great wagon races with ours. We had a block long, dead end, gravel hill next to our house that ended in a street where the speed limit was 40. So you had to ditch the wagon before you hit the busy street. We'd get those wagons going and you know they were so

lovetoknow.com

undependable. That tongue would just get to shaking wildly and we'd flip out onto the gravel. I remember sitting on the side of that road just picking pea gravel out of my knees.
Lynn: And as soon as you'd get cleaned up you would run right back out there.
Terry: Nobody had pads or helmets.
Lynn: Nope, just cut offs and tee shirts.
Sara: I remember having scabby elbows, a skinned face, and scuffs on the heels of my hands.
Terry: We would ride on the handle bars of bikes or ride on the back fender. I knew many kids who got their toes in the

spokes. I did that and a lot more but I never broke any bones.
Lynn: Neither did I but I always wanted to. My sister broke all of her toes at one point or another. She was constantly stubbing and tripping. She was the most beautiful girl who was as clumsy as could be. But I never broke anything even though I was such a tomboy.
Terry: I had bruises all over.
Lynn: But I did get sprains.
Terry: My dad said I was never going to be able to wear a dress anywhere because I had so many bumps and bruises on my legs.
Lynn: Did you have scars?
Terry: Yes, I still have big scars on my legs.
Lynn: Me too.
Sara: I never broke anything either as a kid but I smacked my head a couple times really hard. I think I probably had a concussion at least once. The kids in my neighborhood hung a swing on a big tree on the edge of a hill. We got the great idea that if we hung a swing on it we could swing out over the edge. Of course, being kids, we didn't think about the swinging back. And so we tied a bunch of rags onto the knot in the end of the rope. The first kid jumped on it. He swung out and it was wonderful. But when he swung back, he smacked his head on the trunk of the tree. So then the next kid got up and did it again. We went through three or four kids and it happened to everyone. Pretty soon we had all these kids lying on the ground, dazed. What you did when you were a kid is you said, "You're alright, you're okay, you don't have to go home." If you went home your mom would probably come investigate and the fun would be over. So we'd try and talk the kid out of going home. Eventually somebody did go home and told. The grownups cut the swing down.

Lynn: Even though kids were getting hurt, it was too much fun and there was the chance that the swing would work eventually.

Terry: Bill and I were always doing acrobatics and stuff so this one time he had me on his feet in the backyard and catapulted me like a human cannon. I ended up landing on my back and it knocked the wind out of me. He didn't want mom to know what he had done so he picked me up and was running me around the yard as I was trying to catch my breath. But Mom saw it all out the window and called us in and put me in bed. Bill was feeling bad for what he had done so he bought me this really cute little wind up music box. He had planned to give to me for my birthday, but he gave it to me early because he felt so bad. I still have it.

Terry's music box

Lynn: It sounds like he could be nice even if his ideas weren't always safe.

Terry: Our elementary school had an upper playground and a lower one and it also had the world's best merry-go-round. Do they allow those any more? Anyway there was only a little hill between the two playgrounds and the hill was probably about five feet high. Bill and I were sledding there one time

blogs.dallasobserver.com

and Bill had this good idea that he would sit forward on the sled and I would sit backwards. I was kneeling and holding on and, as we went down, I fell forward off the back of the sled and I didn't let go. It was icy, so my face just dragged along the ice. I had cuts all over; I even had cuts on my eyelids.

Lynn: It never occurred to you to let go?

Terry: No. I went down all the way on that ice. I was one bloody mess. I went to school the next day with cuts all over my face.

Sara: What the older kids could talk you into was amazing.

Lynn: Steve worked one summer at a drive-in movie theater and he worked in the snack bar. All of his friends worked day jobs, but he worked at night. He wanted to play baseball but he needed someone with whom to play catch. Being a little tomboy and a little sister, I was thrilled to death to play with him. "Hey Lynnie, let's go out and play catch." He would throw that ball as hard as he could. He was 16 and I was 8. I'd catch it and I'd think to myself, "Don't cry. You're tough, don't cry." I sucked it in because I knew if I cried then Mom would come out and Steve would be in trouble and I wouldn't be able to play with him. So I had sprained fingers, jammed fingers and bruises.

Terry: I loved playing with my big brother. Bill used to tell me that if you got hurt you should hit the owie. "It will make you tough," he'd say. One time we walked three miles to go see 'Two Ton Baker the Music-Maker', who was this guy on Chicago television. He was with the *Oscar Mayer* truck for some reason. On the way, we

wikipedia

went by this mud puddle and Bill pushed me into the street and the puddle. He thought that was so funny. Of course I got mud all over my face. I had no way to get it off and there were no bathrooms. There were never any bathrooms in stores like today. Anyway, I had a scarf around my neck so I put that over my face so Two Ton Baker wouldn't see the mud. Baker said, "Are you going to rob me?" I could only say, "Uh uh," while Bill laughed. But I still got my little Oscar Mayer wiener whistle. My brother was mean to me but I liked to hang out with him.

Sara: You wanted to be part of whatever the big kids were doing. I was that way with my sister. I just drove her insane because I wouldn't leave her alone. My mom would have to say to me, "You cannot play with Linda and her friends; you cannot even go near them right now." I remember sitting on the landing looking into the basement when her friends were there. All I could see were their feet, but my mom wouldn't let me go any further.

Lynn: I remember climbing up some bleachers at a basketball game and my sister Pam was sitting at the top with a friend. They were having a heart-to-heart and so I popped up and her friend said, "Do we have to have her here?" She was pretty obnoxious and Pam stood up for me. My brother Steve did all the fun things but I was fascinated with pretty Pam and her friends. Of course, I never got any cuts or bruises when I was with Pam.

Sara: Oh, basketball! I played that in my driveway with the neighborhood kids because there were no organized sports for girls – just the *GAA, Girls Athletic Association*.

Lynn: Girls' basketball was only played on a half court.

Sara: You could only dribble three times and then you had to pass the ball.

Lynn: And even in *GAA* we were playing the same people all the time so it wasn't a big deal.

Sara: Did you play with marbles?

Terry: We used basketballs! Marbles would be hard to bounce and you can't make a basket with them.

Sara: No, marbles. The game with the little glass balls, marbles.

Lynn: I was pretty good at marbles.

Terry: Oh, that kind of marbles. We'd play in the dirt and draw the circle.

Lynn: Were you good at that?

Terry: Yeah, I was great at drawing the circle.
Lynn: We would carry our marbles to school in a little bag. My mom made my bag.
Terry: I wish my mom had made me a bag. I lost all my marbles.
Lynn: Really? I wouldn't have guessed.
Sara: Did you play foursquare?
Lynn: Oh yeah, four square, two square, holdies and then free ball.
Sara: What the hell are you talking about? We just played plain old four square. Of course, we had fewer seasons to play outside.
Lynn: How about dodge ball? That was a great game.
Sara: Or tetherball, which was a futile thing. Only tall people won.
Lynn: I loved playing tether ball.
Terry: Me too. We had our own.
Lynn: For little people?
Terry: No, it was real people sized. But my favorite thing to do was to sit on the ball and my friends would bat me around until I got wound up tight.

googleimages

Then they'd stop it after I got hit once or twice. I only got a couple of bad cuts from doing that.
Sara: Speaking of cuts, were you a *Mercurochrome* or *Bactine* family?
Terry: We used *Bactine*.
Sara: Me, too
Lynn: My folks used *Mercurochrome* and it burned! First they'd sear the wound and then Dad would use *Mercurochrome* to paint on the

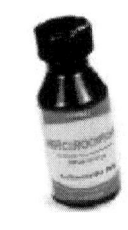

google images

'Bunny Badge of Courage', which was a lopsided orange bunny that he drew on our arm or leg. We wore those with pride.
Terry: And every time you were sick you got...
Lynn: A mustard plaster!
Terry: No, *Vick's Vapor Rub*. If I had a stuffed nose, Mom put some in a *Kleenex* and I held it by my nose and, ahhhh, I could breathe. And if we had a sore throat, she'd have us eat some.
Lynn & Sara: (gasp)
Terry: I'd eat it even if I didn't have a sore throat.
Sara: That explains some things, Lynn.
Lynn: Yeah.
Sara: So what was a mustard plaster?
Lynn: Mom would take...
Terry: Real mustard?
Lynn: Mom would take dry mustard, which is real, make a paste, spread it on two pieces of sheet and slap it on our chest and back. The body would heat them up. She'd check it now and again and when we were a certain shade of red she'd say, "Yep, you're done."
Terry: Finished. Potatoes are done, people are finished.
Lynn: Nope, we were done.
Sara: Speaking of being hot, how did you get rid of a fever?
Lynn: There was the orange flavored baby aspirin. My mom would mush it up in jelly for us to eat.
Sara: My mom would dissolve one in water thinking that it would taste good but, yuck! It was terrible. But my grandmother insisted that the way to get rid of a fever was to put me in bed and put every blanket in the house on me. Sweat it out. Once the sheets were good and soaked she knew the fever had broken.
Terry: My mom put ice in towels and put them under my arms and between my legs. I just knew that I'd be frigid all my life. Don't ask my husband, Ken.
Sara: I ended up with tonsillitis every year so I'd get a

penicillin shot in the butt each time. It hurt like the dickens and the sucker with the safety stick they gave me didn't help a bit. My doctor's office was in his house on Johnson Street in Madison. My mom would call and we'd go around to the alley where there was a back door to the office. It got so that my mom would just sit in the alley, in the car, I'd go in, drop trou' and get the shot. Then I'd get one of those silly little suckers. Did you play doctor?

oldtimeimages

Lynn: Yeah, and I got a spanking for it.
Terry: From your patient?
Lynn: No, from my mom. It was because we dropped our pants to give each other shots and that was looked down upon.
Terry: That was the only time I got a spanking too. Tommy told me to tell Sarah to drop her pants so I did. She told her mom and well, the rest was history.
Sara: We used sticks for the shots, the sharper the better. If we left a red mark then we knew the patient was cured.
Lynn: I had the mumps, did you?
Sara: Yes, but kids don't get the mumps anymore.
Lynn: My mom took a cloth and wrapped it under my chin, brought it up to the top of my head, and tied it there.
Terry: Like Alfalfa in the *Little Rascals* movie. He had a toothache once and they fixed him with that. Did it help your teeth too? My mom completely believed in cod liver oil. If we took that, we'd be healthy forever. So every morning Bill and I got an eye dropper of cod liver oil. We both loved it! You just had to be really careful not to spill any on your school clothes; otherwise you'd either have to change or smell like fish all day.
Sara: I think we used *Flintstone* vitamins. You didn't have to worry about being smelly.
Lynn: All this talk is making me hungry. Who is ready for lunch?

Training Wheels
an original story by Lynn

My brother Steve is eight years older than I am, and my sister Pammy is seven years older. When I was just a little button, they shared a bike that I thought was the best bike in the world. It was a two-wheeler with fat tires covered by wide fenders that were painted with blue and white chevron stripes. It had a plump soft seat and a bell. I'd be tooling along on my hand-me-down tricycle, when one of them, sometimes both of them, would zip past me on the bike. I'd pump, pump, pump, pump trying to catch up with them. Then they'd zip past me from the other direction and I'd pick up my tricycle, turn it around and pump, pump, pump, pump. But I never could catch up with them. That was okay. To me that bike was wonderful.

As we all grew older, we each were given new bikes. Pam and Steve were each given their own bikes, very sleek with thin tires and skinny fenders. I was given a new tricycle. The bike I *wanted* was the bike with the fat tires. My parents understood this, and told me that when both of my feet touched both pedals at the same time, I could have that bike.

They put it in the garage leaning up against the far wall. There it sat, snug and safe, but not gathering dust because every so often, I'd slip into the shadowy garage. I'd squeeze between all the stuff that had collected around the bike. Then I'd climb up and slide my leg between the wall and the bike, careful to keep it tilted towards the wall so it wouldn't fall over. And I'd pretend I was riding the bike.

I was seven years old, the day before Thanksgiving, when I went out to the garage and climbed up on the bike. As I slid my foot down to the pedal, I realized that both of my feet were touching at the same time. I was so excited. I ran upstairs to the kitchen where my mom was cooking.

"Mom! They touch!"
"That's nice," she said without looking up from whatever she was chopping.
"My feet! They both touch!"
Somehow Mom was able to interpret what I meant. "Ohhh! You give us some time to clean up the bike and it's yours."

The day after Thanksgiving I went out to the garage to check on my bike, and it was gone! In its place, on the wall where it had been leaning, was a note addressed to me. It was from the head elf of the bike department of the North Pole informing me that, using elfin magic, they had whisked my bike up to the North Pole to fix it up. Santa would bring it back when he was in the neighborhood on Christmas Eve. Whatever doubts I had about Santa Claus disappeared. I now had had paperwork to prove his existence.

The time between Thanksgiving and Christmas stretched for months that year, but finally it was Christmas morning. I ran to the living room and there, propped up on its new kickstand in front of the tree, was my bike. The elves had done a magnificent job. They'd put on new fat tires, had taken out all of the dents, sanded out all the rust, and had painted the fenders with red and white stripes. They had put on a brand new plump seat. It even had a new bell.

I stepped back so I could take in the beauty before me. Starting at the front tire I panned across the bike, taking in every flowing line, until I reached the back tire. There in the middle of the wheel was a metal rod out sticking on both sides with two miniature wheels that looked like they hadn't fully formed. They looked like the forearms of a Tyrannosaurus Rex.

Pointing at them, I asked in disgust, "What are those?"
Mom replied, "They're training wheels. They'll keep you from falling until you learn how to keep your balance while riding your bike."

"Take them off!" I said. Then Steve said, "I had training wheels on my first two-wheeler." Oh, I thought. Well, if Steve had training wheels maybe I'd give them a try.

We lived in central California at the time, which meant fog for winter. That afternoon, dressed in sweaters and sweatshirts, the family all went out to the driveway to watch me launch my bike. Dad held it up for me, and said, "Okay, climb on."

Suddenly I was a bit nervous. I no longer had the garage wall to keep me from falling, but I trusted my dad and climbed up.

Holding on to the back of the seat, he said, "Start peddling and I'll be right behind you." I started peddling and could hear and feel Dad running behind me, but then he let go. As soon as I felt his hand let go of the seat, the bike dipped to the left and then, 'Tap,' and the bike popped back up. Then the bike dipped to the right, and 'Tap', it popped up. Tap! Tap! Tap! Wobbling from side to side as I rode down the street, I thought these training wheels are fantastic! I love them!

It must have been the year of the bike, because every kid in our neighborhood got a two-wheeler with training wheels. For weeks it was wonderful. All of us were tapping our way up and down the neighborhood block in a wobbly single file line. Our mothers had insisted we ride our bikes on the side of the road to stay out of the way of all the traffic that never came to our quiet neighborhood. I was always the one who was the farthest off the road, because according to my mother the 'side of the road' started halfway into the gutter. This meant I rode at an angle with the right training wheel keeping me from falling over.

Then Cindy had her dad take the training wheels off her bike. The rest of us would be riding in our wobbly line, and Cindy would race past us riding in a straight line. I'd watch her pedal as fast as she could to the end of the block then turn around and zip past us, giggling. I never really liked Cindy. Then Dave's dad took of his training wheels. Then Beth, and Scott, Cindy's little brother who was younger than I.

One by one all the training wheels in the neighborhood came off except for mine.

I just couldn't get my balance. I tried. My dad worked with me, running along my side, yelling, "Sit up tall, Lynnie! Just hold her up!"

My brother Steve took a different approach. "Relax," he'd say. "Don't worry. You'll find your balance." Kind of like the Zen of riding a two-wheeler.

But as hard as I tired, I just couldn't get it. And to add insult to all of this, my right training wheel that had suffered months of abuse to keep me upright in the gutter, had developed a high pitched squeal. So when I rode it was, 'Tap, squeal, tap, squeal!'

This went on and on until June. I was sitting on our front lawn in my cut-offs and favorite Mickey Mouse T-shirt. My friends rode past me on their bikes that had no training wheels, yelling "Hey, Lynn!" I half-heartedly waved back wanting to crawl under the grass and hide. I looked over at my bike that I'd left in a heap on the driveway, a miniature wheel sticking up in the air. Somehow, at that moment, I knew. I can't explain it. I just knew.

I walked over to my dad who was working in the yard, and pointed with my thumb towards the bike, "Take'm off."

Dad looked over at my bike and then at me. "You sure?" "Take'm off." I repeated. Dad went to get his tools. That's when Steve came out of the house as if he knew, too. I can clearly remember him sitting at the top of the steps, in the Lotus position, smiling. It was as if he was saying, "Yes, Cricket, now is your time."

Dad took the training wheels off, then held the bike up. "Okay," he said. "Climb up." All of a sudden, I wasn't so sure. My heart was heavy in my chest and I was having a difficult time taking a full breath. But I looked at that bike and thought, I can do this. So I climbed up and said to Dad, "Don't let go."

Dad said, "Just start peddling, I'll be right behind you." So I started peddling, calling, "Don't let go."
"I'm right behind you."
"Don't let go!"
"I'm right behind you."
"Don't let go!"
"I'm right behind you."
"Don't let go!"
"I'm right behind you."

Then I realized that Dad's voice sounded far away and that he was a half a block behind me!

The bike dipped to the left, then on its own it popped up, and I was riding without my dad, without the garage wall, without training wheels. I was slicing a straight line down the road with the wind blowing against my face. I was free to make my own way.

I didn't think I'd ever have the need for training wheels again, but I was wrong. I've needed training wheels of one kind or another many times. There were my parents, teachers, siblings, and friends. The next time I needed bicycle training wheels was when our son Daniel received his first two-wheeler. As I stood in the driveway watching him on his shiny black and silver bike, wobbling from side to side with those funny little wheels sticking out in the back, I knew that he was finding his own balance, discovering his own freedom, making his own way.

Broad Chatter
Playing in the 50s
Terry remembers

Until I was in sixth grade, I played mostly with boys. They were just more fun. Tommy lived next door to me from the time I was three until I was seven and a half. I'd go over to his house (which was identical to mine, two story brick) and, instead of knocking, I'd yell, 'Yo, Tommy". Out he'd come, ready for the day. And it was always an all day thing since his mother would lock the door the second he was out. She'd let him in for lunch and then again at dinner but other than that, Tommy was on his own.

No one in the neighborhood had swings or a jungle gym, there was no park, and the elementary school was about seven blocks away so we never even thought of going there. But we'd find the best things to do. One year a new house was being built on the corner so the dirt pile, basement, and framed in building were our playhouse for a few months. Our moms knew we were playing at the building site and no one was concerned or worried about any dangers. We were close enough to hear them when they yelled for us to come home. When the house was finished, it was like losing the world's best playground.

When I was six and Tommy was five, we were allowed to cross the streets. Now we had a huge neighborhood to explore but our favorite place was a wooded area about two blocks away. There we'd build forts and trails, play war, and play cowboys and Indians. Tommy was great fun until the winter when he kind of had polio. I say 'kind of' because he never had to go to the hospital but a woman would come to his house to exercise his legs. I was told Tommy 'kind of' had polio and it was left at that. It was during this Tommyless winter that I started playing with Sarah, a girl and a tattletale. Sarah wasn't nearly as much fun as Tommy and, once he was on the streets again, she was the reason for my first real spanking. I'd gotten swats before but this was an 'over dad's knee' real spanking. Since I now had Tommy again, I really didn't want to play with Sarah but she was always there. One day when she asked to play with us, Tommy whispered to me, "Tell her to pull her pants down and then we'll play with her". So I did and Sarah ran home. Mission accomplished! All was well until my mom came down the street where we were looking for bugs in another empty lot. She grabbed my arm, swatted me on the butt, and said those dreaded words, "Wait until your dad gets home." Tattletale Sarah.

Also during Tommy's convalescence, I played with Marcia who was three years older than I. Marcia liked to comb my long hair and enjoyed coloring books…ugh. Eating dinner at her house was a horror. Her mom would fill a huge glass to the top with milk but you weren't allowed to drink any of it until your plate was clean. Then you had to drink down the entire thing! I seldom cleaned my plate at home. I was seven years old and weighed about 35 pounds. I didn't have a big appetite and having to eat without drinking was torture. I ate there twice and learned my lesson. Because she was older, Marcia had lots to teach me. I distinctly remember the time she was snooping in our bathroom cupboard and found a box that I had never noticed before but later I figured out held Kotex. Marcia said, "This is what people use when they want a baby." I was horrified! My little brother, seven years my junior, had just been born! I couldn't fathom that my mom would want another one of those crying, attention grabbing creatures.

We moved to another suburb when I was eight, and once again my best friend was a boy, Bill B. He was an only child and had the coolest stuff, from a reel-to-reel tape recorder to an arcade quality bowling game in his basement. His parents would let us play 'driving' in their car, but our favorite game was to play war in the cemetery which was right in our neighborhood. My older brother Bill would join us. We played football, baseball, keep away, and rode our bikes everywhere. In the winter we went sledding and ice skating at the lagoon, or right on the street if there had been an ice storm. In the summer we rode our bikes two miles to the town pool; in the evening we played flashlight tag throughout the neighborhood. We were always outside.

But my favorite playmate was my brother Bill; I would be overjoyed anytime he was willing to play with me, which wasn't very often since he was four years older than I was. I would do anything he told me to do. We would often catch lightning bugs in jars and then smear the glowing part on our wrists and fingers. Once he told me bees were just as much fun to catch and smear. I tried once and didn't play that again. He is also the one who told me to put my tongue on the light post that was on the corner. Of course it stuck and my mom had to put warm water on my tongue to get me loose. I didn't learn that lesson very well, however, because he talked me into putting my tongue on a metal ice tray several times and I always did it. With Bill I got stuck in trees, got my breath knocked out of me while doing 'acrobatics', shot bb-guns in the basement, and played near the third rail, which electricity ran through. "Go ahead touch it; let's see what happens," he'd say. Real fun!

When Bill and I were in Murphysboro, my dad's home town, we played with our cousin Donny who was the same age as Bill. The three of us would wander through town, play at the Court House where Donny lived (his dad was the sheriff), ride ponies through the streets of the little town of Ava, burn ants with magnifying glasses, look for frogs, and generally get dirty, wet, and muddy. Great boy games! But I was still the little girl in their eyes and especially in my grandmother's eyes. Often the boys got to go places simply because they were boys.

One time they got to go to a nearby farm to dig up bones—human bones! The two sons of the farmer had been digging a tree stump out of a field and discovered an Indian burial ground. Now this was the late 50's, times and attitudes were very different from now. Archeology professors from Southern Illinois University excavated the area and took most of the skeletal remains back to the university; there was no discussion at all of leaving them or returning them to the tribe. After the university had what they wanted, the farmer opened the site to the public. For a dollar, you could dig in the area and keep any bones that you found. Uncle Gov took Bill and Donny to the site but my grandmother said it was not something a little girl should see, so I was left behind. The boys brought back several 'treasures' and I was terribly envious. I hated being a girl! However, in looking back with perfect 20/20 hindsight and the huge changes that society has embraced, I am now glad I wasn't there. Growing up in the 50s and 60s was, for the most part, wonderful but there are some things that were best left there.

Do You Remember?

- Playing checkers and Chinese Checkers

Flickr Florida Memory 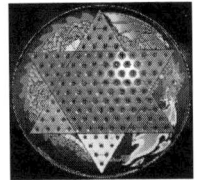   *Flickr Chris Blakeley*

- Playing board games like *Monopoly* and *Clue* and *Bingo*

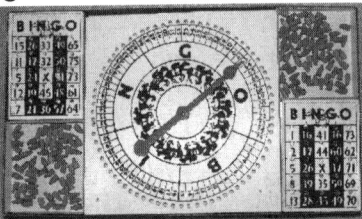

Flickr Joe Haupt

- Playing outside! Everything from Jacks to Jump ropes

Sara

- Flashlight tag
- Statues
- Mother May I
- Annie, Annie Over
- Red Light/Green Light
- Capture the Flag
- Kick The Can
- Cowboys
- Winter games
    - Pie
    - Pom, Pom, Pull Away
    - Crack the Whip

Flickr Doc Searls

Did you play with any of these toys?

Google Images

pelhampacesetter.com

Flickr Howard Dickman

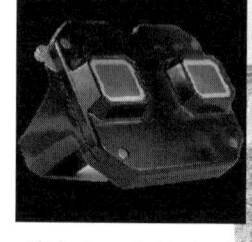

Flickr Francis Mariani

Flickr freeparking

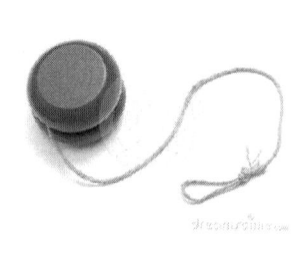

Dreamstime/googleimages

Flickr bixentro

google images

Holidays

The one thing women don't want to find in their stockings on Christmas morning is their husband.   Joan Rivers

Marry an orphan: you'll never have to spend boring holidays with the in-laws.
George Carlin

Terry at Christmas

Sara, Lynn and Terry have just come down from the attic and are having lemonade in Terry's kitchen. Their heads are still full of all the memories they sorted through up there.

Lynn: When I was kid the Fourth of July was a big deal! We had this really big front yard on a corner lot.
About two blocks over there was a stadium where they had the fireworks display, so we had front row seats. The whole neighborhood would gather on our lawn. We did sparklers. We'd write our names in the air with them. Sometimes the fireworks were so close the canisters would fall down around us.
Terry: Did anybody die?
Lynn: No

Flickr BenKAdams

Terry: Rats. That would have been a memory. I was often in Murphysboro, Illinois for the Fourth of July and we would make homemade ice cream with the crank thing. Everyone would take a turn cranking until, at the end, my Uncle Gov had to finish.
Sara: In Madison the fireworks were at the Vilas Park Zoo. Thousands of people would come in during the day and by evening it was just packed with people. I remember the fireworks

going off and then you would hear the big cats howl. So to me the fireworks were "Boom" and "Howl". I look back on that and think what a bad idea that was. Those poor animals! When we got home later we would do sparklers and those snakes that you'd light and they'd leave a black spot on the cement.
Terry: And caps. We'd get caps and set them off with a hammer.
Lynn: One fourth of July, my little brother Johnny had those sheets of caps, and he rubbed them together between his hands and they exploded.
Terry: And your mom just said, "Bet you're not going to do that again."
Sara: Summer was also prime vacation and swimming time. My mom was always afraid we would get ear infections so she made us wear those rubber swimming caps.
Lynn: I remember wearing those – it was something about our long hair clogging up the pump or drain in the swimming pool. Boys didn't have long hair then, so they didn't have to wear them.
Sara: You had to stuff all your hair in and it was so tight. Sometimes they'd have a big old flower on them somewhere.
Lynn: And then you'd peal that cap off and you'd have this nasty red ring around your face.
Terry: And you'd be tan everywhere except where the cap came down. But that's better than my husband

Sara at the beach

Ken's experience. He took lessons at the old YMCA in La Crosse, Wisconsin and the boys couldn't even wear a suit--they swam nude! When I took lessons they used to try to get us to blow bubbles out of our noses. But I'd always wear nose plugs so I could never make the air come out of my nose. I'd just go (strange noise).
Sara: Yep, summer was swimming season. Everything was so hot – we didn't have air conditioning.

Lynn: In central California it'd average between 110/120 degrees. All of us kids insisted it was cool to go barefoot even though the asphalt was hot enough to melt the calluses off the bottom of our feet. We'd stand on the grass looking at the heat waves hovering over the asphalt. And then we'd run across it as fast as we could and would get about half way across before it began searing our feet. When we'd reach the other side we'd collapse on the grass rolling around in pain. Then we'd play a little bit and decide we had to go back across the street.
Terry: Why didn't you put your shoes on before you crossed?
Lynn: It wasn't cool. Hey, I had an image to maintain.
Sara: We'd play under the rhubarb making hollyhock dolls. And we'd play up in the apple tree where there was always a breeze.
Terry: I was climbing an apple tree one time, with one leg up and the other on the ground, and this dog came along, lifted his leg, and peed on me. My shoes squished all the way home.
Lynn: You should have gone barefoot. At the end of summer was my birthday so I always got new school shoes and clothes for as gifts, no toys.
Terry: Then in the fall would come Halloween. I loved Halloween! Did you make your costumes or buy them?
Lynn: Made them.
Sara: Me too. For several years I went as a hobo, old pants with patches. We used a burned a cork to make a beard and mustache on my face, and I had battered old hat. Oh my gosh, I just realized.....I

Terry as half boy and half girl

was going as a homeless person.
Lynn: And everyone had a jack-o-lantern outside.
Terry: But all the houses had a light on too, unless people truly

weren't home - not like now when they fake not being home. We went to every single house and got something.

Lynn: And it didn't matter whether or not we knew the people.

Terry: We didn't have an adult with us. They were at home handing out the candy. We didn't have to be back until 9:00, and we had school the next day.

Sara: There were homemade treats. Caramel apples, taffy, and cookies. Mrs. B made popcorn balls every year.

Terry: My classmate Roger lived at the end of our block and his mom would have a haunted house every year in their basement. We'd go right into the house. No one gave a second thought about us going in any house, whether it was for Halloween or to sell *Girl Scout* cookies.

Lynn: We used pillow cases for our treat bags so we could carry a lot of candy.

Sara: And then when you got home you'd pour it all out and trade with your brothers and sisters. Okay, since we're in this fall thing, what do you think of when I say Thanksgiving?

Terry: Crayons

Lynn: Why?

Terry: Because we made the turkeys by tracing our hands. But Christmas and Thanksgiving were always the exact same meal. Always a turkey.

Lynn: I always wanted the drumstick. A whole

Flickr pds209

drumstick. And they'd plunk it down in front of me.

Sara: It was huge - like a *Flintstone* drumstick.

Lynn: I'd eat about six bites and then I was full. We had a tradition...

Terry: Burnt cabbage.
Lynn: You remember! Sara, it's this French cabbage dish that takes 24 hours to cook, until the cabbage is a dark brown color. My dad named it burnt cabbage. But Brent calls it chou brûlé.
Sara: That sounds much nicer.
Lynn: It does, doesn't it? It's French for burnt cabbage.
Terry: What did your moms put in their dressing?
Sara: Sage,
Lynn: Onion,
Terry: Celery,
Lynn: Bag of guts,
Terry: That was the turkey's *Cracker Jack* prize.
All: And day old bread.
Sara: We'd tear it up into pieces.
Lynn: I always knew when it was a few days before Thanksgiving because mom would flop two loaves of bread, in the wax paper wrappers, on the kitchen counter.
Terry: Why do they put croutons in a sealed bag when they are already stale?
Lynn: That's a pretty good question.
Sara: It really is. We'd go to my Grandma Schumann's. She had this little tiny house, but everybody came to her and so we ate in shifts. The men ate first then we'd clean those plates and then the women would eat. For me it was always a dilemma which group to eat with. If you ate with the men you got the freshest, hottest food. But if you ate with the women they ate more dessert.

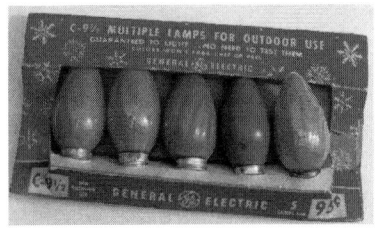

Flickr ErinM

Terry: And Christmas stuff wasn't out in the stores until after Thanksgiving.
Lynn: About a week after Thanksgiving my dad would put up the outside lights. This was before they had the clips

63

you could attach to the house. It was an all day affair and it involved every tool in the garage. The entire front yard was a staging area, but when he was done, we'd all go out to admire them. They were so perfect I'd feel like saluting.

Sara: My dad would say, "going to go up to the attic and get the Christmas stuff." It was the same stuff every year but it was thrilling. We had this fake fireplace in our living room which most of the time was weird, but at Christmastime it was perfect because that's where we'd hang our stockings. They weren't fancy store bought things; they were our regular knee socks. But my favorite part was the tree. We had to put on the tinsel, one 'tinse' at a time. And then in the old days we had to take it off one 'tinse' at a time.

Lynn: To save it for the next year.

Sara: Sometimes we even strung it back on the card.

Terry: My dad would do the one strand thing. And then one year he wanted a flocked tree. But he was going to do it himself. My dad always figured that if one can of something was good, 12 was better. So he used 12 cans of snow! The tree was gorgeous. But 12 cans! And this in a house where the mom didn't like messes. That was the last time he did that because the next year he got one of those metal trees, the aluminum ones. Ours stood on a revolving stand with turquoise spot lights on it and it only had turquoise balls; there were little ones at the top, middle sized in the middle, and big ones at the bottom. But gag me, I thought it was ugly even back then.

Flickr 1950sunlimited

Sara: The one with the color wheel? I thought those were pretty cool.

Lynn: I used to walk through the Christmas tree lots in California and Hawaii and I'd imagine I was walking through a pine forest. I so wanted it to snow. And then I moved to Utah and we'd get Christmas tree permits and go up in the mountains — it was much easier in the lot. After a couple of hours of wallowing in thigh deep snow we'd settle and we'd bring home the saddest looking trees.

Sara: In Wisconsin there were Christmas tree farms all over the place. We'd go and chop one down each year. On Christmas morning we had a stereo with the arm-thingy and mom would pile six albums on that spindle and then they'd drop KAPLUNK and they'd play one after another all morning long.

Lynn: My favorite Christmas carol was *Mele Kalikimaka.*

Terry: What?

Lynn: (sings first line) "On a bright Hawaiian Christmas day". But I have to admit that it wasn't very Christmasy seeing pictures of Santa on a surf board with his fat belly hanging over a lava-lava.

Terry: I'll stick with Bing Crosby and *White Christmas.*

Lynn: One thing that said to me that it was Christmas time was the TV ad about shaving and Santa was riding on the razor

Sara: Oh the *Norelc*o ad.

Lynn: Yeah, I'd see that ad and we knew it was Christmas season.

Sara: At Christmas time we'd get these stencils that were made out of waxed cardboard. Then we used this stuff called *Glass Wax*, which was for furniture and left a white sheen. So we'd pour that on a sponge and we'd make these little scenes all over the picture window. It was a big deal; you had to think about it – where you wanted to put everything. And we were really proud of it when we were done.

Terry: We sprayed fake snow in the corners of the windows.

Lynn: You lived in the Midwest....it snows here.

Terry: But snow didn't really stick in the corners; that's just in the movies. So we had to get it from a can.

Lynn: In central California, winter was fog. We'd have one snow day a year. We'd load up the car early in the morning and drive to Tehachapi Mountain. It would take about three hours to get there and we'd go sledding. By the end of the day our hands and feet would be frozen, but I loved it.

Sara: We played outside all the time in wool clothes and rubber boots. Heavy and not very warm. But we hated coming in. I loved skating and sledding in the winter.

Terry: We had two great places for sledding and skating. We went sledding at Boys' Hill. I don't know why it was called that 'cause girls could sled there too. It was a huge hill which was perfect for going down but not so good for the hike back up, but worth it. We skated at Northside Park Lagoon. There was a tiny log shelter house with a fireplace and hot chocolate and candy bars for sale. We hardly ever went in the shelter. We skated from right after school until dark when Mom would pick us up for supper. Crack The Whip was our all time favorite game.

Flickr joebackward

Sara: One of my favorite memories of winter and Christmas was the Christmas records. Mom and Dad had lots of them; well, at least three which was a lot then. But my sister and I had a lot of other records.

Terry: Yes! I had a carrier for my records; it's still around here somewhere. I swear I had every song that was popular. No matter the time of year or the event I had the song. Here it is!

Sara: Do you have any songs in there about getting older?

Terry: Probably not – we were kids. But, let's look and see. Maybe we can make one fit. Here's one from *West Side Story*. Now it would be:

Tonight, tonight I hope I'll sleep all night.
Tonight I won't get up to pee.

Sara: Oh that's cool, but I don't exactly remember those words. Let's try it with some of these other records...
Lynn: OK - *Stop in the name of* …. (silence)
Terry: What? You've got to go on, Lynn. You have to think of something about getting older.
Lynn: I'm working on it.
Sara: OK I've got a Christmas one to *Away in a Manger*:
Today at the computer,
No place for granny.
I looked up my boyfriend
From 1963.
He still has those jug ears ,
Though now they grow hair,
And he became a Republican,
There goes my love affair.
Lynn: *Great balls of...*
Terry: Great balls of what, Lynn? You've got to think of something. Like this one from *Sound of Music*:
When my knees creak,
when my back hurts,
when I've got to pee,
I simply remember my favorite things
And then I can't find my keys.
Lynn: Do you know the way to …..
Sara: *Chantilly Lace and a wrinkled face*
And saggy boobs hanging down
Lynn: *Splish Splash*... oh. my gosh, I am having a flash.
Terry and Sara: Yes, Lynn! Now sing it!
Lynn: *Splish Splash, I am having a flash.*
Terry: Way to go! Here's a new rendition of *Leaving on a Jet Plane*: *I'm leaving on a Hover Round*

Don't know if I'll be ever found
Sara: *And another Christmas one...*
And so I'm offering this simple phrase
To girls from 50 to 92,
Although it's been said many times, many ways
Getting older is like...
Terry and Lynn: *Cheese fondue!*
Lynn: *I'm not sure I like it that my brain is in sync with yours,*
Terry: *But how about this one....I'm on a roll now.*
Over the Hill and through the woods
Terry: *Straight to old age we go.*
Sara: *Our skin is all wrinkled; it's too hard to tinkle,*
Lynn: *Our husbands are getting slow.*
All: *Ooohhh...Over the Hill and through the woods*
Terry: *So how did we get here?*
Lynn: *My glasses are there; my hearing aid's where?*
Sara: *My teeth are on the chair.*
All: *Ooohhh...Over the Hill and through the woods*
Sara: *Hand me my supplement.*
Lynn: *It takes 'way the pain*
Terry: *But leaves me no brain,*
All: *As over the hill weee wentttt!*
Terry: *Yes, we've still got it!*

Things Were Different Then
an original story by Terry

Things were just different then. By the time I was ten years old, I'd run several businesses, gotten my cousin and brother out of jail, and learned the true meaning of love.

We didn't have garage sales. We didn't have anything to sell. We owned only one of anything and if it broke we'd get it fixed. Our clothes were usually hand-me-downs and when we were through with them, we'd give them to the next kid or put them in the rag bag. Different.

But we did have sales. Every couple of weeks, Mary, the girl across the street, and I would look at each other and say, "*Kool-Aid* stand!" We'd run to my house, never Mary's. Her mom was mean. One time Mary didn't clean the fish bowl on time and her mom ground the fish up in the garbage disposal.

But my mom would just say, clean up your mess. So we'd take the little kids' table outside. Mary would make a sign with notebook paper and crayons and I'd make the *Kool- Aid*. It came in little envelopes that cost a nickel. You had to add sugar. The directions said 1 ½ to 2 cups, so two heaping cups would be just about perfect. We'd get the juice glasses; they'd once held jelly and had pictures of cartoon characters like *Tweety* and *Sylvester* and *Daffy Duck*. We'd get a pan of lukewarm water and take it all outside. Mary would man the stand while I rode around the neighborhood yelling, "*Kool-Aid* for sale!"

And the kids would come running. Never any grownups. We never got any of those 'aren't you cute' sales. As soon as one kid would down his glass, we'd swish it out in the lukewarm water and set it up for the next kid. Sanitary standards. And we'd make a killing—30-35 cents apiece.

I also sold comic books. My dad worked for *Woolworth* and each store had a metal rack that spun around and held comics. The deal was that at the end of the month the employees would take any books that didn't sell, tear off the top of the cover with the title and date, and send it back to the company for credit. Then they were to destroy the rest of the book. But my dad brought them home for me. I loved comics. My favorites were *Uncle Scrooge*, *Superman*, and *Archie* with Betty, Veronica and Jughead. But I read them all from *Little LuLu* to *Children's Illustrated Classics*. But every so often my mom would look in my closet and say, "Clean up this mess". So I'd take the table and the comics outside. I'd ride around the neighborhood yelling, "Comics for sale" and the kids would come again. I'd sell the ten cent comics, which later cost 12 cents, for two cents and the quarter ones for a nickel. And I'd really make out. Dollar fifty, two dollars easy.

I was also in the entertainment business. At least once a summer Mary and I would put on a show, often a magic show. We'd make signs—Magic Show, 2:00 Saturday, 1024 James Court. Five cents admission. Then during the week we'd practice our acts for at least forty minutes. On Saturday we'd put up a rope in my garage and then hang a sheet over it for a stage. We'd make *Kool-Aid* again and now *Rice Krispie* bars which we'd sell for three cents so we'd get at least another nickel out of each kid. And at two o'clock the garage would be packed. The show would last ten, twelve minutes, was always a huge success and we'd make at least 70 cents apiece.

Now with all this money I had two places I'd spend it. The first was Mr. Miester's store which was a neighborhood mom and pop grocery where we'd go for milk, bread, my mom's cigarettes—things you'd run out of between your weekly visits to the grocery store 'cause nobody went to the grocery store more than once a week. But I liked his glass candy case.

The other place I spent my money was the picture show. That's what we said, sometimes just show but never movie. And I'd go to the Saturday afternoon matinees—two features separated by cartoons and sometimes newsreels like when Sputnik went off or something. It cost a quarter to get in, a box of popcorn, which would last at least through the first feature, cost a dime and *Milk Duds* were a nickel. Great combination. And the theater was packed, just with kids. Nobody came with their mom or dad. The first time I took my little brother Randy he was three and I was ten. We walked the eight blocks to the theater, watched both shows and walked back home. We were gone at least four hours. My mom loved Saturday afternoon matinees.

The only time I went to an evening show was when I was in Southern Illinois in my dad's home town. They didn't have matinees so we had to go at night and I'd always go with my brother Bill and cousin Donny who were both four years older than I was. For years we played together.

Donny's dad, my Uncle Gov, was the county sheriff so they lived in the courthouse, a huge three story building that took up an entire city block. What a great place to play. They had this one huge room with twelve iron beds for the jury to sleep in case they had to stay over but we'd bounce on each one as we played cowboys and Indians. On weekends we'd play in the actual court room. They never locked it. And we'd pound on the judge's desk with the gavel yelling, "order in the court." And sometimes they'd talk me into going into the basement where the gallows was still stored to play hangman but I didn't like that very much.

But all that changed when they turned ten, double digits, and now they wanted nothing to do with a six year old little girl. That is also the year we discovered our Zodiac signs. Donny was Taurus the bull, Bill, Leo the lion, and me—I was Libra the scale. Now I heard, "You can't be a bull or a lion; you can't even be a fish; you're nothing but a crumby scale." If I whined to the grownups they'd say, "If you ignore them they'll get bored and stop." It doesn't work now and it certainly didn't work then so I suffered in silence.

One day they'd been unmerciful when Donny announced that they were going to the show that evening. "Can I go too?" "No" they both yelled. My Uncle Gov, the sweetest man in the entire world, said, "Now, I don't know why you can't take Terry Lynn with you." Donny grabbed Bill's hand and yelled, "We'd rather be in jail than take a scale to the show." They ran through the kitchen, through the processing area where the prisoners were fingerprinted, and into the women's section of the jail. They slammed the cell door shut and, to their surprise, it locked. Gov walked in. "That wasn't a good idea, boys. Deputy Buck has the only key and he's taking some men to the prison in Elgin. He won't be back until tomorrow afternoon."

At first the boys thought that it was still a real hoot. My mom even brought them bread and water, but after a while the stark cell with its exposed toilet became a bit much and Donny said, "I guess we should have taken the stupid scale." Immediately Gov popped in. "Well, I'll be a suck-egged mule, boys. Terry Lynn found a spare key in Buck's desk. Guess you'll be taking her with you since she's the one that busted you out." YES!

It was only three blocks to the theater but you had to pass two taverns and I got shoved in both of them. I had to pay their way into the theater and they wouldn't sit with me, but I'd gotten to go. And when we got home, did I tattle? No way. Things were different.

Kids were treated differently too. Our parents weren't always trying to entertain us. The world revolved around them not us. Oh, they took us places but usually just where they wanted to go. We lived only 30 miles from Lake Michigan and my parents took us to the beach—once. But one year they did take Bill, Donny, and me to *Riverview Amusement Park*, a huge permanent carnival like a precursor to *Six Flags*. There were side shows, food stands, every kind of ride you can imagine including several wooden roller coasters. But the most famous ride was the Parachute. It was this huge tower that went over 180 feet in the air. It had six benches similar to the ones on a Ferris wheel. Two people sat on each bench and then they would rise in the air slowly with this panoramic view of Chicago and the Lake Front. Then, when they got to the top, and the passengers never knew when that would happen because they couldn't see up, the seat would fall —freefall—for about 100 feet, leaving their stomachs behind. Then the parachute would come out and they'd float down, usually safely. Bill and Donny loved the parachute ride and I loved the sign that said you had to be 'this tall' to ride and I wasn't because I hated heights, even then.

This fear was challenged however the year that I was ten. I was in Southern Illinois for the Fourth of July, just like I was most years. And, just like most years we were doing what the grownups wanted to do on their day off which was make homemade ice cream, grill out, and play cards in the evening. We never did any 'Fourth of July things' like parades or the fireworks. But this year my Uncle Gov asked me if I wanted to go to the carnival in the city park. I'd never gone before and to this day don't know why he asked me but I was thrilled. Not only was I going to the carnival but I was going with my favorite person in the whole world.

We walked around the arcades and had our picture taken with one of those boards with the holes in them that you put your head through. This time it looked like we were prisoners on a chain gang, which I thought hilarious since Gov was a sheriff. Gov bought me cotton candy and we went on my favorite rides, the *Scrambler* and the *Tilt-a-Whirl*. What a great day.

But then, as we were leaving the park, we passed the Ferris Wheel. Gov said, "Do you want to go on that?" My heart sank. My stomach seized up. I was petrified of the Ferris Wheel. But I was a polite child and he'd gone on my favorite rides. How could I say I didn't want to go on the one ride he'd suggested? So I said, "Sure." My legs were like jelly as we stood in line. I don't know how I walked up the ramp when it was our turn to board. As I slid onto the bench, my feet didn't touch the floor. I wouldn't have them to help me brace. The man swung the bar over our laps and secured it; I grabbed it with a death grip, my fingers immediately turning white. I gritted my teeth and closed my eyes so I heard, rather than saw, the man move the lever for the wheel to start moving. As we stopped to let the next people on, the bench moved a tiny bit. Then I heard, "You're not going to make this thing swing are you?" Was that Gov? I opened my eyes and saw his hands on the bar—they were whiter than mine. Without turning my head so I didn't make anything swing, I looked over at him. His teeth were clenched and his eyes were shut. "I'm not going to swing it", I said. "I hate these things."
His eyes popped open but he didn't turn his head either. "What do you mean? I thought you liked this ride."
"Not me. I'm scared to death".
"Well, don't move an inch. I don't want it to swing."
"I won't if you won't."

We both rode that wheel with our eyes shut not moving a muscle. I'm sure the ride only lasted four or five minutes but it seemed like an eternity. And when it was finally our turn to get off and the man raised the bar that was over our laps, I jumped down on shaky legs. I put my little tired hand in Gov's big one and we walked down that ramp. But I had learned that loving someone sometimes means doing something that scares you and I also knew my Uncle Gov loved me as much as I loved him.

Bill and Donnie in jail

Terry and Uncle Gov

Two Things Meant Christmas
an original story by Sara

In my childhood there were two events that signaled the arrival of Christmas. The first came as a result of my father's work. He worked for the *Oscar Mayer* Company in Madison, Wisconsin. It was hard work, with long hours and few benefits. But, one of them was the Christmas party for employees' children. When I look back on this party I realize it had to be planned by people who never had children of their own and had possibly never spent any time in the company of children. Because this is the way it worked...

Our parents dropped us off in front of a downtown theater. They didn't go in with us because no parents were allowed. When we entered the lobby we were met by Santa's elves who handed each of us a red mesh stocking filled with candy, a red ticket, and an Oscar Mayer wiener whistle, even then they understood product placement. Then we were set loose in the theater. Imagine if you can, an entire movie theater filled with 300 or so children, no adults, and pounds of candy. Needless to say it was a raucous setting. At the foot of the stage there was a man who played Christmas carols on a beautiful organ. After eight or ten familiar songs the man and the organ slowly sank into the floor, as if by magic. Then the cartoons began. Usually they were Disney or *Hannah-Barbera* productions and I remember one that I particularly liked. It was Chip and Dale cavorting in Donald Duck's Christmas tree. They were having great fun driving Donald to near manic distraction. I loved those little chipmunks! Following the cartoons came the main feature, usually a cowboy or animal movie, in which the hero always triumphed. By the time the movie ended we children were in full-gear sugar mania and the theater floor was littered with paper wrappers and was sticky on the bottom of our shoes. That's when *Little Oscar* drove the *Oscar Mayer Weiner Wagon* out on stage. He was a little person, dressed in a butcher's white apron and wearing a white chef's hat. The weiner wagon was a full sized car covered with a huge fiber glass hot dog. We went wild! We got out our wiener whistles and blew them until we lost our breath. But even Little Oscar was not the star of the day. He was just there to introduce the 'big man', Santa Claus himself. When he stepped out on stage he was greeted by a tremendous cheer entirely fueled by candy. Each year Santa would pull red tickets from a big barrel and call out the numbers. Those children who held the matching ticket would come on stage and receive a gift from him. Usually the gifts were things such as paint by number sets, puzzles, or *Tinker Toys*. But the last two numbers that Santa pulled were for bicycles! Every year my sister and I would hold our little sweaty tickets praying that Santa would call our numbers. It never happened.

So the year I turned eight years old I decided to take things into my own hands. For three years I had asked the Santa at the store for a bike and he hadn't brought one. So I went to my mother and told her I really wanted a bicycle for Christmas. She simply said, "Ask your father." I went to my father and told him I really wanted a bike for Christmas. He said, "We can't afford it. Ask Jesus." Well, maybe that would work. In our German Lutheran home

Jesus was even bigger than Santa. So I went to my little desk, got out my number two pencil and my blue-lined penmanship paper and began my letter...*Dear Jesus, Please bring me a bicycle for Christmas. Love, Sara.* No, that wasn't quite right. So I crumpled it up and started my second letter...*Dear Jesus, I've been a very good girl this year. Please bring me a bicycle for Christmas. Love, Sara.* I read that draft and it still wasn't quite right. So I crumpled it up and thought for a long time. Then an ingenious idea came to me. I went into the living room where we had our Nativity set displayed. Very carefully I picked up the Mother Mary figure. Very carefully I carried her back to my room. Very carefully I opened my handkerchief drawer. Very carefully I set her in the drawer and very carefully I closed it. Then I sat down to write my third letter...*Dear Jesus, If you ever want to see your mother again...**

The second event that signaled the arrival of Christmas during my childhood was the church Christmas pageant. About a month before the pageant we began practicing our hymns and we were each given a Bible verse to memorize. Our roles in the pageant were mainly determined by the size of the costumes that were available. These costumes had been made by the ladies of the church back in the 1940s and the fabric was chosen by its itchiness factor and by how much heat it could generate – burlap was very popular. Most of the girls were angels and the boys played either shepherds or Wise Men. For many years I remained the same size and so I was the cow in the stable. My costume was a pair of white

long-john underwear with big red spots painted on it. I sang this song:
> *I am the cow with spots of red,*
> *I gave Him my manger for his bed,*
> *I gave Him my hay to cradle His head,*
> *I am the cow with spots of red.*

The two most important roles, Mary and Joseph, were chosen by the Sunday School Superintendent. In our little Lutheran church most of us were blond, blue-eyed Germans with the exception of two recent Italian Catholic converts. So each year as long as I can remember our Mary was played by Rosalie DiSalvo and our Joseph was Tony Fedele. Rosalie looked just like the Virgin Mary when she was dressed in a blue sheet with a silver halo. Her dark hair and olive skin made her seem so exotic. But I knew her to be an early smoker, a frequent curser, and a girl who lost her virginity sooner than most. Tony made the perfect Joseph. He had a five-o'clock- shadow by the time he was in fifth grade and he never spoke unless he was spoken to...a perfect characteristic for Joseph. When the pageant was finished all the players gathered around the manger and sang 'Silent Night' in German:
> *Stille Nacht, heilige Nacht,*
> *Alles schläft; einsam wacht*
> *Nur das traute hochheilige Paar.*
> *Holder Knabe im lockigen Haar.*
> *Schlaf in himmlischer Ruh,*
> *Schlaf in himmlischer Ruh.*

I like to think that when God looked down those nights on his little creations he did so with a nod of satisfaction and a smile.

*adapted from a story "The Bicycle" by Johnny Moses

Do You Remember?

- New Year's Eve
    - Metal spinning noisemakers
    - Cellophane hats
    - Oyster stew with little oyster crackers
    - The neighbors came to your house to play cards or board games
    - Guy Lombardo

    Flickrpds209

- Presidents Day
    - One year we would get Lincoln's birthday off, the next year we would get Washington's birthday off
    - The stories of the cherry tree & log cabin

- Valentines Day
    - We would decorate a shoe box at school for our cards
    - We labored over printing everyone's name and choosing just the right card for each child in class
    - The school party (put on by the PTA ladies) with punch in a punch bowl, using our best manners

    arielsdancestudio

- Easter
    - Colored chicks
    - Getting a new easter dress and coat
    - Hats with the elastic string under your chin

    Google zsloot

- White patent leather shoes
    - Easter corsages
    - We never refrigerated eggs
    - We just used food coloring and vinegar to color eggs or we did them with onion skins

- Christmas
    - Giving the teacher a hankie at Christmas
    - Drawing a name for school gift exchange
    - School Christmas program which included the biblical Christmas story and hymns

- Birthday Parties
    - Bringing penny candy, *Rice Krispie* bars, or popcorn balls for your birthday treat at school
    - Your birthday party was always at your house
    - Playing *Pin the Tail on the Donkey*, dropping a clothespin in a bottle game, and *Bingo*
    - Mom made the birthday cake
    - All your little friend guests dressed up

Sara's birthday

- Veteran's parade on Memorial Day and going to the cemetery to decorate the graves of relatives

- Playing musical chairs and spin the bottle

- Having treasure and scavenger hunts

Pets

Every child should have two things: a dog, and a mother willing to let her have one.

Even though your dog thinks you are the best thing in the world, it may not be correct.

The three women are sitting around Sara's kitchen table looking at old photos.

Flickr Kim Scarborough

Sara: Oh, look. This is my dog Penny. She was the very best dog in the world.

Lynn: It took me a long time to get a dog. Mom kept a spotless house and she was able to pacify my brother and my sister with a parakeet and guppies. Then I came along and I had to have a dog, I needed a dog, and she was smart enough to realize that. So I was given a dog for my seventh birthday. We went to the pound and picked him out. Immediately he tore up our yard. His last act was to chew down a tree about six inches around and drag it up to the door. Then suddenly, he was gone. But I still needed a dog. So I asked for a dog from Santa Claus. Mom read everything on animals and I would give her little clues and hints. Our house was always beautifully decorated and I would buy Mom little pictures of dogs that she could frame and put up on the wall, or I bought little glass holders of the *Collie Collection*. Mom read up on dogs and she looked for dog breeds that did not shed, only grew a certain size, etc. I wanted a black dog and got one for Christmas. I was so excited! And the first thing it did was pooh under the Christmas tree. But Mom got on top of that quickly. He seemed to understand Mom's

authority, he would jump up on everyone but her. He was allowed to stay in the house, but only in the family room.
Terry: So how long did you have him?
Lynn: I ended up naming him Andy and I kept him until I was 19. I was away at college when he developed tumors. I loved that dog. We took that dog on all our house moves. In fact, my dad's company paid big bucks for me to keep Andy when Dad was transferred to Hawaii. It would cost an exorbitant amount of money to bring him because of the quarantine laws, but I told my parents that I would stay in California with Andy if he couldn't come along. So dad talked with the people at the company. His boss came over one night for dinner and said, "Okay, where's this dog?" One look and he was hooked. Andy got to go with the family. Andy became sick during the summer when I was home from college. We realized there was nothing we could do for him.
Sara: Both my mom and dad liked pets, mostly dogs. In one of my favorite pictures of me I'm dressed like a refugee. Mom always made us wear scarves; I don't know what that was all about. Anyway, I'm holding this kitty and the bottom half of the kitty is just swinging.
Terry: That is about the only pet we didn't have—cats. My dad didn't like cats.
Sara: We had other kinds of pets, too. One Sunday, on the way home from church, my mother swerved to avoid hitting a painted turtle on the road. She pulled over to move it out of the way of traffic, but when she got back in

pinterest.com

the car she had the turtle with her. She said, "Your father always said turtles make good pets, so here you go, girls".

She handed it off to us in the back seat. We named her Tina and we kept her for that whole spring and summer. She would sit on our laps with her head out to be petted. She lived in a large metal washtub that we had rigged out with a little island, sand, some rocks, and a few plants. We fed her lettuce and worms and she thrived quite well. A few times she even laid eggs in the sand, but nothing ever came of them. That fall my dad said we had to let her go so she could hibernate. We knew he was right, but we were sad to lose her. So we painted her name and our names on her shell with silver eavestrough paint. Then we took her out to a muddy little lake by Grandma's house and, after several rounds of petting her head and kissing her, we let her go. She swam off for a ways, then turned around and swam right back to us! "See, Dad, she wants to live with us." But he wasn't buying it and he gently put her back in the water. That time she swam out a little further and then, all of a sudden, another turtle's head popped up out of the water. Tina swam in that direction and we never saw her again. We felt greatly relieved that she had found a friend, which allowed us to leave her and not worry too much. I often wondered in later years if anyone ever saw our little Tina with her fancy painted shell.

Terry: We had lots of turtles. We'd buy them at *Woolworth's*. They had a pet department in the back of the store with birds, fish, and a tank of turtles. The turtles would be all piled up in a corner and all looked the same, but we still took forever to pick one out.

reptilesmagazine.com

We bought a plastic kidney shaped tank, also at *Woolworths*, with a little island and a green plastic palm tree. I loved the turtles but they never lived very long. My dad was the manager of a *Woolworth* store in Chicago that had a pretty big pet department including a myna bird. The employees taught that bird to wolf whistle and say, "Where's Mr. Howell?" and the answer, "Over at Miller's," which was Dad's favorite lunch spot. A lot of people wanted to buy that bird, but Dad wouldn't allow it to be sold. However, he never brought it home either.

Lynn: We had a parakeet once that was iffy because of its feathers. My mom made sure that cage was cleaner than any other cage around.

Terry: My mom loved all kinds of animals and was fine with us having them. I have this darling picture of my mom when she was about three. She was clutching a puppy, which was so her. Almost any animal we brought home, she was fine with it.

Sara: My mom was the same way. Both my parents loved animals and we had a lot of pets. No birds, though.

Terry: We had a couple of parakeets when I was very little, but I don't remember them very well. I did, though buy one for my brother and sister-in-law when they were first married. They lived in an apartment that didn't allow dogs or cats and I thought everyone should have a pet. I went to *Woolworth's*, they had everything, and bought a bird, a cage, food, the whole ball of wax. Bill and his wife Sally were coming that evening to spend the weekend with us, so I put the cage and bird on Bill's childhood bed and then went to take a shower. As I started to towel off, I heard a crash. By the time I got to Bill's room, the cage was on the floor and the bird was gone. However, our dachshund Snitzie had a very satisfied look on her face. I'm not sure if Bill liked getting an empty cage for his birthday or not.

Sara: Most of our animals met untimely deaths too,

because they were being cared for by children. Well, not the dogs and cats, just all the little critters we'd drag home.

Terry: That is what many of our animals were, dragged home ones. Once my older brother Bill worked in the sewer plant and one day he brought home this great big, huge bull snake and let it go on the kitchen floor. Mom wasn't freaked out, but he did have to return it to the sewer plant. I think she was more upset by where it had come from than the fact that it was a snake. We had all sorts of animals: flying squirrels, ground squirrels, baby rabbits. We'd trap them or just find them on the ground. Bill brought home a fox, a baby raccoon, and even a crow. I wanted a de-scented skunk but mom put her foot down on that one.

Sara: We dragged things home from this empty lot next door so we had voles, moles, snakes and little birds and she was fine with that, too. The only thing she didn't like was when we brought home a nest of little garter snakes. I think it just freaked her out to see them all wiggling together. So she chopped their heads off with a knife.

mommymoments.ca

Terry: That seems a bit extreme. We had lots of baby rabbits that we fed with doll bottles. I don't remember any of them surviving. But talking about snakes, Bill found a garter snake one time and barbequed it. Mom wouldn't let him use the grill so he used the can that potato chips came in, rigged up a spit, put charcoal in the bottom, and we ate it. Tasted like chicken.

Lynn: We certainly didn't eat any of our pets.

Terry: My neighbor Mary didn't eat her pets but they did have unusual deaths. Her mom didn't like pets but let her have a goldfish. One time, Mary didn't clean the bowl when she was supposed to and her mom put the fish down the garbage disposal and ground it up. But then she let Mary have a hamster. One summer afternoon Mary put the hamster outside to let it air out but forgot about it. That evening the mosquito fogger came by and BAM, dead hamster.

Sara: I'm just surprised that people air out their hamsters.

Lynn: I hope they didn't get any more pets. That wasn't a safe house for critters.

Terry: No, but her mom did bake the best homemade rolls. I wouldn't have given up my dog for one of those rolls, but a guppy, sure.

Mom and Andy
an original story by Lynn

My mom was of the strong opinion that animals should remain outside in the neighbors' yards. She was okay with animals that lived in confined spaces, like birds and guppies, as long as their cages and bowls were regularly cleaned. My older brother and sister, Steve and Pam, were happy enough with the birds and fish who temporarily resided in our house until they ended up in their final resting places, in the northeast corner of our backyard. For eight years these limited parameters of what pets were allowed worked fine in the family.

Then I came along and mucked up the dynamics. I love animals, particularly dogs. While I liked fish and birds well enough, I found it boring that all we could do was watch them. I wanted a companion who had soft fur to pet, who would follow me around, and who would run and jump and fetch and play with me.

I was always bringing home strange dogs that would wander into our neighborhood, insisting they were homeless. I'd hold the dog in my arms just outside the open kitchen door asking, "Can I keep him?" To which Mom would point to the dog's collar and say, "His name is Skippy and he lives three blocks from here. No, you can't keep him."

But that didn't stop me from trying. I spent a good chunk of my early childhood lobbying for a dog. Whenever *Lassie* came on TV, I'd comment how lucky Timmy and his family were to have a dog who took such good care of them. I systematically checked out every book in the school library that was about dogs and left them lying around the house with pages strategically marked that discussed how smart dogs were and how they can protect us and be our friends.

I studied these books, often more than once. I can still remember the first book that I read by myself. It was about a dog.

"See Dick run. See Spot run. Run Dick. Run Spot. Run Spot, run."

It was sheer poetry.

By the third grade, I'd read and reread all the dog books in the library and was losing hope that I'd ever have a dog. But aside from my mom's defect about disliking animals in the house, she was a pretty smart lady. The extreme distaste that Mom had of furry pets that shed hair and left smelly packages all over the yard was trumped by her love for me. She knew that I didn't just want a dog, I needed a dog. It took her time to wrap her mind around this, but she finally managed. One night at the dinner table, shortly after my eighth birthday, Mom announced that perhaps she might consider the possibility of maybe getting me a dog.

I was ecstatic. Her commitment was a bit wobbly but I wasn't about to let this chance slip by, so I cranked up my efforts. Whenever I could, I spouted little gems of knowledge on the superior care I would provide for my dog. "Every day I'll give him fresh water, because water is good for him." "I'll always brush my dog, because dogs like to be brushed and it keeps them clean." "Every day I'll scoop up the dog poop and put it in a paper sack and dump the sack in the trash can so we won't step in it."

I even pulled out the big guns and wrote a page and a half letter to Santa, making the case for a dog. I wrote that my mom said it was okay for me to have a dog so Santa shouldn't be concerned about bringing a dog into our house. Then I carefully outlined the personal advantages for him if he brought me a dog. This was an inexpensive gift because Santa could give me one of the many puppies from his own dog's litter, which meant minimal labor and material cost. And, if I got a puppy, he didn't have to bring me any other gifts that year, again a tremendous savings. In a post script I added that I'd like the dog to be a boy and to have black fur.

After several weeks, I received a letter postmarked the North Pole. I remember it opened with,

> Dear Lynn,
> Ho, ho, ho. It is so good to hear from you.

The letter then went on and on about gifts for my brothers and sister, which I basically skimmed through, until I reached the last line of the letter.

> My dog, Sadie, has just had the cutest puppies. I will bring you the best of the litter.
> Love,
> Santa

It was happening! After all these years I was getting a dog. I kept the letter in a safe place in case the dog didn't arrive as scheduled and I needed proof that a dog had indeed been promised. I had no need to worry. On Christmas morning, under the tree, was a ball of curly black fur with two brown eyes and a red bow around its middle. It seems Santa's dog was a poodle. At least that's what I was told.

Years later, I figured out that Mom had done quite a bit of research; this was long before the days of *Google*, and she concluded that poodles were among the smartest, easiest dogs to train. She determined that it was important that the dog be a 'member' of the family, and, in order for that to happen, it had to be allowed inside the house. I now wonder what kind of agonies Mom went through to get herself to the place where she could accept allowing a free roaming animal into our house. Her love overcame all prejudices and she focused her search on dogs that were the easiest to house break AND did not shed. This last fact was what sealed the deal for getting a poodle.

I didn't care what breed my puppy was, I just knew that he had soft black hair, was cuddly, and he was mine. It was instant love.

As for his name, I'd been planning on calling my puppy Sam, I'm not sure why, but that was the name I'd picked out. However, Sam just didn't seem to fit. I didn't know much about poodles, but I had heard of French poodles. His papers, yep, my dog had papers, listed his sire's name as Andre which my Dad said was French. However, Andre sounded a bit 'foo-foo' to me. Dad said Andrew was the English version of Andre. We were getting close, but Andrew was too formal, so I shortened his name to Andy.

Newly christened, the first thing Andy did was leave a little gift under the tree. Mom was prepared for such a situation. Immediately Andy was swept away to the backyard, and the Christmas tree, skirting, and everything within a six foot radius was sterilized.

When Andy was brought back into the house, he made it as far as the laundry room which connected the back patio to the family room. Newspaper was layered across the laundry room floor and chicken wire was strung up in the doorway between the laundry and the family rooms. This kept my puppy in neutral territory while still allowing him to see and somewhat interact with the family. From early morning until late at night, every half hour Andy was taken outside to relieve himself. This program was strictly enforced.

I spent the next four days with Andy either on the laundry room floor, getting newspaper print all over my bum, or sitting on the family room floor. I would press my face against the chicken wire as I watched TV across the room. Or I was outside trying to stay warm in my sweatshirt urging Andy to go to the bathroom. I still am not sure if the house breaking experts agreed with this strategy but I can bear personal witness that within four days Andy was completely housebroken.

When he was let out of the laundry into the family room, the only other room he was ever allowed in, Andy bounced about, his little tail vibrating back and forth. He jumped up to me, bounced over to my dad and jumped up to him, bounced over to Pammy, jumped up, bounced over to Mom, stopped, walked around her, then bounced back to me.

That pretty well sums up Andy and Mom's understanding with one another. Mom was the alpha. She made sure he was regularly fed, had fresh water and was kept clean. All the things I'd sincerely promised to do, but didn't always manage without reminders. In return, Andy stayed out of her way.

Mom never called Andy by his name. It was always, "Have you fed *the dog* yet? "Be sure you clean up everything *the dog* has left on the grass." "It's time for *the dog* to have a bath."

She made certain that *the dog* had the best care. In her research, Mom had read that puppies should have a bowl of whole milk every day. So each night Andy got his bowl of milk. However, one night we were out of milk. It was too late to go to the store, so Mom told me to,"Just give *the dog* powdered milk."

I hated the taste of powdered milk and said, "He'll hate it."

"One night won't hurt him."

So I mixed up the milk and poured it into Andy's bowl. As I carried it into the laundry room, Andy hopped in a circle around me, his little tail vibrating back and forth with a vengeance. His tail was still going when he stuck his nose into the frothy milk. Then the tail came to a complete stop. His pink tongue darted into the milk once, maybe twice. He looked up at me, took another taste, then raising his front paw, brought it down into the milk and began splashing the stuff out of his bowl. Mom was disgusted with the mess he had made. But I was delighted. Andy had just confirmed that I had one smart dog.

Andy was my best friend. Wherever I went in the neighborhood, Andy was with me. When I'd go to school, he'd sulked around until I came home, then he'd burst into an ecstatic welcome which I reciprocated. At night I'd sit on the floor so he could curl up in my lap as we watched TV together. Dad said Andy and I were a set, couldn't have one without the other.

When I reached adolescence things began changing. I still loved Andy, but there were distractions that took me away from home more often. For his part, Andy remained a loyal friend, always delighted when I returned home.

Then I went away to college. Mom wrote that Andy hardly ate the first couple of weeks. He'd wander about the yard and the areas of the house he was permitted in, looking for me. I missed him too. Being out on my own for the first time, I found myself wanting my best friend more than ever. But I knew it wasn't practical to have a dog with my college schedule.

Andy would nearly explode with excitement when I'd come home for vacations. We had a ritual. I'd pull up in the car, get out and call, "Andy!" He'd come running full speed straight out me. I'd kneel down, but just before reaching me, he'd run circles around me, spiraling in with each cycle until he was dancing about with my arms wrapped around him, my face buried in his curly fur.

My second summer home from school, Andy greeted me but not with the same energy. Mom told me his appetite seemed to be falling off, and he slept more. One day when I brushed him, he whimpered as if in pain. I made an appointment to take him to his veterinarian. Mom asked if she could go with us. The prognosis was not good. We were told that Andy's body was riddled with tumors. There wasn't anything that could be done except to keep him comfortable. We'd know when we'd have to bring him back.

I spent every spare moment I had with Andy. Much of our time was spent with me on the floor by his blanket so he could lay his head in my lap. Early one morning when I walked downstairs to check on him, I saw Mom with him. I stopped at the doorway and silently watched as she gently fluffed his blanket up around him, whispering gentle sayings just for him to hear.

Shortly after that morning, Andy yelped when I softly brushed my hand over his back, and we knew it was time.

I asked Mom to go the veterinarian's office with me. She drove as I held Andy's shrunken body on my lap. She was beside me as I carefully carried Andy, wrapped in his blanket, inside the office. The veterinarian was kind when he came out for Andy, giving us time to say our goodbyes and promising that he'd just go to sleep and leave the pain behind.

Neither of us spoke as we walked back to the car. Nor did we say anything when got into the car. For several minutes we sat in silence. Mom looked down at Andy's folded blanket which was on the seat between us. She ran her hand over it, smoothing the blanket out.

"Oh, Andy."   Then she cried.

Broad Chatter
That Would Make a Good Pet
a memory from Terry

My mom was a great lover of pets so we had quite a variety. Our menagerie included many of the usual ones: several dogs, although just one at a time, plus turtles, birds, and fish. But it was my older brother Bill who added to the variety.

Snakes were one of his favorites. He really liked to catch snakes. When he was only about ten, I remember him waking Dad up one Sunday morning by dangling a snake over his face. That was not received well and the snake didn't stay long. One time Bill cooked a garter snake over coals in a potato chip can and we ate it. When he was in high school he brought home a five foot long bull snake and released it on the kitchen floor. My mom didn't mind the cooked snake but that bull snake was another story.

Under the age of eleven, Bill often found snakes in a field near our house in Hillside, Illinois. I imagine the field had a lot of snakes because there was also a large population of thirteen striped ground squirrels. Bill made a live trap for the ground squirrels. He placed grain and raisins on the ground. Right over the food he would use a stick to prop up a cardboard box. Attached to the stick was a long string. Bill would lie in that field for hours, holding that string and waiting. When a ground squirrel went to the box to nibble on the grain, Bill would pull the string causing the stick to fly away and the box to come down over the squirrel. It worked - once. He proudly brought the little guy home and put him in a bird cage in the kitchen. Bill worked and worked with that squirrel until it would come out of the cage about a foot to get food and then would run back in. We loved that squirrel. However, mom had placed his cage on a stool right next to the furnace vent. In the late fall, when the furnace went on, the squirrel died of heat exposure. At least that is the story I was told.

Later after we had moved to Wheaton, Illinois, Bill brought home a baby crow that had fallen out of the nest. This was in the days when we thought if you touched a baby bird, the mother wouldn't accept it. So it had to come home or die. The crow was young enough that the mother was still feeding it which is what we had to do. We would feed it canned dog food by stuffing the food down its throat with our finger. This became my job when Bill left for summer camp soon after the crow came to live with us. It did well for about a month and then died. Bummer.

Bill sent away for flying squirrels one year. He got two of them and we named them Brett and Bart Maverick. They were difficult to train so they usually stayed in their cage in the basement. But one night, when Bill and Dad were both gone, the flying squirrels got out and somehow got upstairs. Mom and I chased them all around the living room. They would crawl to the top of the drapes and then take off and glide around the room. It took us two hours to catch them and return them to their cage. Another time they got out in the basement and Snitzie, our dachshund, caught one. She didn't kill it but it was crippled for several months before it died. We gave the remaining one to our pediatrician who kept in on an enclosed porch where it could glide to its heart's content.

 Through the years Bill also brought home a baby fox, gray squirrels, and raccoons. My mom made him release all of those. I brought home baby rabbits that we would nurse with doll bottles. They never lasted long. And I had a hamster for almost three years. They are nocturnal animals so it would run on its squeaky wheel all night long. I'd gob *Vaseline* on the wheel but it never was quiet for long. In order to sleep, I finally resorted to putting the hamster and cage in the bathtub with the bathroom door closed.

We also had a lot of dead animals. Bill took a correspondence taxidermy course. He started with small animals: squirrels, mice, shrews, and practiced stuffing them. Our basement always had an unusual, 'icky', dead smell. He made special little models to display this 'art'. He had a squirrel praying before a little bed and a shrew and mouse boxing in a boxing ring. The larger animals, rabbits, pheasant, and raccoon mostly, were just stuffed and either displayed in his room or in the basement. He also had a raccoon pelt and a fox pelt on his bed. I loved to pet them. When I was in junior high school, we went to *Bobby Rivers Dance Studio* every fortnight for social dance lessons. Mr. Rivers always had a Halloween party. In seventh grade, I dressed up like a cave woman. My mom made a shift dress out of burlap and sewed the fox skin to the front and the raccoon skin to the back. I had chicken wing bone earrings and a chicken thigh bone poking through a bun on the top of my head. I looked great and won first prize. I attribute it all to the realistic look I got with the dead animals from my brother's bedroom.

Looking back, I had very tolerant parents, especially my mom.

Broad Chatter
Penny
a memory from Sara

When I was born our family already owned the best dog in the world. Her name was Penny and she was a black cocker spaniel. My mother used to recall that when I was a toddler I often shared my food with Penny. She would sit next to my *Tailor Tot* patiently waiting for me to be generous. We have photos of me eating a piece of toast, then the next shot is me holding the piece of toast while Penny took a bite, and then me taking the next bite. She never begged, but she was always expectant.

I had a real baby buggy that I used to wheel around our neighborhood when I was small. Most often I put my doll babies in it, but occasionally I put Penny in it. I would tell her to jump in the buggy, which she did, and tie a bonnet on her head. I wheeled her everywhere and she never once jumped out of the buggy or pulled off the bonnet.

When we went to northern Wisconsin for vacation we would take Penny along. She loved being in the woods and at the lake. She was an excellent swimmer and I remember how her long hair and even longer ears would spread out around her like feathers. If she got tired she would simply swim up to me or my sister, put her front paws on our shoulders and rest for a while. Then off she would go again.

When Penny was 15 years old she suddenly developed tumors. The vet told my folks that she didn't have long to live and that they would know when she was suffering.

One Saturday Penny couldn't walk anymore and she was whimpering. Dad said we should tell her goodbye. My sister and I were inconsolable. In those days people did not take their pets to the vet to be euthanized. Dad sent us into the house while he got his gun. Mom held us and covered our ears, but we still heard the shot which sent us into even deeper grief and more intense sobbing.

Dad dropped the gun right where he shot it. He came back into the house and never said a word to us. He was also crying and he had burst a blood vessel in his face because of the stress of putting Penny out of her misery. He went straight to his bedroom and did not reappear for several hours. My mother had to call a neighbor man to come bury Penny and to clean the gun. Later Dad would recall that shooting Penny was one of the worst moments in his life and that the memory of it haunted him for a long time.

And Another Thing
Funerals in the Flower Beds
by Sara

When I was a child, animals were a very important part of my life. We had cats and dogs, but my older sister and I also tried to take care of numerous wild animals. These animals came into our lives in a variety of ways: we would rescue them from the jaws of our cats, we would catch them by the local creek or in the weeds next to our house, or we would find them injured in our neighborhood. It's sad to say that we were not very good caretakers. Most of them died untimely deaths.

I remember prying a vole from the jaws of my kitty. It wasn't hurt very badly, so we put it in a cardboard box with a towel and tried to nurse it back to health. We read in our *World Book Encyclopedia* that they ate insects and worms, which we immediately began to collect. What we didn't know was that a vole can eat more than its weight every day. So the few meager bugs and worms we gave it were not nearly enough to satisfy its appetite. It starved to death within two days.

We had a large picture window in our living room and often small birds would mistakenly fly into it and knock themselves unconscious. Several times, when we heard the thud of the little body on the window, we rushed outside to pick up the little dazed bird. Many times the bird would come back to reality in our hands and then fly away. One time however, the bird was only slightly injured, so we brought it inside. Again we put it in a box with a towel and tried to nurse it back to life. I remember my sister was holding it one night when the phone rang. She set the bird on the back of the wooden kitchen chair as she reached for the phone. She thought it would be able to perch there. The poor thing couldn't hold on. It wobbled forward and backward a few times and then fell flat on to the linoleum floor. This second concussion within 24 hours was its demise.

Whenever our nursing attempts failed we held a funeral. We would wrap the little corpse in *Kleenex*, put it in a small box, and take it out to Mother's flowerbed. We would dig a little hole, lay the box in it, sing some songs, say the *Lord's Prayer,* and then cry like our little hearts were going to break as we dropped the dirt back into the grave. Each animal got a name before it died and we always chose a pretty rock to mark its grave. There were so many of these graves that it must have been hard for Mother to miss them as she tended her flowers.

Our Pets

Terry and Snitzie

Snitzie

Andy

Lynn and Andy

Sara feeding Penny toast

Sara and a kitty

Do you know these famous pets?

ericcassee.tumblr.com

dizzyet.wordpress.com

geocaching.com

littleboysblog2.ru

dvdtalk.com

---

*Answers: Ellie May Clampett's critters, Roy Roger's horse Trigger, Tramp from My Three Sons, The Shaggy Dog, Mr. Ed

Television

We were the first generation to be raised with television. It affected everything we did, wore, and talked about. The Three Boomer Broads

I find television very educating. Every time somebody turns on the set, I go into the other room and read a book. Groucho Marx

Flickrpds209

Terry and Lynn have just walked into Sara's house for coffee and a chat. As they sit down, Lynn sees Sara's TV.

Lynn: Look at that television! I haven't seen such a small screen since I was a kid. That certainly brings back memories. We didn't have one that small but the screen was probably the same size— about as big as a handkerchief. Our first television sat in the corner of the living room and was a huge piece of furniture with two doors you could fold open. Inside was a tiny, round TV screen. We also had a piano in the room and whenever my mom would start to play, I'd run into the room and yell "Wait, wait, wait" and I'd open up 'the curtains'.

Sara: I remember the TVs with the big old doors.

Lynn: That's where the world was.

Terry: The world of *Captain Kangaroo* and *Mr. Green Jeans,* and Sherri Lewis with *Lamb Chop*. You know my nickname in college was Lamb Chop. I remember watching *Romper Room* with Miss Nancy. She would hold her magic mirror and she would see Jane and Jennifer and she would see Sally but she would never see Terry.

Terry's PawPaw and his TV

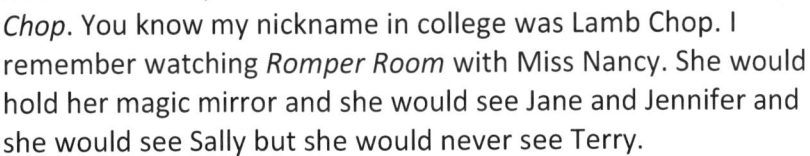

Sara: Or Sara.

Lynn: Or Lynn. We saw the world, but they didn't seem to see us.

Sara: Back then TV wasn't on all time. At midnight they would play the national anthem with a flag flying behind it and then it would go off the air for the night. That target thing, the test pattern, would come on and go 'eeeee'.

Sometimes we'd get up early on Saturday morning. We'd get our cereal and sit in front of the television, but that test pattern was still on 'eeee'.

Lynn: We were the first ones to sit there with a blank stare.

Terry: And we still do.

Sara: We didn't just watch cartoons. There were a lot of half hour series, *Sky King* and his daughter Penny…

Lynn: *Rin Tin Tin* with Rusty. Oh, and *Lassie*. Lassie was so smart, smarter than a lot of the people. There were not very many smart people on that show.

Terry: There were mean people on it, too. It was like they had a sign that said "Mean people come here". I would have sold that farm.

Sara: There were a lot of those half hour series.

Lynn: Well, there really weren't all that many cartoons. There was *Mickey Mouse, Popeye, Casper the Friendly Ghost*. Oh! And *Mighty Mouse*….

All *(sing)*: *Here I come to save the day. That means that Might Mouse is on his way!*

Terry: *If there is a wrong to right…*

Lynn: I think we've got it. You can stop now.

Sara: There were things the family watched all together. Every Saturday night I got my hair set for church watching *Bonanza*.

Lynn: *The Twilight Zone*. I'd sit on the other side of the room and sort of watch, not watch.

Sara: I watched it from my big sister's lap, where I was safe. I remember one episode that was my favorite. It was about a hen-pecked guy that just wanted to read. Then this atomic bomb came. Oh, I loved that one. I think it was called *Time Enough at Last*. I can't remember the name of the actor. But he was famous.

Terry: They always had really good actors on that like. Oh, it was Burgess Meredith.

Sara: Good Job remembering that name, Terry!
Terry: Wasn't he the same guy who did *My Favorite Martian*?
Sara: No, that was Ray Walston.
Terry: Huh, never heard of him. We also watched that, bubble, bubble, bubble thing. You know the champagne bubble guy.
Lynn: Lawrence Welk. When he came on my grandmother didn't look left or right. The world would stop for her as soon as Lawrence Welk walked on to that stage. I liked to watch Bobby dance.
Terry: Little Janet. I liked the Lennon Sisters. I didn't like the Irish tenor guy.
Lynn: He just died.
Terry: You know that really doesn't bother me.
Lynn: My mom would set her day's schedule with what was on TV. She'd have the breakfast dishes done by a certain program and the house straightened by the time the Loretta Young glided in with her grand entrance. Did she glide or sweep?
Terry: Same thing, right? She had those double doors. Nobody had them but her. And then she would twirl around. And she had on a different dress every time!
Lynn: She had the tiniest waist, too. But the best time to watch TV was Saturday morning. I would paddle into the living room and turn on the TV. My older brother Steve would come out of his bedroom and turn it down so low that I had to sit right next to it as I ate my cereal. It took me a few years to figure out that I could turn it back up myself.
Terry: Not really very smart in California, were you? But at least you could eat in front of the TV. We had to eat in the kitchen.
Sara: We could take our cereal in there on Saturday morning.

Terry's Aunt Imy

Lynn: We had those flimsy TV trays. We thought they were great.

Terry: We had those too but we didn't get to use them for breakfast.
Sara: We played outside a lot but there was one thing on TV that could bring me in. It was Captain Bob calling, "What time is it kids?"
All: (sing) *It's Howdy Doody Time. It's Howdy Doody Time.*
Terry: Did you know that Howdy Doody had 48 freckles, one for every state in the Union? Of course that was before Alaska and Hawaii were states. I don't know what they did then.

fiftiesweb.com

Lynn: You are just a little walking Wikipedia!
Terry: I'll have to look that freckle thing up.
Sara: Did your mom watch *Queen for a Day*?
Lynn and Terry: Oh yes!
Lynn: The producers would fill the theater with these poor women with hardship stories. And they'd sob out their stories and then they'd announce, "And the queen for today is..."
Terry: And the spotlight would go around until it landed on this little woman in a dowdy house dress.
Sara: They'd put a crown on her and she'd cry. And they'd say, "We're going to give you a brand new washer and dryer!"
Terry: Oh yeah, like that would fix everything in her life. Those poor women. I liked the *$64,000 Question*. At least the contestants didn't wear house dresses. And I liked the one where that duck came down...*You Bet Your Life*.
Lynn: Groucho Marx. I didn't get his jokes they were nonsensical to me.
Terry: I did. They made perfect sense to me. Then there was *Name That Tune* where they had to hit that rope.
Sara: My favorite game show was *Beat the Clock* because the whole family got to play and often they would get real messy.

en.wikipedia.org

Lynn: And there were shows that our mothers watched all the time, the soap operas.

Terry: My grandma watched *Edge of Night*, *Guiding Light*, and *As the World Turns*. Initially when she watched them they were only 15 minutes long, then they switched to half hour and now they go on forever. But my mom never watched soap operas.

Lynn: Mom would watch them when she was ironing. So she'd watch them about once a week and catch up on the stories and that was about it. I think she watched *General Hospital*.

Terry: My mom watched *Art Linkletter*. Do you remember when they had the little kids on that show? It was called *Kids Say the Darndest Things*.

Sara: He was so good with children. He really got a lot out of them.

Lynn: I dreamed about being on that show. I'd think of all the wise things I was going to say when he asked them, "What would you do with $100?" I was basically going to buy all the land and just make sure everyone had a home.

Sara: Oh, you're so benevolent.

Terry: I remember *The Millionaire*. What was that's guy's name – the millionaire? He'd come knock at your door and give away a million dollars. He was a really rich man.

Sara: Actually it was the rich guy's valet who would knock on the doors.

en.wikipedia.org

Terry: Yeah, he was a chubby guy. They would pull up in the limousine. And a million dollars back then was a huge fortune.

Lynn: Well, it's not anything to sneeze at now.

Terry: Money became a huge hit on TV, like the game show *$64,000 Question*.

Sara: Isn't that the one with the scandal? Where somebody was given the answers?

Terry: Yes. But Joyce Brothers was on it one time. And the word *antidisestablishmententarianism* came up and someone had to

spell that.
Sara: Oh my gosh!
Terry: The way the show went you got to pick your main topic, so Joyce Brothers picked wrestling because it had a finite amount of information; other topics would have been so broad. That way she could learn everything there was to know about wrestling.
Lynn: That was smart.
Terry: Well, she was smart. Smart enough to get $64,000 which was a huge amount in the 50s.
Sara: I would take $64,000 right now.
Lynn: Did you like *Father Knows Best*?
Sara: I liked all those family shows, *Donna Reed, Leave it to Beaver, Andy Griffith*. And then there was *Gunsmoke* with Kitty and Matt. I loved them.

en.wikipedia.org

Lynn: I remember the original *Gunsmoke* started with a shot behind Matt, kind of between his legs and he'd shoot the other guy and you'd see him drop. And then after a while the show started with him riding a horse. The reason they changed it was because of the violence. We were starting that politically correct awareness. But then the violence got much worse.
Sara: I waited all my childhood for Kitty and Matt to kiss, but they never did.
Terry: That's because she was a prostitute.
Sara and Lynn: No, she wasn't!
Terry: Oh come on, those low cut dresses, that mole, hanging out in taverns...prostie. And prostitutes don't kiss. I learned that on *Pretty Woman*.
Lynn: Now that's a source! What about *Leave it to Beaver*?
Sara: June and Ward and Wally and the Beav.
Lynn: And that really obnoxious friend.....
Terry: Eddie. He became a cop. He got shot and everything!
Sara: Well, I don't know about that. There was that rumor about Beaver that he went to Viet Nam and was killed, but that wasn't

true.
Terry: But the cop thing is true. I know; I read it. I wrote it down and then I read it.
Lynn: (ignoring Terry) *77 Sunset Strip*!
All: *Kookie, Kookie lend me your comb.*
Sara: And *I Dream of Jeannie*.
Terry: They wouldn't let her show her belly button. Holy smokes, look what they're showing now!
Lynn: Oh, remember that one show …"to the moon Alice, to the moon".
Sara: *The Honeymooners*.
Terry: You only saw that little tiny room with the sink and the table. She didn't work. They couldn't have had much money. What did she do all day?
Sara: There certainly wasn't much to clean.
Terry: There wasn't much to clean and it didn't look like she was putting on big huge dinners for him either. Like I said, what did poor Alice do all day long?
Lynn: I guess she was cleaning up Ralph's messes.
Terry: But she was the clever one.
Lynn: Like with *Father Knows Best*. Sometimes that show puzzled me. I asked my mom why they call it *Father Knows Best* when the mother came up with the answers. Mom would say, "The father knew best to let the mom solve the problem."
Terry: On the *Honeymooners* they would go into the other room, I'm assuming it was the bedroom, but you never saw their bedroom at all.
Sara: Well, even when we saw a bedroom nobody slept in the same bed.
Lynn: Like *The Dick Van Dyke Show*…Laura and Rob slept in twin beds.

tvtropes.

Terry: Lucy and Ricky…they had twin beds and they were married in real life.

Sara: Then came the really fun shows like the *Beverly Hillbillies*
Terry: I can sing all the words to the Beverly Hillbillies:
Come and listen to a story 'bout a man named Jed.
A poor mountaineer barely kept his family fed.
And then one day he was shootin' at some food,
And up through the ground came a bubblin' crude.
Oil that is, black gold, Texas tea...
Lynn: (interrupting) My sister liked the song to *Rawhide*.
All: (stumbling) Ride 'em up, rope 'em up, do something to them...rawhide!
Lynn: Of course my sister watched it because of Clint Eastwood.
Sara: Rowdy Yates. He was so handsome and so young.
Lynn: Oh yeah, so she'd watch the whole show and then we'd have to sit and watch the closing credits so she could listen to the song. I would be dying because on the other channel the

pinterist.com

Flintstones would be starting and I wanted to hear their song.
All: *Flintstones, meet the Flintstones, They're the modern stone age family...*
Terry: We had all of those TV songs. Today they don't have theme songs so the commercials can be longer– that's what I read anyway. So if they do a theme song with words, it's too long. Our ads were only a minute at the hour and half hour and only 30 seconds at the middle of the show. Think about it, if you were going to get something from the refrigerator during commercials you had to book it. Now it's, "Oh, a commercial, I have time for a shower."
Sara: I liked the *Flintstones* characters, the elephant that was a shower or the bird that was a record player and would say, "It's a living."
Terry: I loved *Bewitched*. (she twitches her nose)
Sara: We all tried that little move with our noses.

Terry: But I liked the first Darrel better.
Sara: Darrin.
Lynn: Yeah, the second one just seemed mad all the time.
Terry: What was the *Dobie Gillis* song? You know, with Manfred Man.
Lynn: You rang?
Sara: Maynard G. Krebs, not Manfred Man. He always said, "Work?" And there was a girl named Wanda.
Lynn: Mom and Dad watched the *Defenders* and the *FBI*.
Terry: I don't remember those.
Lynn: With Ephraim Zimbalist Jr.
Sara: He was originally on *77 Sunset Strip*.
Lynn: Yes, but I'm pretty sure he was on the *FBI* – I'll have to look that up. And then the *Defenders*...
Terry: The *Avengers*?
Lynn: No, the *Defenders* were lawyers. But then there were the *Avengers*, which my mom never got.
Sara: I loved them. I thought they were so cool. I wanted to grow up to be Mrs. Peel. And *The Man From UNCLE*?
Lynn: Mom didn't like that one either.
Terry: My mom liked anything with murders in it.
Sara: *Perry Mason.*
Terry: The bad guys always came clean at the end.
Lynn: Right at the last second.
Sara: That's because Perry was so good. He would make them so nervous they just had to break.

Perrymasontvseries.com

Lynn: Yes, they always confessed.
Sara: Della Street
Lynn: I was always waiting for the romance between her and Perry. Do you remember when you'd turn on the TV and then you would hear the BOOF. And our picture always was rolling.
Terry: We were always adjusting the horizontal hold. Where is that button now?
Sara: They don't have them anymore, dear. Everything is digital.

Lynn: It seems like we could nail it every time with the bar right in the middle of the screen. Feet on the top and heads on the bottom.
Sara: Then we got color TV. The first color show that I remember was the *Wonderful World of Disney*.
Terry: I remember when we got our first color television. Of course we only had one TV and so when we got the color television we were so excited. But it had to sit for twelve hours before it could be turned on. You couldn't just plug it in and watch. It must have had to get acclimated to the temperature in the house. And so here we are, "YES, YES, we got color TV!" But not until tomorrow morning.
Lynn: What a bummer.
Terry: It was dreadful.
Lynn: And who did the adjusting?
Sara: Well, Dad if he was there.
Terry: Oh really? We were told, "Go fix that".
Lynn: It was my dad or my oldest brother, and then it would go down to mom.
Terry: I don't think my mother ever fixed it; my dad would say to us, "Get up and get that". My grandpa would yell, "Down in front!" For the most part he only watched Saturday night wrestling. He'd also yell, "You make a better door than a window."
Terry: My grandma didn't have an outside antenna, only rabbit ears with terrible reception, so when *Bonanza* would come on you'd have to stand to one side holding the antenna and watch the entire program bent over.
Lynn: Now that's dedication.
Sara: Or sad. And remember the TV repairman who would come to the house?
Lynn: He'd have the big box and he'd open it up and he'd have all these tubes, little ones and the great big one.

tgldirect.com

Sara: The picture tube. Sometimes if a small tube broke my dad would take it out, put it in his pocket, and go to the hardware store where they had this board where you could test your tubes.
Terry: Test your tubes? Our next door neighbor, Tommy's dad, was a TV repairman. Then he got TB and had to go to a sanitarium and I thought that was what happened to every television repairman. Why would they want a job like that?
Lynn: I'd want to sit close to the TV but mom would say, 'Don't sit close, it hurts your eyes."
Sara: I recall watching Jack La Laine and doing exercises.
Lynn: Oh yeah, right. He had the chair and the dog.
Terry: And what was that exercise woman's name? The guys all watched her. What was her name?
Lynn: She filled out the leotard a little differently.
Sara: Miss America contests!
Terry: That was a big night. Everybody would sit around and watch.
Sara: You'd root for your state.
All: (sing) *Here she comes, Miss America..*
Lynn: Bert Parks
Terry: (sings) *Here she comes, your ideal.*
Lynn: (sings) *and here we sit, aging well...*(laughter)
Sara: There was no controversy about bathing suit contests or anything.
Terry: Debbie Drake!
Sara: What?
Terry: The exercise lady!
Lynn: You're right. How do we remember that stuff? Well, back to *Miss America*. Their suits were one piece suits, fairly modest. And then their little talents were pretty iffy for some of them.

googleimages.com

Terry: I don't think there's been any Miss America that brought about world peace, but that's what they always wanted.

Sara: That's what they always said anyway. And all of that, for the most part was still in black & white. When I think back on it we didn't really see what color their evening gowns were. They were just fancy, lots of tulle, netting over everything.
Terry: While all that is great, I still preferred *Yogi Bear and Boo Boo*.
Sara: *Heckle & Jeckle*
Lynn: *Cecil and Beany Boy*
Terry: Who?
Lynn: "I'm a-comin' Beany Boy!" You don't remember? Was that after your time? How old are you anyway?
Terry: Four foot ten and one half, Lynn.
Sara: Boris and Natasha,
Terry: *Fred Flintstone* and *Barnie*,
Sara: *Quick Draw McGraw* and *Bobaloo*,
Terry: And there was the *Mickey Mouse Club*.
Lynn: M-I-C-
Sara: See you real soon
Lynn: K-E-Y-
Sara: Why? Because we like you.
Lynn and Sara: M-O-U-S-E...
Terry: Hey, that's Mickey Mouse, isn't it?
Sara: Annette and the Mouseketeers dancing....
Terry: Cubby & Cheryl,
Sara: Spin & Marty.
All: "Meanwhile, back at the ranch."
Lynn: And the good guys always wore white hats. It was all so innocent – now kids can watch 99 channels.

en.wikipedia.org

Terry: And 69 are not good for them. I learned how to spell Encyclopedia from Mickey Mouse. (Terry sings entire encyclopedia song)
Lynn: Let's play that game we played before.
Terry: *Twister*?

Lynn: No the theme songs one, where we guess the name of the show.
Terry: I think *Twister* will work even though we don't have a board or a spinner. I'll just call out the colors. It'll be great.
Sara: (ignoring Terry) Okay, I've got one.
A horse is a horse, of course, of course,
And no one can talk to a horse, of course
That is, of course, unless the horse is the famous ....
Lynn: *Mr. Ed*!! How about this one:
Just sit ...
Terry: On a stool
Lynn: *right back...*
Terry: You naughty little girl.
Lynn: *and you'll hear a tale...*
Terry: A pig's tale
Sara: *A tale of a fateful trip.*
Gilligan's Island!
Terry: My turn.
Green acres is the
Lynn and Sara: *Green Acres*!
Terry: Gosh, you guys are good.
Sara: How about:
Paladin, Paladin, where do you roam?
Paladin, Paladin, far, far from home.
Lynn: *Have Gun Will Travel.*
Terry: And the helper guy was Hey Boy. I gave my hamster his middle name after Hey Boy even though he wasn't Asian.
Sara: What was your hamster's full name?
Terry: Biddy Buddy Watt Hey Boy. I got him in Southern Illinois when I was visiting my grandmother. When it was time to go home, my dad said that little cage wouldn't fit in the passenger part so Biddy had to ride in the trunk....for six hours. When we opened the trunk, he was flat. I blew into him and he came back to life and lived three more years.

en.wikipedia.org

Lynn: You had to ask. And anyway that is his last name.
Sara: I knew there would be a story.
Lynn: Try this one: *Here's the story...*
Terry: *That girl*
Sara: *Of a lovely lady...*
Terry: *That girl!*
Lynn: *Who was bringing up three very lovely girls*
Terry: Those girls?
Lynn: No, *Brady Bunch*!
Terry: My turn
They call him Flipper, Flipper....
Lynn and Sara: *Flipper*
Terry: Boy, you guys are quick.
Sara: It's because you're saying the name of the show right at the beginning.
Terry: Okay, try this one: Bang, Bang! (blows smoke off finger)
Lynn: What?
Terry: Gotcha. *Gunsmoke*!
Sara: That's not the theme song.
Terry: It's my theme song.
Lynn: I still think *Rawhide* was my favorite. (sings)
Rollin' Rollin' Rollin' Keep them doggies movin', movin', movin', Roll'm up, roll'm over, roll'm in, roll'm out. Rawhide!
Terry: I have got to goolie the words for her.
Sara: You mean Google right? Yeah we loved our Westerns! So many of the shows had singing cowboys – Gene Autry, Roy Rogers....
Terry: Didn't Bret Maverick sing?
Sara: On that note I think it is time for another cup of coffee.

Broad Chatter
Twilight Zone
Three Memories

Sara: I remember watching the *Twilight Zone* from the safety of my older sister's lap. Just hearing the opening music and Rod Serling's voice could send shivers down my spine. Sometimes, if it got too scary, I would put my hands over my eyes and just peek through my fingers. But I wouldn't have missed those shows for anything! One of my favorite episodes is called "Time Enough At Last". It's about this little hen-pecked guy, with very thick glasses. The one thing he loves to do in life is to read. But his nasty wife always nags him and tells him it is a waste of time. Well, one day he is in the vault at the bank where he works when the whole world is destroyed. He alone survives because of the vault and when he climbs out through the rubble he finds the marble steps to the library. He begins to gather all the books he can find. He is so happy that now he has 'time enough at last' to read anything he wants. He sits down, reaches for the first book, and his glasses fall off, breaking when they hit the step. For a little girl who loved to read this seemed to be a horrible fate. The show had tapped my emerging empathy and that image has stayed with me all my life.

Terry: My favorite *Twilight Zone* episode? That's like choosing from a box of assorted chocolates-- each one is good. Well, except for the ones with the icky maple cream filling. There were so many great *Twilight Zones*: the guy on the far away planet with the beautiful robot lady, the one where Cliff Robertson was a ventriloquist but it turned out the dummy was the real guy and Robertson was the puppet, the one where the couple kept pulling the fortune teller machine and couldn't leave town, the one where enemy soldiers, Elizabeth Montgomery and Charles Bronson, were the only people left after huge war, *The Monsters Are Due on Maple Street*, *The Eye of the Beholder*…. I could go on and on (I love *Twilight Zone!*) but I'm going to narrow it down to two.

My favorite *Twilight Zone* is *The Invaders*. A woman (played by Agnes Morehead) lives alone in a small, isolated cabin. As she is fixing her dinner on a wood stove, she hears a crash in her attic and finds a tiny spaceship and two small space invaders who she battles. There is no talking in the entire show, just the woman fighting aliens. Finally in the end, after she has killed the invaders, the viewers get a closer look at the tiny ship and surprise! USA is written on the side! Morehead is wonderful in this episode. I usually think of her playing glamorous characters like the mother witch on *Bewitched*. But in this show she has straggly hair, a dirty face, and old brown clothes. The viewer is rooting for the woman the whole show until the final scene. This type of ending is what made *Twilight Zone* so exciting. Another favorite was *To Serve Man*. This time the aliens come to earth. They have a book, their personal manifesto, called *To Serve Man* which one of the humans began to try to translate. While on earth the aliens use their powers to cure diseases, end wars, and make life on earth almost perfect. Humans begin to trust the aliens so, when they were invited to travel to the aliens' planet, many happily sign on. Just as the main character is boarding, the woman doing the translating rushes to the boarding area and yells, "It is a cookbook!" See, another great surprise ending.

Probably my biggest *Twilight Zone* surprise ending, however, didn't come from Rod Serling. We had been watching *The Dummy* (the Cliff Robertson episode) and when it was over, it was off to bed for me. As I lay in bed, thinking of that dummy, my covers moved just a tiny bit. Odd. Several minutes went by and then there was a tug on my covers again. I tried to convince myself that I was just imagining this when they were tugged again. I freaked! My mom came rushing into my room and told me I was imagining it. So I calmed down and was almost asleep when it happened again. I jumped out of bed, screaming. This time my mom pushed my bed away from the wall to prove to me that nothing was there, and there we found my older brother Bill squished between the wall and the bed with a cruel, 'dummy' look on his face. His own *Twilight Zone* surprise ending.

Lynn: For me the all-time benchmark episode of the *Twilight Zone* is called *The Monsters are Due on Maple Street.* Maple Street was the classic middle class American Dream neighborhood, lined with trees and two storied houses. It is a Saturday afternoon, and the neighbors are out mowing their lawns, working on their cars, kids playing baseball, and buying ice cream from the ice cream man. All is peaceful until a light streaks through the sky and seems to land in a nearby area. At first the neighbors thought it might be a meteorite, but there isn't an explosion, so they are confused. Then things begin to happen. The electricity goes out, cars won't start, phones don't work, and there is no water. One of the neighborhood boys talks about the stories he read in comic books. Stories about aliens who sent people to earth who looked just like regular human families but they weren't human, and he said that the light was a spaceship. This scares the neighbors and they begin to accuse one another of being aliens. Sometimes a car would start on its own, or lights in one house would turn on then off which makes the neighbors suspicious, until they completely turn on each other, killing one another. The camera then travels up to some aliens on the hillside talking about all they have to do is stop a few of the humans' machines, turn on and off some lights and power, and let the humans do the rest.

"They pick the most dangerous enemy they can find, and it's themselves," explains one of the aliens. "All we do is just sit back and watch. This world is full of Maple Streets."

The aliens scared me as a kid. Now the story scares me with how fear and prejudice can cause people to do inhuman things to one another.

Cigarettes and Other Dangers

Things I've learned: never lick a steak knife, you really do not need a parachute to skydive unless you plan to parachute twice, and never take a sleeping pill and a laxative on the same night. I'm sure there are more but I just can't think of any right now.

Flickr Fugue

The three women are at Sara's cabin in Northern Wisconsin, sitting around a low table piled with very old magazines.

Lynn: Look at the articles in these magazines; the Cuban Missile Crisis, Bay of Pigs, demonstrations. And the ads! Boy, we were exposed to a lot of dangerous things in the 50s and 60s.
Sara: Cigarettes were a big one. Everyone smoked, at least it seemed that way.
Terry: My parents both smoked and I started when I was 16 or 17. That was when my friend Bobbi called me a slut.
Lynn and Sara: Whoa!
Terry: She wrote it in her diary because I had started smoking. Then our friend Ginny started smoking so Bobbi wrote in her diary that Ginny and I were both sluts. But that was so wrong. Everyone knew Ginny wasn't a slut.
Sara: Did your parents know you were smoking?
Terry: Not for a long time. My folks both smoked so they never knew when I did, because they couldn't smell it on me. And Bobbi finally did smoke and it took her ten years after I stopped for her to quit.
Sara: Some of us had a harder time than others. I always said I was born to smoke. I took to it like nobody's

business. I was twelve years old and sat under an old semi truck with Janet, an older girl, and she gave me a cigarette and I said, "Yeah, I like this." I was hooked from the get-go.

Terry: Isn't it interesting that we had no sex in the early movies but everybody smoked. It was everywhere.

Lynn: We even had the candy cigarettes.

Terry: And ads with Santa Claus smoking.

Lynn: "4 out of 5 doctors recommend..."

Sara: At the beginning of the old *Twilight Zone* shows, Rod Serling smoked. People smoked on the TV shows, the *Tonight Show*, even some news shows. Almost all the grownups I knew smoked.

Flickr farm7.static

Lynn: Dad smoked when I was younger, then gave it up. We had a lot of friends from our church and they didn't smoke either. But some of our neighbors did, and also the people Dad worked with. I remember teachers smoking in the break room. I could smell it on them. All the movies and TV made smoking look so sophisticated.

Terry: It was glamorous and worldly. My mom smoked while she ironed and did housework; she had her cold coffee, no microwave to heat it up, and a cigarette going all day long.

Lynn: I do remember my dad smoking because it took him a long time to quit. So I could smell cigarette smoke a mile away. One teacher would get right up in my face and sniff; she could smell my dad's smoke. But in the movies, the smoke kind of gave this neat effect.

Sara: I always think of smoking when I think of old movies. Humphrey Bogart would be smoking a cigarette and talking romantically to Lauren Bacall, just inches from her face, and then he'd lean in to kiss her....
Lynn and Terry: Whoa!
Sara: You kind of expected her to cough or wipe her mouth or something. Everybody smoked and it was very chic to do it. Of course, Bacall had been smoking too and with women it was the longer the cigarette the better. Sexy?
Terry: I'm with Lynn. It wasn't just being sexy, smoking was sophisticated. That's what our media was showing us. We didn't have sexy clothing to buy as girls but we could get those cigarettes.

Flickr pds209

Sara: It was part of the message of being grown up. That's what grownups did and that's what we bought in to.
Lynn: I was being deprogrammed on that. "This is not something 'we' do."
Sara: My dad smoked cigarettes when I was really young and then he went to cigars, then a pipe, then chew. I'm not surprised tobacco was an issue for me.
Lynn: I remember we would go to the beach and my dad would come up out of the water and he'd plop down on the towel and say, "Right now a cigarette would taste so good! But no..." He wouldn't do it, but there was always that urge. All our neighbors smoked, we just didn't think too much about it. Lighters and ashtrays were often

Flickr Cheryl

gifts.

Terry: I read that in the 50s ashtrays were the number one gift for weddings.

Lynn: Someone gave us an ashtray once but I thought it was a coaster and used it that way.

Terry: We were shut up in cars with cigarette smoke, shut in houses with it, airplanes, restaurants, everywhere and nobody thought anything about it. I even smoked at *Radio City Music Hall* in New York. All the seats had ashtrays set in the back of them.

Sara: Cigarettes used to have coupons and people would buy stuff with them. *Old Gold* had them, *Marlboro* and *Winston* had merchandise.

Terry: There was a lot of advertising for cigarettes. I saw a poster once with Ronald Reagan, the actor, advertising cigarettes. Little did we know then what he would one day become!

Lynn: There were also ads with doctors saying which cigarettes were the best for you.

Terry: And the jingles! "Call for *Phillip Morris*!" "*Winston* tastes good like a cigarette should." Not only was it advertising cigarettes but it was also pushing bad grammar!

Sara: Always the teacher, aren't you?

Lynn: I liked the *Marlboro* man. He was rugged, tough, and hot!

Terry: So you liked him better than *Joe the Camel*? Remember, "I'd walk a mile for a *Camel*!"

Sara: Smoking wasn't the only dangerous thing we did in the 60s. Drugs really came into the

Flickr Fugue

culture then.
Lynn: Yeah, everybody started talking about and doing drugs during the 60s. Peyote, LSD, *Metamucil*....
Terry: Oh funny, Lynn said the wrong word. You mean mexilitamin?
Sara: I think you both mean mescaline. But all of those were illegal, except the *Metamucil*.
Lynn: But there were also the legal prescription drugs, diet pills and pep pills.
Terry: My mom took pep pills for two days and then didn't sleep for four days. Boy, did we have a clean house.
Sara: Grace Slick wrote that song *Go Ask Alice* about a girl stealing her mom's prescription drugs. And the book *Valley of the Dolls* was about that too.
Lynn: But by the end of the decade...
Terry: 1969
Lynn: Smoking pot was so common place. I'd walk down the hall in my junior high and could smell it in the bathroom.
Terry: Wacky Tabacky
Sara: Weed
Terry: Mary Jane
Sara: Acapulco Gold
Lynn: I heard those words.
Terry: We used to be hip.
Sara: We used to be cool.
Lynn: We used to be young.
Terry: That's true but there are things that I'm glad we left behind.
Sara: She's right. The mosquito fogger and DDT!

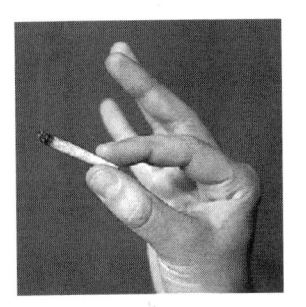

www.nola.com

1950sunlimited

Lynn: What are you talking about?
Terry: Oh, I forgot, you lived in California. I suppose you didn't have mosquitoes in California. But we did!
Sara: And one way we got rid of them was the mosquito fogger truck.
Terry: It would come at dusk and spray out this fog of chemicals. Maybe DDT? I don't know, but we'd ride our bikes back and forth through the fog.
Sara: Can you imagine what that was doing to our brains?
Terry: I know, but I loved it!
Lynn: That explains a few things.
Terry: One time Mary, the girl across the street, put her hamster in the yard to air it out but then forgot about it. That evening the fogger truck came by and the hamster died.
Lynn: We didn't have hamster killing foggers in California but there were other dangers. What about the whole cold war thing? I think it all started with Sputnik. Did you stand out in your yard and look for the satellite in the sky?
Sara: Of course. I loved the idea of a satellite but the cold war brought lots of scares. Like the bomb shelters. Bomb shelters were always on *Twilight Zone*.
Lynn: A neighbor a few houses down from us had a bomb shelter in their back yard. It was this little domed building. It

Flickr pds209

seemed weird at first but after a while it was just part of the neighborhood.
Sara: We had air raid drills at school as often as we had

tornado drills. And they showed those Civil Defense films about living underground.

Lynn: Yeah, there was always this unseen sinister threat, but I was never quite sure of what. I only knew that if I got under my desk, I'd be safe. A nuclear bomb might drop right on top of us, but our desks would protect us.

Sara: I had this picture in my mind of a bomb coming down from the sky, like one of those cartoon bombs, and it would explode and I wouldn't be able to get home to my mom and dad.

Terry: Pretty scary for little kids. Guess they didn't really explain the whole thing to us or maybe we just weren't very smart. In 1969.

Broad Chatter
The Red Threat
three memories

Lynn: Air raid drills were serious. At least that's what my 4th grade teacher, Miss Merriweather, conveyed. She told us to put away our history books because our principal, Mr. Newman, was going to come in and talk to us about something very important. I wondered who was in trouble this time and hoped it wasn't me. I never got into trouble. I was one of those kids who made the naughty kids sick.

Mr. Newman's speech was short and to the point. He told us about the Soviets and their bombs and how we needed to be prepared. I remember thinking that the stuff those Soviets tried to do to us wouldn't work even if they decided to drop their dumb bomb on us. We knew what to do.

We listened for Miss Merriweather to give the signal. "Under your desks," she called in her soft Alabama drawl which sounded almost musical to my Californian ears. I rolled off my chair, dropped onto my knees, and scooted under my desk. The underside of the desk was shaped like a fat belly; its round middle bumped my shoulder and head. But this wasn't a time for comfort. The instructions were to squeeze every part of my nine year old body under that desk. So I tucked myself into the tightest ball possible.

It's interesting how different the world looks when you are under something that you've spent months sitting over. The drab bandage color of the metal casing and legs of the desk created a tiny universe filled with dusty wonders. There was the desk leg with the worn spot that I constantly kicked and worried with my hard soled shoe. This was something Miss Merriweather was always reminding me not to do. Small pieces of confetti-like paper littered the floor, having filtered down from above when I carefully tore my papers along folded edges. There was a fine dust around the edges of the desk's metal frame, and transparent tendrils of dust dangled above me.

Hey, there was my yellow crayon that I'd been looking for last week when I was coloring my paper Easter basket. It must have rolled under the desk's brace when I unknowingly dropped it. I worked my fingers under the brace until I was able to prod the crayon from its hiding space. I was tempted to reach my hand up and around the desk's fat belly, carefully lift up my desk top, and drop the crayon inside so I'd have it the next time I needed the color yellow. But then I remembered that everything above the desk could disintegrate in the bomb's intense heat. I had to keep all parts of me and my crayon under the desk to be safe.

Miss Merriweather called out, "All clear," and we clamored out from our caves and resumed our seats. Miss Merriweather and Mr. Newman praised us, reminding us how important it was to get under our desks as soon as we heard the signal. Their solemn expressions and serious words worked their way into me. I looked down at my hand and unfolded my fingers from around the yellow, stubby crayon and imagined it as a pool of dripping, yellow wax. That's when I became scared.

Sara: When I was a child we regularly had air raid drills in school. The alarm would sound (the same siren as for a tornado drill) and we would file, in an orderly fashion, into the hallway which ran the length of the one story building. We would sit with our backs against the wall, our knees bent, put our hands over our head, and finally put our heads between our knees. We sat quietly this way until our teachers told us it was safe to get up and return to our classrooms.

We watched Civil Defense films in school as well. They usually started with a picture of an exploding atomic bomb and then a stern voice would tell us how to survive the fallout. The best way, of course, was to retreat to a home-built fallout shelter. This was often portrayed as a tiny cement bunker filled with shelves of food and water and a few cots for sleeping. The food was all in cans as was the water. Sometimes we saw families playing checkers and looking content in the shelter while they listened to the news from the surface via the radio. I recall the men in our neighborhood meeting several times to discuss building such shelters. In the end none of them did and I believe my father was of the opinion that surviving the holocaust would be worthless.

My personal vision of all this was that someday the Russians would send a bomb that would land in the school playground. This bomb, in my child's mind, looked like the bombs we saw on TV cartoons. My greatest fear was that I would not be able to get back to my home and my family, and that all my skin would burn off. It was a terrifying vision that left me on edge all of my childhood. Whether we were bombed or not, we all lived with that dark fear of the total destruction of our world. When I drew pictures of it, I always used my black and red crayons.

Terry: Geese. I was petrified of geese during the Cold War times. Just geese. Oh, I'd seen the TV show about the atomic bomb turning everything first into a skeleton and then dust. But I'd watch the sky for geese. I'd seen films at school instructing us to get under our desks and cup our hands over our necks. But every day as I walked to school I'd listen for that telltale, frightening honking sound. I practiced, along with my classmates, getting under my desk just as the films had shown us. But I'd flinch every time I saw a bird.

Geese, you say. What was scary about geese? Mary, the girl across the street, is the one who told me about the geese. Mary was a year younger than I was but she was wise beyond her years. We played together, fought with each other (She once bit me right through my jeans and you could count the teeth marks. And my mother didn't say anything to her mom!) and, of course, talked a lot—we were girls. When I didn't have a boy to play with, Mary was my go-to pal.

One day on the way to school, Mary told me that her dad said the government was constantly checking the radar for atomic bombs coming from the USSR. That was comforting until she said that on the radar, flocks of geese looked just like planes carrying bombs. And, she continued, if the government thought the USSR was sending bombs to us, then the US would send bombs to them. The Third World War would start and everything would be destroyed. It could all happen because of a silly flock of geese!

So I watched for geese. I listened for geese. I was afraid of geese. I spent a good part of my childhood worrying about geese. Atomic bombs, not so much. For me it was geese.

Not Always Like Donna Reed
an original story by Terry

Our parents made us think our world in the 50s was pretty safe. They wanted us to be safe, to be innocent. Oh, we had the atomic bomb that was going to burn the flesh off our bones, but if we went under our desks, nothing would happen. They gave us broad warnings: every stick will poke your eye out, or falling out of a tree always results in a broken skull. But they didn't talk about lots of other things. No one talked about Mrs. Peterson having to run to a neighbor in the middle of the night and, in the morning, having a black eye and bruises. Or why Andy Smith was 12 years old and still in a first grade reading group learning about *Dick and Jane.* Or why Sarah's mom stole flowers from the graves in the cemetery and then gassed herself in the garage. We thought we were safe and they wanted it that way; everyone wanted to believe they lived just like *My Three Sons* or *Ozzie and Harriet.* I spent my summers in *Mayberry*.

Of course, I wasn't on the TV show, but my Mayberry could have been the prototype for *The Andy Griffith Show*. My Mayberry was Murphysboro, Illinois. It had the same kind of Main Street with locally owned stores; the only chain store was *Woolworth's* and, since you knew the first name of everyone who worked there, it didn't seem like a chain.

My Uncle Gov was Andy Griffith; he was the sheriff, had the same Southern accent and gentle way of dealing with people. And while Deputy Buck was much more competent than Barnie Fife, they did have a guy that was the perennial prisoner just like Otis. On the show Otis was the one who would let himself in and out of jail. Uncle Gov had Ernie. Sometimes Ernie would be locked in but most of the time, he could let himself out whenever he wanted. You'd walk in the jail kitchen and he'd be cleaning the refrigerator or helping dish up food trays for the prisoners and then he'd go back to his cell to take a nap.

I guess my grandmother was Aunt Bea; she wasn't as plump but I think they probably both smelled of baked pies and *Evening in Paris Toilet Water.*

And me? I was Opie. I'd roam all over town, anywhere I wanted to go. I even had my own cane fishing pole just like Opie. In the beginning of each show, they'd show Andy and Opie coming from their fishing hole. My fishing hole was a tiny lake called Carbon Lake. Aunt Imy and Uncle Gov had built a small cabin on the lake as had ten other couples. The cabins were so far apart you couldn't see any of them but there was a lodge where the members would meet once or twice a week for a shared meal and cards. The lodge was right on the edge of the lake. The cement front porch ended right in the water; there was no beach and the only protection was a railing made out of pipe. I'd play and fish on that porch with the only warning being, "Don't fall in; you'll drown." Even though I wasn't a swimmer, I was never asked to wear a life jacket. But I knew I'd surely die if I went off that porch, so I'd lean against the railing as far out as I could with my cane pole and sometimes I'd even catch something.

One time my family was at the lodge also. My mom, dad, and two brothers had come from the suburbs of Chicago to bring me back home at the end of summer. Now reality returned and I was once again in charge of watching my annoying little brother Randy. One day we were on the porch, no life jackets, only that threat of death, and Randy was being a real pest. I saw a turtle swimming about ten feet off the porch. With my nine year old brain, I decided it would be great to catch the turtle for Randy. I wasn't trying to entertain him. I thought it was a snapping turtle and just liked the idea of handing it to him. My thinking didn't go beyond that to any consequences that might occur if I actually succeeded. So I grabbed my pole but there was no bait. Most of the men were out in their little row boats and had taken the bait. I ran into the kitchen where the women were preparing supper and I spotted the raw hamburger. Great! I knew turtles loved raw hamburger. That is what we always fed the many turtles we had gotten at *Woolworth's*. We kept them in one of those clear plastic turtle bowls with the island and the green plastic palm tree and our turtles loved raw hamburger. So I put the hamburger on the hook, leaned out over the pipe railing and threw it out. Of course the hamburger dropped off in mid flight. Back to the kitchen I went, looking for something that would stay on the hook. I spotted dill pickle slices. I went back to the porch with my new bait. I threw out the hook and the pickle stayed on! I got a bite! I hauled in my catch but instead of the turtle, I had a pound and a half bass, the biggest bass that had ever been caught in that tiny lake. Of course all the men spent the rest of the fishing season with pickle bait, but I was the only one who was ever successful. And Randy and I didn't drown. We'd followed the rule. We were safe.

That same week, my older brother and my cousin Donny, went frog hunting one night. Right next to the lodge was a marshy swamp and you could hear it was filled with frogs. My mom gave them the rule, "Mind your p's and q's", a very good, general, all purpose rule. The boys were back within minutes, white as ghosts. Bill had stepped on a water moccasin, a very poisonous snake. The only reason he hadn't been bitten was that the snake was in the process of swallowing a fish. As the boys told the story, the grownups hardly batted an eye and their card game didn't stop. They just said, "Guess you'll watch where you step the next time." Follow the rules and you'll be safe.

Yes, we were safe. Nothing could happen. We had all the broad rules and that would save us. As I wandered Opie-style all over Murphysboro, I had main two rules. Don't take candy from strangers and don't get into a stranger's car. Silly rules. I didn't know any strangers in Murphysboro.

Like Opie, I was usually alone. For some reason there were seldom any kids my age around so I always wandered by myself. Except for the summer I was ten. That year I had Uncle John. He was my grandmother's only brother in a family of five siblings. And he was much loved. John was a coal miner and so the two previous summers that I'd spent in Murphysboro, he had been working. But this summer he was laid off. Now he too was wandering around town looking for odd jobs to make a little cash. And he would let me tag along. Once or twice a week he'd go to a coal mine to see if they were hiring and he'd take me with him. I loved going to the coal mines. The buildings were all unpainted wood that reminded me of the towns in cowboy shows like *Have Gun Will Travel*. The offices always had pinup girl calendars. I was intrigued by their skimpy outfits and interesting poses and thought they all must be famous movie stars.

The best part, though, was that Uncle John was such fun. He was always joking and laughing and he told wonderful stories. My favorite took place when he was a boy. If he did something wrong, his mom, my great-grandmother Ma Lilly, would make him put on one of his sisters' dresses and then she'd push him out the door for the entire day. He'd race down to the culvert and hide there until it was dark enough to run home without anyone seeing him. I laughed every time he told me that story.

One day I stopped by his house on my travels about town. His wife Lila had canned peaches before she went off to work at my grandmother's restaurant and John was carrying the jars down to the cellar. Of course I helped. When we got them all on the shelf, we stood back to admire the beautiful orange jars shining in the sunlight coming through the cellar window. Uncle John put his arms around me and rubbed my chest. I didn't like it and squirmed away. I wasn't sure what had happened or if I'd just imagined it. Maybe his hands had just slipped as he was taking them away. I didn't say anything. What would I say? He then turned, went upstairs and off we went to repair the toilet at the neighbor's house.

About a week later, Lila told me that Uncle John was going to a coal mine and that if I hurried over, I could probably go with him. I raced the seven or eight blocks to their house so I wouldn't miss him. When I saw his car in the yard, I knew I was on time. As I burst through the door, John yelled, "Hey Terry Lynn, just in time! We'll be leaving as soon as this television program is over."

I went into the living room and started to sit on the couch when he said, "Come sit on my lap." I was never much of a lap sitter, but I had those other rules, the politeness rules. Do what grownups tell you to do. It was respectful especially in the "yes, ma'am and no, sir" south. So I sat on his lap and his arm came around me—tight. He placed his other hand in my shorts. I didn't say anything; I didn't know what to say. When he was finished, he pushed me off his lap and went into the bathroom and told me to stay right there. I stayed—the politeness rule. I thought at the time he'd gone into the bathroom to wash his hands. I had been taught to wash my hands after touching that area. When he came out, it was as if nothing had happened. "Let's get this show on the road," he said. I followed him. We got in the car and went to the coal mine. I sat as close to the door as I could and said nothing the entire trip. John chatted away and told stories, just like always. When we got to the coal mine, the buildings didn't look like cowboy towns anymore, they just looked old and dirty. The calendars looked different, too. They didn't remind me of the pretty movie stars that I thought they were but something bad and dirty. The whole way home, as I sat tight against the door, I kept thinking, "Wait until I tell my grandmother. Wait 'til I tell MawMaw".

But when I raced into the restaurant, she said, "Did you have fun? Isn't that John just the best brother anyone could ever have?" What could I say? I didn't have the words. My mother had never told me that wonderful, fun great Uncle Johns could be worse than strangers. She just didn't tell me.

You're a Boomer if you know the sayings in the ads for these cigarettes:

Classic_film Flickr	farm8.staticFlickr	farm4.staticFlickr
Tareyton	**Winston**	**Phillip Morris**

*Answers are at the end of the chapter

Do you remember?

- The constant threat of Communism and Khrushchev
- *Silent Spring*, Rachel Carson's book as a first call for environmental protection
- The first Earth Day
- No emission controls on cars
- Dumping and littering at will
- " Keep America and anti-littering campaign beginning in 1953

pds209 Flickr

pds209 Flickr

144

- The Cuban Missile Crisis
- Use of DDT
- No fire, carbon monoxide, or radon detectors in homes
- Sugar-laden food and then the introduction of saccharin
- Emptying car ashtrays anywhere and piles of butts in parking lots or along the side of the road
- No seatbelts in cars
- Bears eating garbage at the dump
- Burning home garbage
- No safety caps on medicines

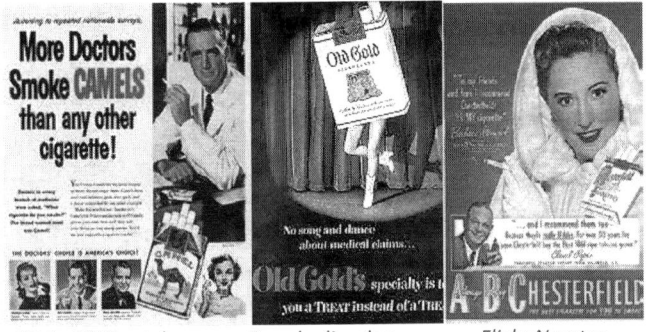

Flickr 1950s style *Google digadoo* *Flickr Nesster*

*Tareyton – "I'd rather fight than switch"
Winston – "Winston tastes good like a cigarette should"
Phillip Morris – "Call for Phillip Morris"

Fashion

I dress to kill. Unfortunately my cooking is similar.

It ain't the jeans that make your butt look fat.

Women will never be equal to men until they can walk down the street with a bald head and a beer gut and still think they are sexy.

The reason women don't play football is because 11 of them would never wear the same outfit in public. Phyllis Diller

Flickr farm9.static

Still at the cabin, Lynn is sitting in the main room looking again at the old photo albums and magazines. Terry comes in singing to the tune of *Wouldn't It Be Loverly*: "All I want is some perky breasts, not like these hanging down my chest." Lynn quickly interrupts her.

Lynn: Terry, did you notice the dates on these magazines? 1968, 1953. Hey, is that make-up you've got on? We're at a lake in the middle of nowhere. This is supposed to be a get-away.
Terry: I did this for the two of you. You wouldn't want to see me without it. As my mom used to say, she looked like the *Wreck of the Hesperus* without makeup. That's a ship, you know.
Lynn: Yes. But it feels so good to get away.
Terry: Have you been out to the lake?
Lynn: Oh yes, in my flannels. My mom would have been appalled. I can't recall ever seeing her dressed like this, flannels, sweatshirt, uncombed hair.
Terry: Mine, either. My mother took a bath every single day at 4:00 all of her married life.

Lynn: Getting ready because your dad was coming home.
Terry: Yes, she even got dressed up in good clothes. And, when I was under 7, Bill and I had to take a bath every day after she was finished.
Lynn: My mom looked darn good but I was questionable. However, when mom was a kid, it was baths once a week on Saturday night and she remembered picking out toe jam towards the end of the week.
Terry: We had to take a bath every other night.
Lynn: We took one every night.
Terry: We weren't dirty or anything. We took a half bath on the nights in between.
Sara: We called those 'bird baths' where you just do it with the washcloth. We only took full baths twice a week. But we never filled the bath tub up.
Terry: I had it full, right up to that drain thing so that whenever you moved water would go down the overflow.
Lynn: I hated to bathe. When I was old enough to bathe myself, Mom would say, "Lynnie, go take your bath." And I just played in the bathroom until I figured enough time had gone by. But she soon caught on to that. Then she said, "Lynn, you go in there, take off your clothes and get into the tub." So I'd take off my clothes and sit in the dry tub. But she caught on to that, too, and said, "Lynn Anne, get in the tub and run the water." So I'd take off my clothes, sit in the tub and watch the water go down the drain.
Sara: Such a literal kid!
Lynn: I have since changed.
Sara and Terry: Good!
Sara: But you know when we were little, people dressed up more. Women would wear heels to go shopping…
Lynn: Yes! We'd go downtown to shop!
Terry: Shopping wasn't for entertainment. When we went

shopping, it was all business. My favorite was the shoe stores. Still is!
Lynn: Did the salesmen x-ray your feet?
Terry: That's why I liked them. Those big x-ray boxes! We'd put our feet in these little slots. There was a place on the top for you to look and one for your mom and one for the salesman. You could wiggle your toes and see the bones move. I wanted them to x-ray me every time, but they set limits.
Sara: Yeah, for all the radiation that was running through your little feet. Terry, did you ever wonder how tall you'd be if your feet hadn't been x-rayed so much?

Flickfarm6.static

Terry: (Terry makes a face at Sara) And I always liked the shoe polish display. It was a metal rack with those little tins of polish. And then they got the white polish with the little ball on the end. That was cool.
Lynn: We used *Vaseline* to shine up our patent leather shoes.
Terry: You used *Vaseline*?
Lynn: Yeah.
Terry: So you had leaves and dirt stuck to your shoes?
Lynn: We didn't coat the shoes with it. We'd just use a dab to shine them up for church.
Sara: We always dressed up for church. I wore my good dress with crinolines and kid gloves.

Flickr Florida Memory

Lynn: And women wore hats more often back then.
Terry: I went to Mrs. Milliner's with my mom to have a hat especially made for her.
Lynn: You mean the milliner who made the hat?
Terry: Yes, Mrs. Milliner.
Lynn: The lady who made the hats was called a milliner.
Terry: Yes, Lynn. That's what I said, Mrs. Milliner. Gee.
Lynn: Never mind.
Sara: Sometimes at church, women who didn't have a hat would put hankies on their heads and if they didn't have a hankie, they'd just use *Kleenex*.
Lynn: My grandmother always had an embroidered hanky for when she was 'going out'. Then at home, she'd use *Kleenex*. She just shoved them in all the nooks and crannies.
Sara: They'd stuff them up their sleeves...
Lynn: Right in between the girls...
Terry: With the girls again. Did you bring them along?
Lynn: Always!
Terry: Mom always had a *Kleenex* under her pillow. She was as neat as a pin but, if she used that *Kleenex* in the night, she'd put it back under her pillow. Ugh.
Lynn: I do that now. (Terry moves away from Lynn)
Sara: They put *Kleenex* in the waist of whatever they were wearing.
Lynn: There were just these little bulges all over.
Sara: And young girls would stuff their bras with *Kleenex* and toilet paper. Then there were those 1960s padded bras that had sponge-like things in them. They were inches thick, so you had no real boob, you just had padding.
Terry: When they took them off they'd shrink from a size C to a AA. My mom never told me that not everything was

going to be real. But speaking of bras, Ken says the most popular bra size in the nursing home is 38 long.

Sara and sister Linda

Sara: (ignoring Terry) When you think about it, in the 50s all our clothes were different from what they are now but I think the winter clothes were really strange. For one thing, everything was heavy.

Terry: The snow pants were wool. They didn't really keep any wet away. And our boots were just rubber which is not warm. My feet would get so cold.

Sara: And my wrists! I can remember them getting chapped because snow would get in between your mittens and your coat and, because it was wool, the snow would just ball up and lay on your skin for hours.

Terry: Didn't you eat it out of there? Did you ever put bread bags on your shoes?

Sara: Yes! That way we could get them on without help.

Terry: Then, when we came in from playing, we always had to go straight to the basement to take off our snowy clothes and you couldn't see a thing because you had been out in that bright snow. Snow blind.

Sara: One year, I don't know what came over my mother, but she bought red plastic snow pants for my sister and me. The whole idea was that they'd keep the wet out, which they did. But then we'd go out in the cold and the dang things would crack. And every crack was a leak. But she must have paid 'good money' for them. She made us wear them although we hated them. They made a horrible swishing noise and people laughed at us.

Lynn: 'I paid good money for that.' That is a phrase I don't hear much now.

Sara: Here's something else you don't hear about anymore, house dresses. (she points to a photo in an album) Lynn, this your mother, right? And that's exactly what she's wearing, a house dress. Women did housework in dresses. And they never wore those dresses to go anywhere; they were just for home. I hardly ever wear a dress now. In fact I just got these new pants. How do they look on me? They're the first pair of low-rise flares I've ever bought.
Terry: No, they're not, Sara. You had pants just like those in the 60s. They were just called hip-huggers and bell bottoms in our day.
Lynn: You're right. If we had just held onto our clothes from the 60s, we'd be back in fashion. Of course, we wouldn't be able to fit in them.
Terry: I couldn't wear pants to school all through high school. But the skirts got shorter and shorter each year. Thus, the skirt checks.
Lynn: Mine stayed just below my knees for years.
Terry: The school officials hated the short skirts but we loved them! In college I even had two dressses that had matching panties that you wore under them - in case things got too high. Twice I accidently tucked my dress in the pants. One time, at a restaurant, a man stopped me and said, "I like your little pants but you might want to take your skirt out of them!"
Lynn: That never would have happened to me!
Sara: We wore the short skirts too. Remember I told you about rolling up our skirts after skirt check. They got higher and higher each year.
Terry: We were so cute and daring!

Sara: That must be when we first changed to panty hose. We couldn't possibly have been wearing garter belts with such short hemlines.

Lynn: Oh my word, garter belts! And the nylons always got snags and runs in them.

Sara: Remember using clear nail polish to stop a runner?

Lynn: It would dry right on your skin.

Sara: When I got home I'd peel off the nylon and about three layers of skin.

Terry: I used *Elmer's* glue. It dries clear, you know.

Sara: (ignoring Terry) But, we wore a lot more underwear in those days.

Lynn: Quite an arsenal. We had those industrial strength, huge, old white bras.

Terry: Or the pointy ones.

Lynn: We'd put on garter belts with nylons or even girdles. We'd encase it all in a full slip and then we'd put on our clothes.

WikimediaCommons

Terry: Do they even sell full slips anymore?

Sara: I have no idea.

Lynn: I just bought one the other day.

Terry: Where? At an antique store? But just a few short years after all that, we were going braless.

Terry and Sara: Letting it all hang out!

Sara: My mother hated that. It just wasn't right and certainly not ladylike. But it sure felt good.

Google imageconsultingschool

Terry: Still does!
Lynn: I never went braless. (Sara and Terry mouths fall open) My girls have always known the wonders of being lifted and separated.
Sara: Just think, in the six years between my sister and me, we went from her in bobby socks and poodle skirts, listening to 45s at a sock hop, to me in a fringed vest and miniskirt going to rock concerts. That was the beginning of the British invasion. Everything that came from England was cool. All the fashions went through this huge shift to Piccadilly Street. Fashions like big plastic jewelry, pale pink lipstick, go-go boots, and paisley on everything!
Terry: Really short skirts and fishnet stockings. (Terry looks at Lynn) I know you didn't wear those either, did you?
Sara: Your skin used to poke up through every hole in those fishnets. The one fashion that became really big in the 50s and 60s, and is still with us today, is our jeans.
Lynn: There have been changes to them also. They've gone up and down, high waist to low waist, skinny to bellbottom, pleated to holey. Now the boys have them hanging down to their knees. Why has that fad lasted so long?
Sara: I don't know. Just think how bad it feels is when the crotch of your pantyhose gets stretched out like that.
Terry: I was walking back to the parking lot from school one day and the elastic in my underwear gave out. I was wearing a dress and my underpants started falling off. I had to hold on to them and walk like a duck. Just like those boys.
Lynn: I saw a kid trying to run

astrologybylauren

across the street the other day and he was holding his jeans up to his chest.

Terry: Ken heard about a kid who was trying to run from the police. His jeans fell down and he tripped on them and that's how the police got him!

Sara: I think James Dean made jeans famous. You know, in that movie? The one about the two boys?

Lynn: The brothers.....

Terry: The Brothers Kilimanjaro?

Lynn: No, not them.

Terry: Butch Cassidy and the Sundance Kid?

Lynn: They're not brothers.

Terry: They might be. Maybe they just had different mothers. But anyway, they wore jeans, at their waist. Do you remember the first time you wore jeans?

Lynn: I'm sure I had denim diapers.

Sara: I bet we're the first generation to live and die in jeans.

Terry: And eat *Twinkies*.

Sara: What are you talking about?

Terry: They might have been gone forever too, just like James Dean.

Lynn: *East of Eden*!

Terry: Who?

Lynn: The James Dean movie. I knew it would come to me eventually.

Sara: I wonder what I did with those jeans I had in high school. I cut the sides and sewed in strips so they'd be bell bottoms. They were great. I wish I still had them.

Terry: Why? They certainly wouldn't fit you anymore. You have definitely outgrown them. And I don't mean you've gotten taller.

Lynn: We've grown out of more than just jeans. Even with all of the lifting and separating we do now, everything is definitely heading south.

Terry: And east

Sara: I've got some west going on here.

Lynn: Whatever direction we're heading, there are some fashion statements for us 'older' folks that I hope I never see.

Sara: Like, don't wear *Depends* with your thong underwear.

Lynn: Or skinny jeans with your saggy ankles.

Terry: How about no nose rings with bifocals?

Lynn: Or an unbuttoned disco shirt and heart monitor.

Sara: Those old guys in Europe need this one, no Speedos and beer bellies.

Terry: Or short shorts and cellulite, miniskirts and support hose.

Lynn: Walkers and stilettos

Terry: Be careful, that's one I'm planning on!

(Sara and Lynn roll their eyes at Terry. Lynn picks up one of the old magazines, Sara flips through a stack of old albums, and Terry grabs an old newspaper. While they silently read, their thoughts are revealed.)

Lynn: *Clothes have really changed since 1958. Look at that picture. How can she breathe?*

Terry: *Go figure. Obituaries were about dead people back then too. This one says she passed peacefully, age 63. Well, she lived a full life, wait a minute…..63?*

Sara: (looking at Grace Slick on an old Jefferson Airpane album) *Look at that little outfit she's got on. I'd look good in that.*

Lynn: *Oh wow, a full body girdle. She'd have to have one of those on to look like that. How does she sit down? Well, maybe she doesn't.*

Terry: *I wonder if everyone died, who would cut my hair.*

Sara: *I'm too old now to pull off that look. Maybe….*

Terry: *I wonder what happens if you get scared half to death twice?*

Lynn: *The woman in this ad just stripped the floor wax wearing a dress and high heels. I guess that is her 'house dress'; mine is a torn t-shirt and jeans.*
Terry: *The obituary says this woman was married for 33 years. Well, the secret to a long marriage is not to get divorced.*
Sara: *I'd look good in that outfit. I wish I still had some of my stuff from the 60's.*
Terry: *I want to die like my grandpa—in his sleep, not like the passengers in his car.*
Sara: I'm just as cute as Grace Slick. Oops, did I just say that out loud?
Terry: I heard you in my head because I'm psychotic.
Lynn: What?
Sara: I think you mean psychic.
Terry: Yeah, I've got ESPN, and while the voices in my head may not be real, they sure have fun ideas.
Sara: Enough of this sitting around. Terry, get your stilettos on and let's go down to the lake! That's why we're here, you know!
Terry: Great! I'll go get them.

Furs
Terry remembers

Fur coats were a big thing in the 50s and 60s. Besides stores that exclusively sold furs, department stores like *Marshall Fields*, *Macy's*, and even *Sears* carried a huge selection of fur coats. Both my grandmother and Aunt Cat had full length mink coats and wished they had more of them. They would go into the department store in Murphysboro, Illinois and try on minks monthly. They also loved diamonds.

My mom's sister, Loretta, had a mink collar that actually had the animal's head, legs and tail on it. It had glass eyes and there was a clip under its chin. Loretta would wrap this animal skin (it did have felt on the bottom) around her neck and then clip the tail to the head so it would stay on. This creature fascinated me much more than my grandmother's huge mink coat. Loretta always sent it to the cleaners for 'storage' during the summer. I suppose that was so it didn't draw flies or something.

My mom was an excellent dresser when she wasn't wearing house dresses. She wore pants in the late 30s, saved for months as a young woman to buy a bolero jacket, and was always on top of the fashions. But I never heard her say she wanted a fur coat. Then one Christmas my parents made a pact to just buy small things for each other. On Christmas Eve the man across the street who worked in the fur department at *Field's* asked Mom how she liked her mink jacket. The secret was out. Later that afternoon I heard her crying as she was taking her bath. When I asked what was wrong, she explained that she'd kept the pact and had only bought insignificant things for Dad and he had gotten her that expensive present. I only saw my mom cry twice and that was the last time. I don't remember Christmas morning or her opening the gift, but she did wear that jacket often. I'm not sure if it was because she liked it or because Dad had gotten it for her.

You're a Boomer if you know who these models are:

Flickr farm9static *Flickr farm6static*

*answers at end of chapter

Do you remember?

- Pill box hats
- Cat's eye glasses, granny glasses
- Balloon and sack dresses
- Saddle shoes
- Box-pleated skirts you had to iron
- Clear rubber overshoes and shoe bags
- Joe Namath wearing pantyhose
- Colored knee socks
- Pedal pushers
- Aprons
- Nurse caps and white shoes
- Gloves that went past your elbow
- Sanitary napkin belt

Flickr Uppityrib

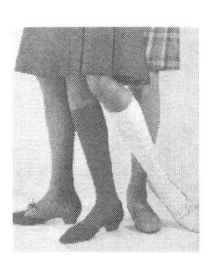

Flickr Bess Georgette

- Nehru suits
- Mary Janes
- Mod dresses
- Striped elephant pants
- Big sunglasses
- Wooden platform shoes
- Jumpsuits with really wide legs to look like a skirt
- Teachers wore ties and high heels
- Tuxedos with ruffled shirts for prom
- The *Maidenform* bra ads
- The first bikinis

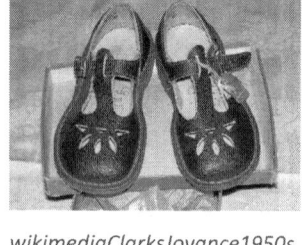

wikimediaClarksJoyance1950s

Flickr classic_film

Wikimedia 1971

Jean Shrimpton, Twiggy

160

Cars

Mapquest really needs to start their directions on #5. I'm pretty sure I know how to get out of my neighborhood.

Flickr 1950s unlimited

The Broads have returned for another day of cleaning out Terry's attic.

Terry: Ken says all this is junk and needs to go but I believe that junk is something you've kept for years and throw away three weeks before you need it. Maybe we should just go downstairs and have some lemonade. Anyone with me?
Sara: No, Terry. This is going to be interesting. I love this trunk. Was it your grandfather's? And look at this old driver's license. Terry, was this your first one?
Terry: Yep.
Sara: Pretty cute. Terry Howell. Eyes hazel, hair brown...
Terry: Can I ask a stupid question?
Lynn: Oh yes.
Terry: When a man is completely bald, what color do they list as his hair color?
Lynn: Clear. You know when I took my driver's test, I was so nervous. I was sitting behind the wheel and the tester was this little clear-headed guy who sounded just like Maxwell Smart. "Well, Miss Lewis, take a right turn directly ahead."
Terry: I had to have a pillow to sit on. I used to be short; I'm not as tall as I look.
Lynn: (laughs) Oh, you're serious.
Terry: So I had to go to Driver's Ed with my pillow every day. There were three of us in the car and when I was

driving I wasn't allowed to talk. The instructor claimed I talked with my hands. What was this man thinking? Is it true that you never really learn to swear until you learn to drive?

Lynn: According to my dad, it's when you're the teacher.

Sara: I don't remember the third person in my car, but one was this girl named Gisela. Gisela had a way of chattering while she drove. I think she was nervous. She'd chatter her way through stop signs. So the instructor was always over there with that brake thing, saying "Gisela, Gisela, GISELA!"

Terry: It was so great to finally get a driver's license. Freedom! My mom didn't drive for many years, so she was pretty much stuck at home. And we were often stuck with her.

Lynn: In the California suburbs having a car was a survival essential; we drove everywhere.

Terry: Sometimes we'd walk to catch the bus or the train and mom did grocery shopping with my aunt and uncle. Mom took lessons when I was ten and but even then she didn't venture very far from home.

Lynn: Mom drove everywhere and we had two cars for as long as I can remember.

Sara: My mom was like Terry's. So were lots of moms in our neighborhood. That's why we had all the home delivery guys. Remember the milk man who delivered the milk,

wikimedia

eggs, and cheese? We had a wooden box outside the back door where we put the empty bottles and we'd leave a list for him. And the *Omar* man, too.

162

Terry: Omar? Like the hunchback?
Sara: You mean, Igor? No, *Omar* delivered bread. I don't know if that was the name of the bakery or maybe it was his name.
Lynn: Our bread man had the best chocolate-covered donuts. Will you pass the cookies?
Sara: My favorite delivery guy was the *Fuller Brush* man. He would come once a year and lay out all of his brushes.
Terry: The one I liked only came around a couple of times a year. He had a bicycle and he'd ring his bell and as soon as the housewives would hear that bell, they would run outside chasing him with their knives.
Sara and Lynn (they look amazed)
Terry: He was the knife sharpener guy.
Sara: The bell I liked was the ice cream truck bell. I wish I could have driven one of those! I have always liked driving and cars. I've got a Hybrid now but it is nothing like those cars of the 50s and 60s. I loved them!
Lynn: We had an emerald green Buick. It was massive. It took half a block just to park that thing with its big fins on the back. Boy, that was a nice car.
Sara: We had a Desoto. My sister used to call it Cloud Number 9, because it was so heavy and big and rode so smoothly. That car probably got eight miles to the gallon. Of course gas was only twenty-five cents a gallon back then.
Lynn: But people were earning less. My dad was only bringing home about seven grand a year and that was good money.
Sara: My parents' first mortgage was $6500. It took them fifteen years of sacrifice to get it paid off.
Lynn: My dad sold his hunting rifle for $300 to make the down payment on their first house.

Terry: In 1969 my dad bought a brand new car for under $2000.
Lynn: You know what bums me out. We didn't get the *Jetson* flying cars.
Sara: But now we have tiny little Jetson-like cars that we plug in.

Flickr x-ray delta

Terry: But I wanted to fly.
Lynn: Most of the cars we now have are boring.
Terry: That's because they all look the same. You can't tell one make from one model. When we were kids, each car looked different. My dad had a long Oldsmobile once that was black on the bottom with a pink top. One of my mom's happiest days was when it got stolen and he bought an all white one.
Sara: Two-tone cars! And I remember those hard top convertibles where the trunk opened and the entire roof came up, over the seats and bang! It would land on the windshield and you latched it down. So now it was a hard topped car. They were really cool.
Terry: Did you ever have that little metal rod that stuck out and told you where the curb was?
Sara: A curb finder. And cars used to have little vent windows.
Terry: I really wish I still had those. I loved them.
Lynn: On really long trips, Mom and Dad would just be talking and they were always, constantly throughout the entire trip adjusting those vents.

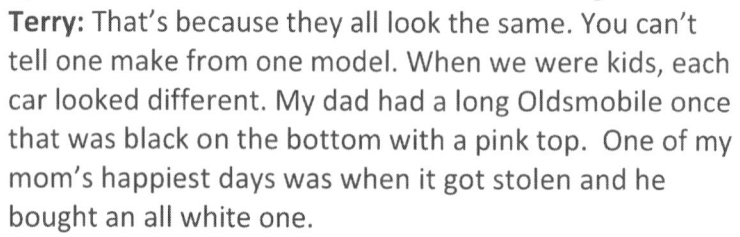

Wikimedia

"Have you got enough air back there?"
Terry: There was no air conditioning.
Lynn: That old Buick had our first air conditioner. It didn't come in the car, it was added on. You had the console and then in the middle section, under the console they added on this unit; it had these little eyeball things that you could turn out and the cold air kind of shot out. Whenever our dog went into the car he'd lay right in front of it.
Terry: Our first station wagon had a back seat that faced backwards. We always wanted to go in the 'way back'. But can you imagine how dangerous that back seat was? We were facing backwards and had no seatbelts! My family got that car when my brother Randy was little and the back window was electric, the rest of them were all roll downs. Randy would always sit back there and, when mom would park, he would roll down the window and crawl out. That panicked Mom so she had it disconnected. The next time the car was in the shop and she picked it up ,they said, "We noticed the back window wasn't working so we fixed it for you."
Sara: We used to ride down in the wheel well, up in the back window, or sit on my dad's lap and pretend to drive. Like you said, there were no seatbelts.
Lynn: And all the cars had a bench front seat so you could fit four people up there which we often did.
Sara: And it wasn't uncommon to sit on laps when you were a kid to make room for adults.

Wikimedia

Lynn: We'd stack people up like cord wood.
Terry: There was that dimmer button for the lights in the car.
Sara: Oh yeah, on the floor and the choke button.
Lynn: Stick shift
Terry: Four on the floor
Sara: White wall tires. Ugh.
Lynn: The littlest kid in the family always had to scrub the whitewalls with a soapy *Brillo Pad*.
Sara: We never went to the car wash. We always washed the car at home, with the hose, in the driveway.
Terry: Once I drove into the wrong end of a car wash. People get so excited. The lady in the other car was just screaming. I was just as surprised to see her.
Lynn: At the filling station the guy would come out and Dad would say, "Fill'er up with regular" and then he'd check your oil, show dad the dipstick and say, "You're down a quart." Dad would reply, "10W40". It was like they were speaking a foreign language.

Flickr Tommy & Georgie

Sara: Yeah, guy talk. Then they'd check the air in your tires.
Terry: And he'd wash your windows.
Lynn: That was my dream job, washing the windows. In fact, when stations went to self-serve and I got to wash my own windows, I thought it was pretty cool.
Terry: I've got a whole house full of dirty windows. Come over and knock yourself out, Lynnie. Actually full service gas stations were great for the customers but

not always good for the workers. Ken worked at the *Clark* station over on South Avenue in La Crosse. He hated it in the summer when the mayflies came out because then you'd have to clean all those bugs off the lights and the grill too. He said it was just gross.

Flickr x-ray delta

Lynn: Summer time for us meant Sunday drives. Did you take rides on Sunday afternoons? I loved those. My dad would sit in the driver's seat with just one hand loosely on the wheel and all four of us were in back, unbuckled.
Sara: I used to like to stick my head out the window.
Terry: My brother Randy often stood in the front; he was the youngest and they let him do that to keep him quiet. But one day Dad was driving along and Randy turned the key off. The power steering and everything else was gone. It was a little bit of a panic.
Sara: We didn't have any DVDs in the car and we couldn't stop at every *Kwik Trip*; gas stations were few and far between.
Terry: All the kids in my family had to sit in the back seat and be quiet, because you weren't supposed to disturb Dad. My mom wouldn't let us have pencils because if the car stopped quickly, you'd poke your eye out. So the only thing we could have was crayons or you read a

book, that was it. Or we'd play White Horse. If Dad saw a white horse on his side, we had to give him a nickel and if we saw one on the other side, he had to give us a nickel. He always saw more so he always won. And he took our money!

Lynn: We did a 'count the cow' thing.

Sara: Not in Wisconsin. You'd be counting in the millions. We'd play ABC. I see something that begins with A, I see something that begins with B.

Lynn: Or the sign game where you find words on signs that started with the letters in order.

Terry: We sang songs all the time.

Sara: Oh yeah, we did too.

Lynn: Mom would sing us songs from when she was a girl. They were so sad. I'd tear up every time. I remember one about a mother whose two year old died and there was this line about her missing the little fingerprints she used to clean off the windows.

Terry: Yuck! We sang happy songs like *Mares Eat Oats* and *You Are my Sunshine*. Happy stuff.

Sara: My dad's favorite song was *K-K-Katy* but I liked *Everybody Loves to Eat Worms*.

Lynn: Did your dad ever say, "Don't make me stop this car!"

Sara: Or "You don't want me to come back there!"

Terry: Once I learned to drive I didn't take rides with the family much anymore. I was almost always allowed to have the car but I was restricted as to how far I could go. So I'd tell Mom I was going to the library but really ride past potential boyfriends' houses. My friend Shirley's dad checked the speedometer but Ginny's dad taught us how to turn it off. So we 'tooled' all over town and beyond.

Sara: We used to do the same sort of thing. I would tell Mom we were all going over to somebody's house and then one of us would get a car. The big thing in Madison was to go up to the square and 'drag the square'. Just drive around and around it all night long. You'd pull over and sit on the hood and then boys would come along.
Lynn: We called it dragging Main.
Sara: Just driving in cars; we did a lot of that because gas was so cheap.
Terry: Thirty-five cents a gallon.
Sara: I just remember getting three dollars worth of gas and you could drive all night.
Terry: I always had to make sure I replaced the gas I used because mom never liked it if you brought the car home almost empty.
Lynn: Right.
Terry: But a few dollars worth would take you forever.
Lynn: When we moved to Hawaii one of the things they told my folks was that people didn't need a large car because gas was so much more expensive and you didn't go very far. So they bought a *Mustang* the first year they came out.
Terry: 1969
Sara: No, 1964.
Lynn: Yep, a 1964, 2x2, fast-back, honey gold. It was the coolest car and I was in the sixth grade. Mom would pick me up in it and I thought I was pretty special. Well, my mom had never had a speeding ticket and she was so proud of that. My dad would get a ticket about every third week. We were driving somewhere as a family,

three of us stuffed in the back, Mom was driving and still in second gear and she was pulled over by the police for speeding. We were all like, "Throw the book at her!" We were so pleased and she

Flickr Maia C

was so disgusted. It was the only ticket she ever got.
Sara: I love it. She was winding that little engine up pretty tight.
Terry: The *Mustangs* were cool cars.
Sara: Still are, even the new ones.
Terry: When you see the new ones now, how can you even tell it's a *Mustang*? Hey guys, we've almost cleaned out one trunk. Just eight more plus all these boxes and we'll be finished with the attic.

My First Car
an original story by Terry

I had the greatest car as a teen. Well, it wasn't really mine; my name wasn't on the title but for all practical purposes, like driving it, it was mine. Some people called her a bug or a beetle, but I always used her real names, *Volkswagen* and VW. Mine had a cream colored *Karmann Ghia* body and a black cloth top. Yep, a convertible. She was beautiful.

My dad purchased her in the summer after my freshman year in high school. Dad was the manager of a *Woolworth* store in downtown Chicago and the parking ramp that he used raised their rates to two or three dollars a day. So he got the idea to buy the *Volkswagen* and park her in the alley behind his store. Perfect plan. He bought one of those little driving caps and would drive to work with the top down. He looked cute. But then the *Volkswagen* got broken into, twice. What was he thinking? This was an alley, in Chicago! And then fall came. In those days the *Volkswagen* heater ran on the motor. The faster you went the more heat you got. But my dad was driving to and from work in rush hour, bumper to bumper, stop and go traffic; the fastest he went was twenty-five miles an hour and he was freezing. So about the first of November he parked *VW* in our garage and there she sat.

My mom didn't know how to drive a standard transmission. Mom had come into driving late in life. Like many moms in the 50's and 60's she didn't learn until she was almost 40, and she wasn't what you would call a natural. I remember her coming home from one of her paid driving lessons. She was making a left turn into our driveway and had on the right blinker. Either the instructor didn't see this mistake or he thought, "I just can't deal with one more thing", he didn't say anything. When he left, I told her she'd used the wrong blinker. And she said, "No, Terry, I have it memorized, down for right and up for left." Not a natural.

My dad decided he'd teach her how to shift and, wonder of wonders, they stayed married. My little brother Randy and I were in the backseat for her last lesson. Mom was stopped at a stoplight on this ever so slight incline with cars all around. She had never gotten the clutch/gas pedal rhythm and after stalling it three times, she pulled up the emergency brake (we used them then) and said, "I'm done with this D-double-M thing." And that was the end of her lessons.

Now Sunday afternoons were spent with my dad teaching me to shift. I already knew how to drive a car; I'd driven the riding lawnmower for years and my friend Bobbi, who was ten months older than I was and already had her license, would take me to a subdivision and let me drive her dad's big yellow boat of a *Bonneville*. Yes, we called it the *Yellow Submarine*. But when you think about it, an unlicensed driver, a newly licensed driver, and a neighborhood full of hundreds of kids, it was a recipe for disaster. But I didn't kill anyone that I knew about.

And then on the day of my sixteenth birthday, I got my license and from that day on *VW* was mine. I'd drive her the six blocks to high school, park her in an empty lot across the street (there was no student parking then), and all day long she would call my name. After school, we'd pack five, six, seven kids in that little bitty car. If it was above 32 degrees, we'd put the top down and tool around town in hats, scarves and winter coats. We were cool. One time I picked up this kid from my typing class and his two friends. As we drove around, a car full of hoods started following us. We were scared so I pulled into a strange driveway to fool them in to thinking that it was mine, but they followed us in and blocked us from leaving. The kid from my typing class yelled, "Lock the doors. Roll up the windows!" We all stared at him; the top was down! But then we started laughing at him. I think that kid, John Belushi, started his comedy career that day.

Sometimes *VW* took us on adventures. I'd tell my mom I was going to the library and I never lied. We went to the library and drove through the parking lot. Then we'd head for the 'Crack Station', so named because of the way the head mechanic wore his pants. We'd get a dollar's worth of gas and we could go anywhere. But usually we'd go the thirty miles to downtown Chicago. Just as we got to the Loop, I'd take a left on Wells Street and head for Old Towne where the hippie shops were. We'd buy psychedelic posters, dangly earrings, and other stuff that I couldn't show my mom, but we'd always be home within ten minutes of the library closing so I could continue using that excuse.

As sweet as she was, *VW* was sometimes temperamental. It always seemed to happen when we were at the *Big Boy Restaurant* making a twelve ounce *Coke* last for two hours. It would be time to go home and she wouldn't start. But she was a stick, no problem. I'd push in the clutch, put her in first gear, my friends would push and vrooooom, off we'd go. Home before curfew.

Then in the late spring of my senior year, we were all sitting around the dinner table in our assigned seats, when my dad said, "I ordered a new car today. Trading in the *Volkswagen*." My heart went into my stomach. I lost my appetite and I never lose my appetite. "I know you are disappointed, Terry," he continued, "but your mom doesn't drive it and you are off to college in a few months." Freshman couldn't take cars to college then. "The new car will come in about two weeks."

So for two weeks, *VW* and I did all our favorite things: tooling around town, going to Old Towne, hanging out at the *Big Boy*. And then one day I came home from work. It had been Jenny's turn to drive and she had a really cool car, too. It was a little blue *Ford Falcon* with an awesome smell. One time she was driving with a bottle of whiskey in the trunk and she went over the railroad tracks too fast (also not a natural driver) and the bottle broke. To hide the smell we sprayed the trunk with an entire can of *Right Guard* deodorant so after that it always had this manly, musky, whiskey smell and her mom and dad never asked where the smell came from! Whatever! Anyway, in *VW*'s place was a cream colored *Oldsmobile 88* hardtop. I took the old car (I was not going to be sucked in by that new car smell) to the used car lot and there she sat, all alone. I hugged her, we reminisced, I cried. I did that for about four days and then she was gone, someone else's little *VW* with the cream colored *Karmann Ghia* body and the black cloth top. I hope they were nice to her. And I hope she was temperamental for them too!

Riding Around in Our Automobiles
an original story by Sara

When I was growing up it was the golden age of automobiles and we did everything in our cars. When I was a child, it was common to go for a Sunday ride as entertainment. We had no purpose for these trips and no specific destination. We were just sailing along with our heads out the window and the breeze blowing through our hair. I remember one car we had in particular. It was a green and white *De Soto* and my sister called it 'Cloud Number 9' because it just floated down the road. These were the days when we could pull into a filling station and, as our tires crossed a rubber hose, a bell would go off inside the station. A boy would come running out to meet us at the pump. My dad would roll down his window and say, "Fill 'er up." The boy would start to pump the gas and then he would wash the windows, check the oil pressure and fill the tires if needed.

Sometimes, on warm summer nights my dad would casually say, "I could sure go for a root beer float", and we girls would squeal with delight because we knew we were going to the *A&W* root beer stand. We'd jump into the car, often already in our pajamas, and head out for a frosty mug of root beer and ice cream. Or on special nights we would go the *Big Sky Drive-In* theater. Often we would leave a bit early so that we could visit *Peppermint Park*, a small amusement joint near *the Big Sky*. I loved this place. They had a ride with big cups to sit in and with a big wheel in the center. The harder you cranked the wheel the faster you would spin around. It was exhilarating and more than a bit nauseating. They also had trampolines. These were constructed of thick red rubber webs stretched over large rectangular holes in the ground. So we would step onto them and start to jump. Down into the pit we would go and then up into the air, over and over again. There were no safety rails and the pits were surrounded by gravel. We had different safety standards in those days. But my favorite ride at *Peppermint Park* was the *Hover Craft*. We'd sit in a plastic molded seat attached to a saucer-like disc. The man would come around and switch on a button and a bladder beneath the disc would inflate. The discs were sitting on an old go-kart track and once inflated all we had to do was lean one way or another to make them go. And those babies could really cook! I believed that eventually all real cars would operate this way.

Once dusk began to fall we headed for the drive-in. We'd pay our admission at a little booth and then my dad would set about finding the perfect spot to park. He'd pull into the upward-facing slot next to a speaker post. My mother would pull the speaker into the car, hook it on the window, and then crank that twelve pound thing up and turn it on. Scratchy noises would fill the car, which meant it was working, and then off we would go to the refreshment stand. I remember getting *Buttercup* popcorn – the type that was advertised on the screen by a dancing popcorn box singing:
> *Buttercup, Buttercup*
> *Popcorn at its best*
> *Served in a king-size cup*
> *It beats all the rest!*

Back in the car we would change into our pajamas because by the time the second feature began we were usually fast asleep.

When I was old enough to drive myself, gas cost around twenty-five cents per gallon, so for a buck we could go just about anywhere. We often went to downtown Madison and 'cruised the square' for hours. We would circle the Capitol building with hundreds of other kids, pulling over if we met someone interesting, usually boys from the other side of town. Or we did Chinese fire drills. If the stoplight turned red just as we got to it, we would all jump out of the car, run around it one time hooting and hollering, and then try to jump back in before the light turned green.

In my teen years we also went back to the drive-in theater, but with different purposes. On 'Buck Night' we would pack as many friends as possible into the car and our admission was only one dollar. But on regular admission nights, we would often stop a mile or so before the theater and put some of the smaller friends in the cavernous trunk of our old car. This tactic saved us a few bucks that we could now use to buy the *Buttercup* popcorn. The drive-in was also a place where I went with my boyfriend. On those nights it was a lot less about watching the movie and a lot more about 'making out' or 'parking'. Parking was common in my day. There were places all over town where a young couple could pull in, look at the stars and at each other. My boyfriend at the time had a *Gran Torino*. I remember many nights straddling the console between the bucket seats in all sorts of awkward positions. The steamy windows of the car were a sign of our teenage lust. I knew many a girl who lost her virginity in those big old cars. They were

like rolling motel rooms. As John Prine sang:
Who ever thought
That me and my girlfriend would ever get caught
We were sitting in the back seat just shootin' the breeze
With her hair up in curlers and her pants to her knees.

But my most daring adventures in the car actually occurred with my mother and her family when I was quite young. You see I was born into a gang. I really had no choice. By being born a female into my mother's family I was automatically 'made'. We were sort of a German Cosa Nostra. The leader of the gang was my maternal grandmother, Wilhemina Carolina Fredericka Schumann, but everyone just knew her as Minnie. And the gang was known as Minnie's girls. There was my aunt Esther, the eldest girl, who was a nervous little thing with eyes like a hawk. She could spot trouble a mile away, a convenient talent for a gang member, and she was known to us all as 'Guard Dog'. Then there was my aunt Lorraine. She was a lovely woman with a child-like innocence, another good trait for a gang member. We all called her 'Baby Face'. My mother, the middle child, was known as 'Bubbles'. For years I thought this name was due to her effervescent personality, but later I learned that it had something to do with some dancing she had done during the war for the GIs. And me, well, I was 'The Kid' and it was assumed that someday I would take over the business.

We pulled our job twice a year. The gang would arrive at our house under the cover of pre-dawn darkness. They would pull into our driveway in their silent *Edsels* and

Studebakers. When they emerged from the cars they were dressed in the gang garb; cotton print dresses they had sewn themselves, cloth coats with rhinestone broaches and clip-on earrings to match. They were solid women who wore corsets and black horn-rimmed glasses. They came armed with thermoses of black, German coffee, the kind that's ready when the spoon stands up in it. They also brought fry cakes, the only donuts I knew as a child. The dough had been deep fried in a cast iron skillet and then rolled in white sugar.

I would jump into the back seat of Cloud Number 9, among their ample bosoms, and we would head south toward Illinois. We never committed our crime in Wisconsin. 'Guard Dog' drove and Minnie rode shotgun. It seemed like Minnie's girls had no fear. They chatted as if we were on a holiday. Sometimes the car windows would get so fogged over that I would have to rub a spot with my mitten to see outside. After a while Minnie called out, "State line!" and the women all snapped to and began to apply their disguises. Out came the bullet shaped cylinders of lipstick with names like Flamingo and Vermillion. Next the jeweled compacts full of loose powder were opened and soon the car was filled with talcum and sweetness.

About this time we arrived at crime central. 'Guard Dog' pulled up to the curb and let us all out; she remained in the car so we could make a quick getaway later. I remember stepping out onto the curb in front of a large building. I looked up and over the door of that building were these words - Land of Lincoln Oleomargarine Warehouse. That's right we were oleo smugglers! This was during the days when it was illegal to buy, sell, or own oleomargarine in the dairy state of Wisconsin. And we were there for the express purpose of buying contraband, which we would then transport over state lines and distribute to our friends and relatives. These were the same women who took me to church and taught me my prayers! But they were tough, they had no remorse. They said that everyone did it or they bought it from those of us who did.

Once inside the warehouse Minnie's girls went to work. They took out their lists of clients and bought the correct amount of oleo. Then when we stepped outside 'Guard Dog' squealed up to the curb and we began to load pound, after pound, after greasy pound of the contraband into the huge trunk of our *De Soto*, until the back end dropped close to the pavement and we bottomed out as we left the parking lot.

The trip home was a bit quieter. I don't know if the girls were tired or had a guilty conscience. But this time when Minnie called out, "State line!" the women sort of ducked their heads and looked away from the windows. Several times I remember 'Guard Dog' spotted Johnny Law as we bounced back to Wisconsin. But the cops never stopped us. I think they knew they would be in big trouble if they messed with our gang!

When we arrived back at my house the gang divvied up the loot and went their separate ways. That evening, under the cover of darkness in our windowless basement, my mother and I would counterfeit the loot. You see the oleomargarine came in one pound bags and was manila colored. But in each bag was a golden capsule; it looked sort of like a vitamin E tablet. We would knead the bag until that capsule burst and spread that sunshiny, buttery color throughout the bag. The next day my mother would openly and fearlessly deliver the goods to everyone on her list.

We never talked about our crime sprees. But at holiday times, when the whole family gathered around Minnie's table, one of the men would say, "Pass the butter." Furtive glances would pass between the gang members and then we passed the oleo. As the men smeared it on thick slabs of bread, we'd nod to each other with knowing looks.

You're a Boomer if you know what these are:

Flickr retro me

Flickr aldenjewell

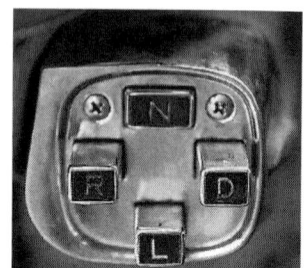

farm4.static

Answers at the end of the chapter

Do You Remember?

- Plastic car seats
- Rope across the back of the front seat
- Deep wheel wells front and back
- Carburetors
- Cars you could shift without a clutch
- Running boards
- Only AM radios
- 8 track tapes and the player we installed ourselves

x-raydeltaone

- The first motor scooters
- Windshields with a blue stripe across the top
- Antennas you would manually adjust
- Trunks you had to open with a key
- Paying cash at the gas station – no credit cards
- Pump 'dinged' for every gallon of gas you put in
- Fins and cats eye lights
- The song, *See the USA in your Chevrolet, America is asking you to call.* It was a full song with several verses and was the theme song for the Dinah Shore show.

Google Mathias Degen

- No air bags
- 58 Chevy was "the" car to own
- The first *VW Beetles* and how they became Love Bugs
- Large, hard plastic steering wheels with metal horn rims

Fotopedia dbking

- When we called them "filling stations"
- *Get your kicks on Route 66*

---

*Oscar Mayer Weiner Wagon, car dimmer switch on the floor, push button gear shift

Beauty

Remember the first time you pulled a hair off your collar and realized it was attached to your chin?

On their way to lunch, the three women pass a vintage clothing store and decide to pop in.

farm6.static Flickr

Lynn: Go-go boots! You know, our fashion sense was dominated by the British invasion but so was our hair and make-up. We looked completely different in the 60s from the girls who were teens in the 50s.
Sara: Just about everything was different. We had….
Terry: Long straight hair! Did you iron your hair?
Sara: I didn't have to; my hair was very straight.
Terry: I ironed my hair and it was straight but I did it anyway.
Lynn: Mom wouldn't let us do that. She'd say, "You're going to burn it off!" I had straight hair but I used a straightener. That stuff made my hair stick straight!
Terry: Well, that all started

Flickr classic_film

184

with that one model from England. Stringy, the one like the branch.
Lynn: Twiggy?
Terry: Whatever, it was a tree thing. Anyway, she was the first super model, and the first one whose name I knew. Probably the only one whose name I know. But back then you had to straighten your hair. If you didn't iron it, you used rollers and slept in them all night.

Google anhistoriclady

Lynn: You could barely move; and they hurt so much. Remember the ones with the brush inside? You would just bury your face in the pillow and, of course, then you couldn't breathe. Then we used those sponge rollers because they were supposed to be the kind you could sleep on. But they still had those plastic little snaps and they would dig into your head no matter how you turned.
Terry: But finally we got those hair dryers.
Sara: Oh, the bonnet ones. But they took forever!
Lynn: I took off the bonnet and then I could just blow the air out the hose.
Terry: Oh, so you were an early blower.
Lynn: And the perms?
Terry: Yeah! We did those at home.
Lynn: That's because they were *Toni Home Perms.*
Terry: I never thought of that.

Flickr pds209

Lynn: Those things were brutal. It's amazing we aren't all bald. And you would have the different sized curlers for the tight or loose curls.
Sara: They smelled toxic.
Terry: I was madly in love with the boy across the street. He was really cute but very shy. I was getting a perm one day and I was sitting in the den with those curlers in my hair waiting those unbelievably long 30 minutes, and the stink was all over the house. He knocked on the door and asked me to go play miniature golf and I said, "What?"
and he had to say the whole thing over again. Well, he had five sisters so he obviously knew I could not go, but he had been practicing and practicing his little 'speech' and repeated it. But I still couldn't go because I had this stupid permanent on my head.
Sara: Finally, when you couldn't stand that toxic smell and the pain any longer, your mom would put on the neutralizer and the burning stopped. It felt so good!
Lynn: But then you couldn't wash your hair for 24 hours and the smell was still there. When I got one, my hair was just ZING for about two weeks and then finally the curls would start relaxing.
Sara: Mine would always just get frizzy and after two weeks it would be straight again. It was the most useless thing for my hair. It just didn't work for me.
Terry: One time I did get a permanent at a local beauty shop. It was owned by the lady who lived across the street from us. Oh, and her sister... she had a son who was supposed to go to Yale, but instead he went to jail. So she moved to Viola.
Lynn: Is that where the beauty shop was?
Terry: No, they didn't have a beauty shop in Viola then.

Anyway I wanted to get the 'flip' hair style, remember those? And I ended up with tight curls all around my head, looking just like George Washington.

Sara: What was she on?

Terry: It's a he, and he's on the dollar bill.

Sara: Did you have those really old curling irons? The ones without the plugs? I remember one that my mother used. She put in the gas jet of the stove. When she'd do her hair, you'd smell burning hair all over the house.

Wikimedia

Lynn: You'd get the little burn scars.

Sara: Or did you put the tape on your face to make spit curls?

Lynn and Terry: Yes!

Terry: The pink tape. And if we didn't have that we'd use scotch tape.

Sara: You'd go to school the next day with these welts on your face. That had to be pretty.

Lynn: Ripped skin, burned hair, toxins,it was dangerous to be beautiful back then.

Farm4.staticflickr

Terry: Yes, but you wouldn't want to be like Queen Isabella.

Lynn: Why?

Terry: Queen Isabella was 55 years old when she died, and only took two baths in her entire life.

Sara: Wow! Just wow.

Terry: Men did different stuff to their hair too. One of my neighbors always put *Brylcreme* on his hair. You could see the comb lines in his hair, but my mother always said that it was really because he only washed his hair once a year. I don't think that was really unusual then but I wonder how he picked which day.
Lynn: Did your moms try different beauty aids from stuff around the house?
Terry and Sara: Oh yeah.
Lynn: Mayonnaise?
Sara: Mayonnaise?
Lynn: I think it was supposed to be a hair conditioner, or was it used as a skin cream?
Sara: My mom used to rinse her hair with vinegar because it was supposed to be good for brunettes. Lemon juice, if you were blond.
Lynn: Or you used an egg.
Sara: Or beer.
Terry: No, we drink that.
Lynn: We had lots of different products. Most are probably banned now.
Terry: Did you know that Napoleon wrote a letter to Josephine saying, "I'll be home in three days. Don't bathe"?
Lynn: I'm not quite sure what to make of that.
Sara: They must have had terrible acne. I remember when I first had an onset of acne. I was 13 and I'd scrub my face like crazy. The stuff we used to treat it was just nasty. It was sort of like it just burned your skin right off.
Lynn: They called that the gentle cleanser.
Sara: Somehow I thought that as I grew older skin eruptions would disappear, that you grew out of acne.
Terry: Yeah, I had one just the other day!

Sara: My mother never told me that I'd have menopause and acne at the same time.

Terry: But there wasn't much about 'beauty' that was gentle, especially back then. I loved watching my mom get ready to go out, which happened about once every two months. She used make-up which fascinated me. And she'd pluck her eyebrows herself. But now that I think about it, I don't remember her plucking anywhere else.

Sara: Maybe she wasn't old enough yet. But I am and I'm always worried now that I'm missing one of those 'monster hairs' that grow in overnight.

Lynn: Oh yes! What a pain.

Terry: I don't remember my mom having to chin pluck even when she was older. Maybe she did it in secret. Although I was in my college roommate's wedding and her mother's 'monster hairs' were about three inches long! She finally plucked them the day of the wedding. My mother didn't tell me about those hairs.

Lynn: My family is kind of hairless people so my mom didn't talk about it either.

Sara: My mom did. The last time I was at my mom's she said, "Check my face and check my eyebrows," before we went to this little party. And my husband, who can't grow any hair on the top of his head, can grow wild eyebrows overnight.

Terry: Ugh, men with hairs in their ears or up their nose. Boy, I'm glad I'm not a guy with those hair problems. One Christmas we gave Ken one of those nose/ear hair remover things; I bought it for him for $10 as a joke. He thought it was the best gift he'd ever gotten.

Lynn: I remember my dad would shave and then he'd get the edge right up in his nose. And he told us there was a girl in his high school who had hair up her nose and that she was so pretty until she leaned back. So I'd go into the bathroom and check myself out.

Sara: Or mustaches on women. I remember our boys went to this babysitter for years and years. Later our youngest son said he suspected she might be a man because she had a mustache. He couldn't quite figure that out when he was little.

Terry: And now lots of us have mustaches!

Lynn: My grandpa used to have this saying, "Eat some of this. It'll put hair on your chest." And when I was little I wanted that hair so I ate whatever he suggested.

Sara: Do you remember shaving for the first time?

Lynn: Oh man, do I! Shaving and *Right Guard*. Bad combination. This was when we moved to Hawaii and we were living by the beach. My older sister convinced my mom that I, at 12, should be allowed to shave because we wore bathing suits all the time. I was so excited. It was one of those double-edged razors.

Terry and Sara: Yes! Lethal!

Terry: You'd use one of them and then you walked around with little scraps of toilet paper stuck to you all day.

Lynn: So I also shaved under my arms; my mom showed me how. We didn't use shaving cream, just soap. I probably did it 6 or 7 times to make sure I got every little hair. And then I thought, "Well, I have to do the whole thing." So I took a can of *Right Guard* and sprayed it...

Terry and Sara: Owie, owie, owie!

Lynn: I just screamed and went running from one room to the next. I think they were ready to call the paramedics. My mom didn't tell me not to use the deodorant right away after shaving. We had just gone from the roll-ons to

the sprays. That was the advent of the sprays, before we even heard about the ozone layer.
Terry: But I think the roll-ons hurt too.
Lynn: There was just a lot of alcohol in those things.
Sara: My sister and I used our dad's razor, and he hated that because when he'd try to shave it would always be dull. But finally I got a Lady Remington, the electric shaver.
Lynn: The little pink ones. You got them for Christmas.
Sara: They worked for crap, they didn't cut jack. I remember thinking you were supposed to use aftershave on your legs which was a similar bad mistake.

The Remington Princess

Flickr 1950s unlimited

Lynn: I used to have a uni-brow so I shaved it, which didn't help at all.
Sara: The first time I shaved my legs was because my older sister marched me into my mother and said, "Teach her how to shave her legs! Her legs are so hairy!" I looked at my legs and yes, they had hair, but they always had. Obviously it was repulsive to her. My sister was of the generation where they not only plucked, but they curled their eyelashes with that little tool. Remember that little thing?
Lynn: Yeah, you'd catch your lid in there.
Sara: Then you used blue mascara and ratted your hair and used lots of hairspray. And set your hair on juice cans. I almost forgot about those!
Terry: The sixties were the beginnings of piercings, too. In

high school everybody got pierced ears, well, just the girls. I used an ice cube and a potato. My friend Jenny did them for me and she got them crooked so I had to have one done twice.
Lynn: Now everything is pierced – noses,
Sara: belly buttons,
Lynn: tongues and lips,
Sara: eyebrows,
Terry: and ears.
Lynn: I'm not sure you've noticed but I don't have pierced ears. I was chicken. However, I wore those stupid clip-on earrings for years.
Sara: Those hurt so bad.
Lynn: You can get national secrets out of people with those things.
Sara: Enhanced interrogation.
Terry: We also used the ones that screwed into your ears.

Flickr Annie Pilon

Lynn: You'd wind them into your flesh until the blood stopped flowing and the whole side of your face would go numb. Or with the clip-on ones, you'd be talking to someone and all of a sudden one would fall off.
Sara: I'd wear those earrings to dances. Those dances remind me of boys' cologne. I remember slow dancing with boys and smelling *Hai Karate, English Leather, Jade, Brut...*
Terry: And *Old Spice*.
Lynn: That's what grandpa wore.

Terry: That's what Jim P. wore to Homecoming.
Sara: How old was he?
Terry: He was a senior.
Sara: Senior citizen?
Lynn: But the 60s were when the fake hair came in. My sister Pammy had false eyelashes and she had a fall.
Terry: Did you she hurt herself?
Lynn: No, it was up on top of her head. And she'd take off the eyelashes and leave them on the bathroom counter by the sink; they looked like little caterpillars. Sometimes she'd leave her fall at the foot of the stairs to take up with her later, but usually she'd forget to take it up. I'd be walking up the stairs late at night and wouldn't turn on the ights, and I'd step down.

Flickr Jamie

Terry: Thought it was a rat, huh?
Sara: We were improvising lots of fake stuff then. Some girls used Kleenex in their bras, but one girl in my junior high went further. Once, as she went up to the board, an orange fell out of her shirt. Now she would just have implants.
Terry: My friend Ginny was dancing with this new guy after a basketball game and her fake hair (we used the technical term—fake hair) fell right off. The guy just walked away. I'm sure he didn't know what to do. I think he thought she was falling apart.

Broad Chatter
Playing at the Beauty Shop
a memory from Terry

When I was growing up, I didn't know any mothers who worked. Moms stayed home so that when you walked in the door after school and said, "I'm home!" your mom would say, "How was school today?" Moms were home. Moms didn't work. That was my reality.

I was almost an adult when I finally realized the three most important women in my life, besides my mom, all had jobs. My grandmother owned a restaurant, my great Aunt Cat was the candy lady at *Woolworth's*, and my Aunt Imy owned a beauty shop. I was with these women all summer long when I would visit my grandmother. But they never said they were going to 'work'; they went to the three places that I thought were the most wonderful places in the world. How could that be work?

I probably spent the most time at Aunt Imy's beauty shop. There was so much going on there and I was allowed to not only help out but also be the recipient of all that 'beauty'. The shop was on the north end of the main street in town, Walnut Street. As I walked there from Maw Maw's restaurant, I passed two shoe stores, a department store, an appliance store, two drug stores, and a women's clothing store. All of these were locally owned businesses. The *Woolworth* store was the only chain store and, with its wooden floors, counters with glass dividers, and bins filled with candy that was scooped up, weighed, and put into little white bags, it seemed like a local business also. I would stop in the stores and shops on a regular basis. The owners all knew who I was and never minded this little girl who wandered around town all by herself.

The *Beauty Shoppe* had once been a jewelry store so the door was between two large windows and one of my jobs was to set up displays in those windows. I would study the photos of the hair models and decide which ones deserved a place of honor in the window. But my favorite display was a plastic bird with a cup of water. Once you set the bird in motion, he would bob down to the cup as though he was getting a drink. Everyone loved that bird!

As you walked through the door and past my displays, the smell of shampoo, hair spray, and permanent wave solution was almost overpowering and I loved that smell. There were two molded plastic chairs in front and a table with magazines: *Look, Life, Saturday Evening Post*, and my favorite, *True Confessions*. On the left side of the room were three stalls divided by partitions that were smoked glass on the top and vinyl on the bottom. On the right were four chairs with hair dryers attached. Way in the back were the three sinks (that were called 'bowls' by those of us in the know) where the customers' hair was washed. On the right were sinks for washing the combs and brushes. And, for a young girl, each of those places was a grand place to 'play'.

Aunt Imy, Pearl, and Sharon, who had started as an apprentice, were the three beauticians. They would arrive at seven in the morning. Most of their customers got their hair 'done' once a week and the business women would come right away in the morning before they went to work; obviously they weren't moms, at least in my eyes. Every week their hair was washed, set with brush curlers, and dried under those dryer hoods. After they were combed out, they were given a mask to put over their faces to protect them from the hair spray which was put on in copious amounts. Every three to six months they would get a permanent, a stinky, smelly process that took several hours and would take place in the late afternoon or more often on Saturday. Getting your hair dyed was rare. I remember walking in just as my aunt was going blond for the first time. As I peaked around the partition, she was in a green stage and everyone was a bit worried. It all turned out okay and after Imy made the plunge, more and more customers joined the ranks of dying their hair. My grandmother, who had white hair, went for the blue stuff which was supposed to take the yellow out by replacing it with blue. Not a good look in my opinion.

My duties, besides being the window designer, were comb washer and hair sweeper. I really wanted to answer the phone and write appointments in that huge book but was not allowed near it. I was also the errand 'boy'. I'd run across the street to the one drug store in town with a soda fountain and get cherry or chocolate cokes for the customers and beauticians. They always put them in glasses, no plastic or paper cups, and then I'd return the glasses every few days. Occasionally I was sent to 'the restaurant' (my grandmother's) to get 'beauty shop burgers' for everyone. These sandwiches were loaded—tomatoes, onions, pickles, even a boiled egg and are still the best burgers I've ever eaten. But my favorite errand was to go to the *Dairy Queen* which was about a mile away. Someone without a customer would drive me but I'd take the orders and the money and get everyone, including me, a chocolate shake.

One day, and only that once, my Uncle Gov, Aunt Imy's husband, let me wash his hair in the bowl. I put the plastic cape around his shoulders and lowered his head into the neck slot. The bowls really weren't any different than they are now and I loved using the spray hose. But there is really a skill involved with that hose because not only did I get Gov's head wet but also his entire back. He just smiled and said it felt kind of good. He was truly the best adult in the entire world!

For the two years of Sharon's apprenticeship, I was her guinea pig. I got my eyebrows plucked every two weeks whether I needed it or not. Does any eight year old really need plucked eyebrows? She also did my fingernails at least twice a week! I'd soak my fingers in a little bowl, then Sharon would file my nails, trim my cuticles, and finally apply the polish that I'd picked out, *Love that Pink* or *Cherries in the Glow*. Of course I wasn't allowed to wear lipstick so I could pick any color and not have to worry about matching my lips as was the fashion then.

My dad had never wanted me to cut my hair so it hung below my waist. The summer I was ten, Aunt Imy decided I needed it cut and she didn't discuss this with my parents. I picked out a DA, Duck's Ass, which I thought was very daring. My hair went from below my waist to as short as my brother's. I thought my mom would have a heart attack when she saw it, but my dad, who loved his sister unconditionally and thought she could do no wrong, said how much he liked it. Mom didn't talk to him or Imy for a week.

Probably the best part of hanging out at the *Beauty Shoppe* was the other women and their conversations. I was always allowed to listen in on the news, gossip, complaints about husbands, and joys and worries of raising children. I learned a lot from listening in; mostly that it was important to connect with other people and the *Beauty Shoppe* was a great place to connect. Men had their taverns, but the women ruled the beauty shops.

So, as I said, during my childhood I didn't know any moms who worked. I knew women who had fun all day, who talked and laughed, who shared joys and sorrows, but work? No, this was way too much fun to be work.

You're a Boomer if you know what these are:

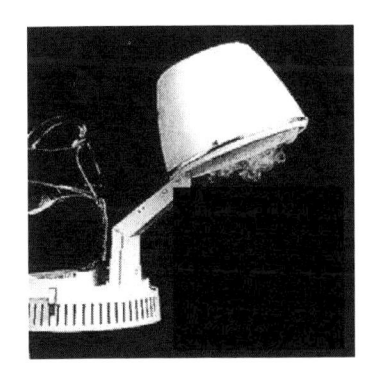

Wikimedia

dreamstime.com

What were Spoolies?

Answers at the end of the chapter

Do you remember?
- Dippity Doo
- Blue mascara
- Velcro rollers
- Vanity mirrors and dressers
- Metal hair *Klippies* and hairpins
- Clear plastic rain bonnets
- Flip, DA, French twist hairdos
- Getting an "updo" for prom
- Jewelry boxes with dancing ballerinas
- Headbands and hair bows
- *Evening in Paris* and *Chanel #5*

1950sunlimited

199

- Cold cream
- Foam turbans to sleep in and not ruin your hairstyle
- Ratting your hair to make a beehive
- The *Breck* girls
- Powder puffs and loose powder
- Frosting your hair with the holey bonnet and a crochet hook

1950sunlimited

*Beauty Salon Hair Dryer, Home permanent rollers

Google Creative Commons

Sex
*I don't know much about sex---
I've always been married*

*Marriage is a 50/50 relationship—
I cook, he eats.*

The three women have gotten to the restaurant for lunch and, as usual, are reminiscing.

Terry: Did you guys have to go to that movie at school about how the body changes? My mom took me when I was in fifth grade and then, whenI was in sixth grade, she said we should go back and see it again.

Flickr Robert Valdemar

Lynn: Why was that?
Terry: I think it was remedial. After that time, my mom asked me if I had any questions about the movie. They told about everything that was happening to our bodies but they didn't tell us how the baby got there. I asked her about that and she said, "Terry, think about it. A woman looks like this (She made a circle with her right index finger and thumb) and a man looks like that (She stuck out her left index finger), now don't those things go together?" And that was the end of it until she asked me one day to get a female plug at Peterson's hardware. I didn't know what she meant so she went back to the,

Flickr romana klee

"Think about it, Terry." I didn't know until then that I had so much in common with hardware.

Sara: I think at my Mother-Daughter Tea the movie was actually a film strip. That DuKane thing.

Terry: Beep!

Sara: I don't remember anything beyond that. I never made the connection between that film strip and birth. But I did have Debbie who told me about what you did with boys and it just sounded disgusting. The first time she told me about French kissing I thought I was going to gag.

Lynn: When I was in the 7th or 8th grade, I was reading a biology book about walruses, when I said, "Oh." I bet I reread that paragraph seven or eight times. Then one night after that I was sitting next to my mom, we were watching TV, and I told her about the walruses and she added a detail or two and that was about it.

Sara: My dad and I went fishing and on the way back we were walking through this cow pasture and there was a cow bellering. I said, "Dad, what's wrong with that cow?" And he said, "Well, let's just sit down for a minute and watch her." She delivered a calf right then and there. I was so impressed; I was wide-eyed. But I didn't connect that to me and I didn't know how the calf got in her.

Terry: When I was thirteen and I got my period for the first time, I stayed home from school for about three days. I was freaked everyone would know! My mother had saved a magazine which she gave to me. It had to do with a beaver dam, that's all I remember...moving into womanhood and beaver dams.

Lynn: So we have beavers, cows and walruses.

Terry: The beavers are the only one that really works with all that.

Sara: Nothing was working for me!

Terry: I had a theory when I was a kid that it had something to do with the belly button. It took me a while to let go of that.

Sara: I bet a lot of children believe that because that's the most obvious thing and it's sort of in the right place. But moving on, were your parents affectionate in front of you?

Lynn: Very. My dad would look at Mom across the table and he'd tap his finger (taps finger three times) and she'd tap back. I...Love...You.

Terry: No, it's "Knock three times on the table if you want me". Was that their signal for the night?

Lynn: I don't know. But I never thought of that until now! Thank you for ruining it for me! I just thought they were being romantic. When I told my son the facts of life he listened intently; I had the encyclopedia out and showed him some pictures, no walruses in this discussion. I went through the whole thing and then I asked him if he had any questions. He said, "You and Dad don't do that, do you?" It took me a while when I was young to figure out that, oh my word, my parents did this.

Sara: That's a scary moment when you actually realize your parents had to do 'that' in order for you to be here.

Lynn: My parents did it at least four times!

Sara: I only have proof of my folks doing it twice.

Terry: Well, my kids are adopted so they didn't have to think about Ken and me doing it at all!

Sara: Yep, no proof there.

Terry: Although Ken drove Megan crazy when she was in high school by saying, "Mom and I are going upstairs to do the nasty."

Sara: Still no real proof!!

Lynn: Sometimes we'd walk into the room and my parents would be, well, we called it 'making out'.

Sara: My folks were affectionate, too. They would hug and kiss and hold hands in front of us. They were always physically affectionate but never inappropriately.
Lynn: And what would you do?
Sara: We'd look away or pretend that it was awful, but I think it really was very reassuring to me. In my heart-of-hearts I always liked that display because it was so obvious that they loved each other. And I liked looking at old pictures of them when they first met and at their wedding pictures. That was a very romantic thing for me. But I wasn't envisioning them doing anything but holding hands and getting married.
Lynn: Mom would tell the story about how they met. Dad was overseas for years and mom dated like crazy and even had a few marriage proposals in there, but Dad would write her these letters. He was pretty romantic. He would write all these things like, "staring out into the night thinking of the diamonds in your eyes." They maintained that romance right up until the end.

Sara's parents

Sara: Did she keep those letters?
Lynn: She kept some of them. I remember Dad was a pretty good writer. When they became pregnant with Steve, which was pretty much on their honeymoon, he wrote a letter from the baby. He called the baby 'Gadget Lewis'. It was pretty cute. It was nice because I expected the same thing when I got married, and I have a very affectionate husband who I appreciate.
Sara: My mother told a few stories about their early years together. When they first met she tried to trick my dad.

She was living with her two sisters, her sister-in-law, and a bunch of kids in this little cramped apartment. Dad was coming for his first date with her. It was a blind date; he had never met her before. He took the bus to Mom's apartment and my Aunt Lorraine was on the same bus. When Dad asked the bus driver about the address, she realized that this was the guy who was coming to date her sister. So she got off a block early, ran to the apartment, burst in yelling, "He's coming; he's on the bus!" So those women decided that, when he got there, they wouldn't tell him which one was Evelyn. He sat there while they teased him and then finally he said, "Well, I think I'll take you to the movie." And he pointed at my mother. He had seen a picture of her so he really knew all along. Mom loved that little story.

Lynn: My mom said my dad was a ladies' man before he was married and then he met my mom and she was this sweet, innocent little Mormon girl. He met her on a blind date, too. He was in the Air Corps stationed above Salt Lake City and he had a good friend who wanted to go out with mom's best friend. She was afraid to go out with him alone. She said if he would do a double date, she'd go out with him. So the guy talked my dad into going. That afternoon my dad ran into an old girlfriend. He called my mom and said, "I'm sorry I can't make it. I'm just really sick." Then the old girlfriend ditched him for someone else so he called my mom back saying, "I'm feeling so much better."

Sara: What a stinker!

Terry: Like Maxine says: Marriage can be fun some of the time. Trouble is, marriage is all of the time.

Lynn: Dad said when he saw her, he swears she was wearing a skirt and ankle high stockings but she always said, "I was not! I was 18 years old."

Terry: My folks met at a dance. They went to dances all the time. Mom had won many jitterbug contests; she was little so they could throw her all around, plus she was a really good dancer. She had several marriage proposals before my dad, but when they met, she ditched all the other guys and the dance contests for Dad. They did continue dancing together all their married lives. Anyway, World War II started and my dad joined the Navy so they eloped and didn't tell anyone for a while. My grandmother (Dad's mom) told Mom one day, "It's a good thing you're waiting until after Bud gets back from the service. All these people are getting married in a rush now, but it's much better if you wait." Mom felt terrible because she was already married to him. They finally told everyone when he came back from boot camp just before he was shipped to the Pacific. I have a photo of him kissing her good-bye.
Sara: Do you remember your first kiss?
Lynn: Oh yes. I was a tomboy, about nine years old, and a bunch of us were playing war. I was captured and there was this boy who was supposed to guard me in their fort. He said, "If you give me a kiss, I'll let you go." So I thought, "What the hey." I gave him a little peck and then I picked up his gun and shot him!
Terry: Good girl
Sara: My very first kiss was when I kissed this boy, Lon, in Kindergarten and he pushed me in the ditch. I was in love with him all through elementary school.

Flickr Bunky's Pickle

Lynn: Even after he pushed you in the ditch?

Sara: Yeah, it was true love, L-U-V, love.

Terry: I had this cute neighbor boy, Dick, who I had loved forever, but he was shy. Finally one day, he caught up with me as I was walking to school and asked me to Homecoming. I was thrilled! I always picked up my friend Ginny on the way to school and I was in such shock that, when I got to her house, I told him good-bye and went in. Later I realized I could have walked the whole way with him. Duh me.

Sara: And then the pill came along and all of life changed. The whole sexual revolution.

Terry: When I started college no one even thought of living with a guy, but by my junior year it was very common. Although I didn't even give it a thought. My dad would have had a heart attack.

Sara: And look at us now. No one even blinks an eye about people living together.

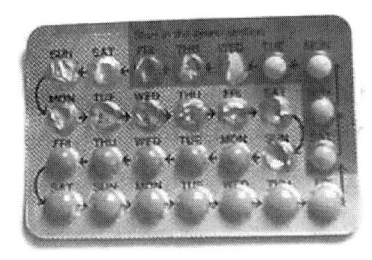

Wikimedia Commons

Lynn: My house is a bit different. Both Brent and my dad, if he were here, would still have a heart attack

Sara: But the sexual revolution brought so much more to women than living together.

Lynn: The whole idea that women could do important things outside the home. Since women could regulate their families, they could regulate their lives - have careers.

Terry: We got the *Pill* and so women could have sex without having to worry about getting preggers.

Lynn: That's a word we should have left behind. In fifth

grade we were asked what we wanted to be. Boys were saying lawyers, doctors, astronauts. And girls were saying secretary, teacher, mother, and...
Terry: and baton twirler! (all do a hand gesture)
Lynn: What I wanted to be was a farmer but I couldn't say that. So what I said was that I wanted to be a farmer's wife.
Sara: The wife or the daughter. You had to fit into the roles that were open to you. My typing class was all girls because that is what we were expected to be, secretaries and then wives.
Terry: Actually, I really wanted to be a stewardess.
Sara: That was only for women then, now it's men too and they are all called flight attendants.
Terry: No, I didn't want to attend, I wanted to stew.

Flickr James Vaughan

Once Santa brought me a stewardess hat, wings, food tray, silverware, passenger chart-thingy and Peter Lawford was always on my plane. I really wanted to be a stewardess.
Lynn: So why didn't you?
Terry: (stands and gestures)
Lynn: Oh, you couldn't reach the overhead compartments.
Sara: Santa didn't bring you stewardess arms and legs.
Lynn: We did get a lot of the things we wanted from the women's movement. But we've still got a ways to go, like equal pay.
Sara: Some things from the sexual revolution, though, have backfired, like deadly sexual diseases. And now with reality shows, oh oh, television again, they're taking life and sex

to the extreme with shows like the Kardashians or *Desperate Housewives* or *The Bachelor*.
Lynn: I think those are definitely backfire shows.

Broad Chatter
The Girls Who Knew It All
three memories

Sara: I came into an understanding of sexuality pretty late in life. Even after I had begun menstruating I didn't understand that it had anything to do with having babies. It wasn't until I took 9th grade Biology class that I started putting the pieces together. I was also a tomboy and didn't have any interest in boys until about that same time. As a child I saw boys only as friends or competitors. I didn't have any brothers so I had no concept of a boy's anatomy.

But there was a girl in my neighborhood who 'knew it all' at a very young age. She wanted to date, get married, and have children and my mother called her 'boy crazy'. She always wanted to play dolls and wedding, which I considered boring. When I was about 12, she began to tell me stories about what older boys and girls did together. I couldn't believe it! Her stories actually scared me. I remember her telling me about French kissing and I thought that if a boy ever did that to me I'd just choke, or maybe even throw up. I was left wondering why people would do that to each other.

Terry: For me the girls who 'knew everything' were few and far between. When I was young, there was Marcia who was three years older than I was and told me about the box (*Kotex*) in the bathroom that caused babies and that was about it. Most of my information came from the *True Confessions* magazine that I read at my aunt's beauty shop. I distinctly remember a story of a girl who had three children before she graduated from high school, on time!

Before I read that story I had thought you had to be married to have kids. I also learned from the *Fredericks of Hollywood* ads at the back of the magazine. There were drawings of pointy bras, push up bras, and bras with strategic holes in them. No adults that I knew ordered from *Fredericks* but I knew I would be ordering from them when I was an adult…..never happened! A few friends told dirty jokes that I either didn't get or got turned around.

Flickr pds 209

One of those was told (allegedly) by Dick Biondi, a DJ on WLS radio. It involved a boy and girl at a ball game. Biondi said the boy would kiss the girl on the strikes and she would kiss him on the balls. Biondi got fired (that was the story going around) because of that joke which I thought was weird because he'd turned it around. I thought the boy would kiss the girl on the balls (her breasts); those were the only ball body things I knew. I was well into junior high school when that happened.

At that same time, girls would run into the bathroom yelling, "Get out of the way. My friend is coming!" and I would look at the door to see who it was.

So, except for undergarments and extreme stories, I was pretty naïve until Jasmine moved to town when I was a sophomore in high school. First of all I'd never known anyone with such an exotic name. Plus she was from California, home of the *Beach Boys* and *Chad and Dean*. How cool was that? But more importantly, Jasmine had 'been around'. She dated older guys and she'd tell us everything that happened. For instance the time she and a guy snuck into the dentist office where she worked and 'did stuff' in the dentist chair. I was intrigued and scared to death. One day she said she could find a cool older guy for me. I really didn't know what to do. I acted excited but inside I was mush. So, I went to my mom. I told her some of the things that Jasmine had done, leaving out the really scary things. Mom came through with flying colors and said I couldn't be friends with her anymore. Now, as innocent as I was, I seldom did what my mom said. I snuck out of friends' houses during overnights, went to parties, took the train to Chicago when I was supposed to be staying at a friend's. But this time Mom was my lifeline. I didn't tell Jasmine exactly what my mom said, but I didn't hang out with her anymore, and in my own head I was able to justify that because of my 'dumb' mom, not my fears.

Lynn: When I was twelve, I had an appendectomy with some complications which resulted in, among other things, my being grounded from any physical activity for the rest of the semester. This meant I couldn't play any sports during P.E. which bummed me out.

Instead of going outside or to the gym, I spent the P.E. period in 'the cage' which was where we checked out clean towels, balls and other equipment. This meant we were busy at the beginning of the period and busy at the end of the period, but for the bulk of the time we just sat on stools and folded towels. It would have been pretty boring, if I hadn't been locked in the cage with another girl who had been sick.

I was in the 7th grade and she was in the 9th grade. I don't remember her name, but I do remember that she seemed to be the oldest 9th grader I'd ever known. She had some mystery illness which she never explained to me, except that I remember having the distinct impression that she wasn't really sick. She just hated sports and had mastered the art of appearing sick whenever it was time for P.E.

We didn't have much in common and she knew about things that hadn't even approached my radar screen. According to her, she was actively dating. I think she was on her 25th boyfriend by then and she'd known several of them biblically. This was the way she explained it to me, which in my innocent mind meant they'd gone to church together.

It was in 'the cage' that I was told my first off-colored joke which I didn't get at all. I told her that I didn't get it, and she kept repeating the punch line over and over as if somehow a glow of worldly knowledge was going to click on inside me. The way she whispered the story made it seem like the joke was terribly dirty. But years later, when I finally knew enough to understand the punchline, I realized that the joke really wasn't all that bad. I wonder what ever happened to her?

Books
an original story by Terry

The new craze in books during 2012 and beyond was the *Fifty Shades of Gray* series. Everyone was reading it. But we Boomers did have our book crazes too. The big one when I was growing up was *Valley of the Dolls*. It was racy, filled with Hollywood soap opera type stories and stores couldn't keep it on the shelves.

I was working at *Woolworth's* in uptown Wheaton (as opposed to downtown Chicago) during that time. Sometimes I'd stock counters (they had these glass dividers that the merchandise had to fit between) but mostly I ran the cash register. On Friday nights and Saturdays this was a fun job. We'd have a line eight or ten people long and I could really show off my skills of hitting the right buttons without looking at them and giving change without the register telling me how much to give. We actually had to count back the correct change in those days! During the week, however, things were often pretty slow. I was in charge of the *Sno-Cone* machine, which is not as much fun as it sounds, but that was about it. I'd watch the customers at the lunch counter as they ordered 7 oz. *Cokes* or tulip sundaes, stare out the window and watch the clock. And then I found a diversion, reading.

Flickr Jacqueline S

During those slow times, I would stand at the cash register

with a book or magazine hidden just below the counter so the manager, Mr. Carlson, couldn't see it. Perfect! There was a pretty good selection of reading material within arm's reach. One of my favorites was these little books of *Playboy Ribald Classics. Woolworth's* never stocked the actual magazine, just these little books of old 'racy' stories. This was a great book to hide under the counter since it was only about 4x6 inches. But my best reading occurred when the book, *Valley of the Dolls,* came out.

The store had many copies and they were so popular that the books were kept on the end of the counter so the customers could impulsively grab them. That made them within easy reach of a bored cashier. I'd pretend to be stacking them neatly and then sneak one under the counter. I read the whole book (a different copy every time) that way, in little bits, sneaking peaks between customers. Soon afterwards Mr. Carlson caught me with a *Ribald Classic* and I was exiled from the cash register and sent back to filling the counters for a while.

My mom read *Valley of the Dolls*. She actually bought the book! She was a great reader, mostly mysteries, but she spent a lot of time reading a variety of genres. At one time she had the book *Tropic of Cancer*, which was another racy book. After finishing it, she placed it on the shelf and told me that when I was eighteen I could read it. It was always there, on the shelf, as I picked out the next *Readers' Digest Condensed Book* that I would read and to this day I've never read *Tropic of Cancer*.

But one day when I was sixteen, I came home from school and found mom reading in bed. As I walked into her bedroom, she stuffed the book she was reading under the pillow. She didn't put it on the shelf like *Tropic of Cancer,* but under the pillow! The next time I was home alone, I searched for the book. I found it in her underwear drawer. It was the book *Candy* by Terry Southern. Of course, this one I read—in short spurts when Mom was gone. It was a really, really racy novel that made *Valley of the Dolls* look tame and I learned a lot from it, mostly, if you want to hide something, put it in plain sight.

and another thing
That Strange Machine
Sara remembers

In grade school my best friend, Karen, and I got curious about the *Kotex* machine in the girls' bathroom. I brought a nickel to school one day and we put it in the machine, turned the metal dial and out came a plain brown box. We grabbed it, ran into a bathroom stall, locked the door, and opened the box. There was this thing in it, a big, soft, cottony thing, and two safety pins. For the life of us we couldn't figure out what it might be. Karen's guess was that it was something you could use to clean your glasses. I thought maybe it was one of those things you put in your dress to absorb underarm perspiration. Karen and I threw the mysterious thing away but we each kept one of the safety pins as a token our daring adventure. In reality, it was a symbol of our innocence and ignorance.

Flickr Leah.Jones

I Vahnt to Take You Out
an original story by Lynn Wing

I always figured my first date would be with someone like Gregory Peck. But no, my first date was with Dougie. Dougie was a high school senior, I was a sophomore. He was about an inch shorter than I was, which wasn't what I preferred, but it really wasn't a problem for me. The problem that I had with Dougie was his life's passion. He wanted to be a vampire. Really. A living dead, "I've come to drink your blood," vampire.

I met Dougie in drama club. He'd go about the room flapping his arms like a bat and squeaking. Or he'd stand with his back against the wall, his arms crossed over his chest and his eyes closed, and when anyone would walk by, his eyes would pop open and he'd say, "Good evening" in true Bela Lugosi fashion. This was before vampires were considered cool. Needless to say, Dougie didn't have a lot of friends. I suppose that I was nice enough to Dougie. When I'd walk into a room, if he was there, I'd say, "Hi, Dougie". And if I was leaving, and he was there, I'd say, "Bye, Dougie." That was all it took for me to become *The Girl* for him. I could tell he liked me, but I wasn't too concerned. I figured he'd be graduating soon and going off to college. And as long as I was never alone with him after dark, I'd be safe. Then the school year ended, and this is exactly what happened. It was the first Monday of summer vacation when the phone rang, 7:00 p.m. straight up. Someone had given Dougie my phone number. He asked me a couple of questions such as how I was doing, and if I liked something or other, which, being in shock, I mumbled out some sort of answer. Then he asked me out on a date for the next Saturday. Fortunately, I had other plans and when I hung up I thought, "I dodged that bullet."

The next Monday, 7:00 p.m. straight up, the phone rang. This time I manufactured something that I was doing on Saturday. At exactly 7:00 p.m., every Monday that summer, Dougie called me. It got so that when the phone would ring, Mom would automatically reach up to adjust the time on the wall clock while calling out, "Lynn, it's for you."
 He would ask me a couple of questions, to which I'd answer with the first thing that came to mind, and then he'd ask me out for the following Saturday.

I don't know if it was Dougie's tenacity that wore me down, or if time had dulled my memory. I remember thinking he really couldn't be all that bad. And perhaps he'd had a growth spurt. All I do know is that on the next to the last Monday of summer vacation, when Dougie called and asked me out again, I said, "Yes."

The next Saturday, at 4:30 p.m., straight down, the doorbell rang. As soon as I opened the door it came to me in a rush why I hadn't wanted to go out with Dougie. For one thing there had been a growth spurt. Unfortunately, I was the one who had grown.

And then there was his 'look.' His hair was slicked back, vampire fashion. And, head to toe, he was completely dressed in black. The only splash of color was the biggest, pinkest corsage I'd ever seen, that he was holding out to me.

Dougie's hands were so sweaty that he couldn't get a good enough grip on the corsage pin, so Mom had to pin it onto my blouse all the while gushing, "How sweet!"

My blouse was one of those peasant style blouses made of a thin, flimsy cotton material, so the weight of the corsage pulled the neckline of my blouse way below where I wanted it to be. Mom ended up pinning it up on my shoulder. But the corsage still pulled the neckline too low for my taste. However, I found if I twisted my head to the left and jammed my chin into the flower, I was able to keep everything from drifting down. And so with my chin firmly placed in the *Barbie* pink flower and my eyes squinting so I could see in front of me, we walked out to Dougie's parents' four door sedan, which, of course, was black.

Dougie opened the door for me and ran around to the driver's side. As soon as he slid behind the wheel he began chatting that, since musicals were my favorite type of movies, he had the perfect movie picked out for us to see, *Paint Your Wagon*. That's when I realized that all summer long, Dougie had been running reconnaissance on me with his innocent sounding questions. And in my half-thought out responses, I must have told him that I loved musicals, which I kind of like, and that pink is my favorite color, which it isn't.

Half of Pleasant Hill, California was at the theater that evening to watch *Paint Your Wagon*. We ended up getting the last two seats located in the center of the front row. As I sat there, waiting for the movie to start, I tried to, inconspicuously as possible, scratch my nose from the tickle of the fern attached to the corsage. As I did, I felt a twinge of fear as I realized that my with my head turned into the corsage and slightly tilted up towards the movie screen, my exposed neck was vulnerable to Dougie. But I knew it was silly to be afraid. If Dougie was going to bite me, it wouldn't be when we were sitting in a packed theater surrounded by witnesses.

Then a new fear took hold. Dougie was sitting in the universal 'I want to hold your hand' position, his hands lightly poised on the armrests of the chair, waiting to make his move. I desperately did not want that to happen. So I immediately put my hands in the universal 'I don't want you to hold my hand' clasp. But Dougie must not have known what my hands clenched in a tight ball meant, because his hand was slowly making its way towards me. I could see that he fully expected me to release my death grip on myself so he could engulf my hand in his sweaty palm. I really didn't want to create a scene, so I did the only thing I could think of doing. I began to twiddle my thumbs.

It worked! Dougie's hand retreated back to the armrest. He leaned over, and whispered, "What are you doing?" I casually looked down at my spinning thumbs and said, "Oh, this? It's a habit. I twiddle my thumbs whenever I go to a movie."

And so I twiddled my thumbs; I twiddled them forwards, I twiddle them backwards, I twiddled them from side to side. For two hours and 38 minutes, plus intermission, I twiddled my thumbs. By the time I was back in the car, the joints in my thumbs had swollen, freezing my thumbs in place, the left thumb sticking straight up like a fat antenna, the right thumb sticking out to the side as if I were permanently trying to hitch a ride. My neck ached from twisting my face into the corsage. But the movie was pretty good, and we still had time to get home before it was dark, so all in all I was feeling that it'd been an okay date.

However, instead of turning left out of the parking lot to take me home, Dougie turned right, and with a big smile on his face said, "When you told me that pie is your all-time favorite food, I knew the perfect place to take you." I sat there thinking, "I told him I like pie?"

We drove across town to this tiny bakery cafe set next door to a large retirement complex. The neon sign read "Grandma Tilly's Homemade Pies - The Flakiest Crusts in Town".

When we walked up to the cafe's glass door the sign read, 'Closed'. I said, "Oh darn, they're closed."

Dougie smiled, and pushing open the door, announced, "No problem."

As soon as we stepped inside the cafe, I heard someone call out, "They're here!" And instantly we were surrounded by a dozen short people with dark hair. It turned out that 'Grandma Tilly' was literally Grandma Tilly, and there was Granddad Jim, and aunts and uncles and cousins and siblings. As they swarmed around us herding us across the floor to a table, I hoped that Dougie's fascination with vampires was not a family trait.

They sat me in a chair at a small round table with a vase holding pink carnations. I could hear Andy Williams crooning *Moon River* on the Hi-Fi, and I knew that I wasn't the only one on a first date. I didn't even have to order.

As soon as I sat down Grandma Tilly set in front of me…. I need to pause the story to share a piece of information. You know how everyone has at least one food that makes them gag, even just the thought of it? For some people it may be raw octopus, others escargot. For me, it's raisins. When I was six, I became violently ill after eating a raisin salad, but that's another story.

Anyway, there I was, sitting across from Dougie who was beaming, his family circling way too close, and Grandma Tilly placed in front of me a huge wedge of the house specialty, deep dish raisin pie. I thought, "Can it get any worse?"

That's when Granddad Jim rammed a sparkler in the center of the pie, and with a flourish of his cigar lighter, lit that baby up. It seemed like it took 45 minutes for the sparkler to die down, but during that time I was able to work out a strategy of how I was going to eat the pie without tasting it. I'd wolf it down. After all, it worked for my dog.

As soon as that sparkler puttered out I scooped up my fork the best I could without a thumb, chunked out the biggest piece of pie I could spear, jammed it into my mouth, and swallowed it whole. Immediately, I chunked out the next piece, and the next, and the next, clearing the plate in less than one minute.

As soon as I'd gagged down the last chunk, Grandma Tilly said, "Why Dougie, you're right, this girl really does love pie! Granddad, you go get her another piece."

I was halfway through the second piece, when I knew I was going to be sick. I stood, the back of my legs tipping over the chair, and managed to gasp, "Bathroom."

One of the cousins pointed across the room, towards a hallway. I lurched down the hallway into the women's room. The raisins didn't come up, but they were rumbling about with a vengeance in my stomach. The thought came that, "Maybe I'll feel better if I splash some cold water on my face."

Have you ever noticed how handy opposing thumbs can be? Particularly when something is stuck, like the cold water faucet in that women's room at that very moment. Not being able to get a good grip on the faucet, I started hitting it with my palm, and it must have been already weakened because at the fourth smack that handle spun loose and a gush of cold water hit me. That the sink was set low for short people so the stream hit me directly below my belt and just above my thighs. Using both palms, I frantically worked to get enough of a grip on the handle until I was able to ease the flow of water to a trickle.

I stood there, in the pool of water, my soaked pants dripping cold water, thinking, "I can't go back out there in this vulnerable state to a family of possible vampires."

Then I remembered. As I was running to the women's room, at the end of the hallway I had briefly caught sight of an entrance to a store. It was a bit of a blur, but it looked like it might be a women's boutique, and if it was, then maybe they would have pants. I had the ten dollars in my purse that my mom had always insisted that I was to keep with me in case of an emergency, and this definitely was an emergency.

Luck was with me. It was a boutique, full of clothes perfect for all the little old ladies that lived in the retirement complex next door. The salesclerk was so happy to have a customer that she didn't seem to mind that I was dripping on the floor. I asked her if they had any pants, and smiling she said, "We have a lovely selection of slacks." I bought the only pants I could afford, a nice polyester pair with a floral pattern that was two sizes too big for me. But the elastic waistband made it easy for me to hold them up without a thumb, and the pink matched the color of my corsage.

By the time I hobbled back to the cafe's dining room, the table had been cleared and the family was gone. Only Dougie and Grandma Tilly were seated at the table. She was reaching over across it and patting Dougie's hand. As soon as she caught sight of me, she stood. At her full height this woman came up to no more than my chest, but when she unfolded herself from that chair I had the distinct impression of a mama bear protecting her young.

"Oh," she said, ice tinging each word, "You didn't leave. When you were gone so long, I went to the girl's room to check on you and all I found was water all over the counter and floor."

"Ah, yeah," I mumbled, "There was an accident."

We didn't stay long. Dougie was silent as he drove me home.

I felt terrible. I sat there with my chin resting in the wilting orchid, my thumbs frozen in place, my wet jeans soaking through my purse onto my new floral slacks, and I thought, "Why didn't I let Dougie hold my hand? So what if I don't like him?" And when Grandma Tilly set the raisin pie in front of me, all I needed to say was, "I'm sorry I don't like raisins, but that lemon meringue looks fantastic."

By the time we pulled up front of my house, I'd determined that the next time Dougie asked me out, I was going to say yes, right away. And I was going to show Grandma Tilly and Granddad Jim that I'm a nice girl.

But Dougie never called me again.

I heard through friends that a week after our date Dougie left to attend Stanford University on a full-ride scholarship. Later, I learned he made a fortune during the 1990's with a dot com company he'd founded. To the best of my knowledge he never became a vampire. But he does have a blog about vampires with a million plus following.

I wonder what my first date would have been like if it had been with Gregory Peck. No vampires. But then, he never owned a dot com company.

You're a Boomer if you recognize these sexy women:

Flickr pds209 *Flickr pds209* *Flickr pds209*

*Answers at the end of the chapter

Flickr pds209

Do you remember?

- Barbara Eden in *I Dream of Jeannie* was not allowed to show her belly button.
- Laura Petrie (Mary Tyler Moore) and Rob Petrie (Dick Van Dyke) were married, but had twin beds. So did Lucy and Desi in *I Love Lucy*
- Baby Doll pajamas
- The first topless swim suit in *Life* magazine
- The conservative swim suits in the Miss America contest

Flickr James Vaughan

Flickr pds209

- Ads to increase your bust size in women's magazines
- Pin Up girl calendars

Flickr Tropic-7

How we went from this definition of "sexy" In the 1950s...

...to this one in the 1960s

Flickr pds209

Flickr pds2

*Sharon Tate, Raquel Welch, Diana Ross

The Green Thing

Every litter bit hurts

Flickr classic film

Don't blow it – good planets are hard to find.
Time Magazine

Don't throw that away; we'll find a use for it somewhere.
Ken's dad

The three women are in Lynn's kitchen cleaning up after lunch.

Lynn: I've got a bag for the bottles, one for the cans, and we'll put the compostable garbage in the woods.

Terry: That's a pretty green thing to do.

Sara: You know, I've been doing that all my life. That is just how I was taught to take care of things. I guess my folks were green before it was 'in' to be green.

Terry: I think we were all green back then. We just didn't know it.

Sara: Mom had this old pan and that was where all the food scraps went. Then they'd be put into the compost pile for the garden. She did that all year 'round.

Lynn: You are right. We were green in the 50s and 60s.

Sara: It wasn't because we were thinking about the environment. It was just that's how you got rid of your trash. We were green for lots of things. We had pop machines. You got the whole bottle and you

Pinterest.com

229

pried the top off right at the machine; there was a bottle opener and the caps fell into a little well. When you were finished, you returned the bottles and they were filled up again. So the bottles were sometimes scratched on the outside. We got money back when we returned the bottles but it was usually used to pay the deposit on the filled ones we'd buy.

Lynn: I remember trying to get Grandpa to drink his *Dr. Pepper* so we could fill up the case. We'd put it in the wagon and would walk two blocks to this place where we could turn them in. We were really pushing soda pop on Grandpa and raking in the dough.

Terry: You got two cents a bottle.

Lynn: In 1969?

Terry: No, that was in 1959, Lynn.

Lynn: We only had paper grocery bags. Actually, we'd get paper bags at every store we went to, department stores, dime stores. It was all paper.

Sara: We also used brown paper bags as book covers for our school books. That way the books would stay nice for the next year's students. But, because of the paper cover, we could decorate each book in our own special way.

Terry: I loved making each book look different. Well, you had to since they all had the same brown paper cover.

Sara: We also had a burn barrel and everything that went in the kitchen trash bag had to be burnable. So we'd burn the bags with the stuff right inside.

Burnbarrel.org

Terry: We had one before I moved to Wheaton. No one had them in Wheaton. We also had a clothes line at that old house. Everyone in our neighborhood in Wheaton just had dryers.
Sara: My mom always used a clothes line. It made the clothes smell so sweet.
Terry: I have one now. It is my favorite household chore. Actually, it is the only household chore I like.
Lynn: Talking about laundry, our moms washed the baby's diapers because we didn't have the throw-away kind. Then they turned them into cleaning rags once the baby was potty trained. They were the best for washing windows!
Sara: Kids got hand-me-down clothes from their brothers or sisters, not always brand new clothing.
Lynn: Maybe people were tougher then. We certainly used fewer powered things and did more walking. We walked up stairs, because we didn't have an escalator in every store and building. We walked to the grocery store and didn't climb into a gas guzzling machine every time we had to go two blocks.
Terry: We used less of everything. We had one television in the house, not one in every room. The TV had a small screen; now the screens take up an entire wall.
Lynn: In the kitchen, we blended and stirred by hand because we didn't have blenders and food processors to do everything for us. When we sent packages in the mail, which was the only way to send anything, we used wadded up old newspapers, not *Styrofoam* or plastic bubble wrap. Although, I do love to pop those bubbles.

improvephotography.com

Sara: We drank from a fountain when we were thirsty instead of using a cup or a plastic bottle. Or we drank right from the hose when we were outside. We refilled pens with ink instead of buying a new pen. We replaced the blades in a razor instead of throwing away the whole thing when the blade got dull.

Lynn: My mom didn't take us everywhere either. She made us walk unless it was something really far away. She always said she was a mom not a taxi service.

Sara: We didn't depend on our cars as much or any other motorized thing. We all had push lawn mowers, for a while anyway, until we finally got a power mower. When my dad got a riding mower, I ran over two little pine trees with it. But I guess by that time he wasn't thinking about how much he was spending on gas; he was just thinking of saving time.

Lynn: I did love the sound of those push mowers. It was kind of a 'flop, flop, flop' sound.

Terry: You had to sharpen the blades or you'd have short and long patches of grass.

Jeffs60s.com

Lynn: Now we have mowers that mulch,
Terry: and aerate.
Sara: They even eat weeds.
Lynn: And they have windshields.
Terry: Do you like washing them too, like car windshields?
Lynn: No, that would be a waste of water. I remember in 5th grade we were talking about things you couldn't sell and one of them was water.
Sara: We thought "How would you sell water? It would be like selling air."
Terry: Speaking of green, what about those stamps?
Sara and Lynn: *S&H Green Stamps!*

Terry: What does S&H stand for? Stick 'em on and Hand them in?
Lynn: Stanley & Harvey
Sara: It makes me think of S&M! But did you get the little books?
Terry: Mom had a specific drawer just for them.
Sara: You'd sit down at night and paste those things in the book. Sometimes you had a big stamp that was worth fifty of the little ones.
Terry: I loved it when the books were full and you could get actual 'stuff'. After a while there was an *S&H Green Stamp Store* in the next town so you could touch the merchandise before you decided what you wanted.

sodahead.com

Lynn: We also got free items when we bought things at the store.
Terry: Yes, when you went to the grocery store you got silverware or dishes just for buying groceries.
Lynn: There was a special every week.
Terry: So you'd get your gravy boat one week and a plate the next.
Sara: We also got towels in our laundry detergent and we got dishes at the gas station, too.
Lynn: You got little appliances, like toasters, when you got an account at the bank. Now they charge you for a checking account.
Terry: We got free toys in our cereal boxes too. And it was a real toy not like the *Cracker Jacks* today. Have you seen the toys now? They are just a cardboard thing with maybe a riddle on them. We got toys!

Lynn: A whistle that would really whistle.
Terry: Occasionally you had to send away for something, but usually it was right in the box.
Sara: When the cereal box came home from the grocery store and if it said, 'Prize Inside' we'd go for it. We had this big metal bowl that would hold one whole box of cereal. We'd dump the cereal in there and scrounge around until we found the prize.

blog.redfin.com

Terry: We weren't allowed to dump it out so we'd push the sides together to peer in. One kid would be the pusher and one would be the grabber. There was always an argument because the grabber got the toy.
Sara: My sister and I took turns. But it was fun just to see what the toy was, no matter who got it.
Lynn: It was so much fun to get something free.
Sara: When the box was empty, my mom took it to the burn barrel.
Terry: It is interesting that people are so conscious of being green now, but actually the whole concept just skipped a few generations. I'm glad it's back.
Sara: My folks would fit right in.

Broad Chatter
Growing Up With People from the Depression
three memories

Terry: When WWII was over, my parents and older brother moved from small town Southern Illinois to the suburbs of Chicago. They had a strong desire to become successful and 'move up' in the world. So many of the habits from the Depression were left behind as they worked to keep up with the 'Joneses'. Our first homes had burn barrels and clotheslines but, when we moved to Wheaton, these things were looked down upon and completely discarded. My parents, mostly my mom, kept the fear of losing everything which they had seen happen during the Depression. They had their house paid for in five years. My mom told me about rich people from her childhood losing their homes in the 30s and she wanted to make sure this didn't happen to us. Mom was a saver. Putting money in the bank came right after paying bills. If I wanted a new dress for a dance, I was told I had to wait until the end of the month to see what money was left.

My husband's family, however, always lived with the Depression mentality. Maybe it was because they were young adults in the 30s while my parents were just beginning their teen years. Or maybe they lived in a town that wasn't as concerned with appearances.

Flickr Melissa

Whatever the reason, they reduced, reused, and recycled long before anyone used those terms. Helen had a burn barrel, a clothesline, and a worm bed where she put all the food scraps. When fishing, she and Len never threw back any small fish. They were put in the garden for fertilizer. Len used peanut tins for all his nails and screws even though that meant he had to open each one whenever he was looking for a specific nail. Helen had a two foot stack of saved *Styrofoam Mc Donald's Big Mac* containers because, "you never know when one might come in handy." They poured over the Sunday ads and made a list of the best deals. This meant, on grocery shopping day, they would drive all over town trying to save money. They didn't seem to be concerned with how much gas they were using as long as they got the cheapest price on milk.

I have been influenced by both families and, of course, the recycling movement. I love stashing money in the bank, felt relieved when I got my house paid for, love hanging out laundry both for the smell and for knowing it reduces electric use. I don't save *Mc Donald* containers and I use jars for my nails, but I like to find alternative uses for things. It just feels right.

Sara: My mother and father were financially conservative. They both had vivid memories of when the banks crashed and money was scarce, even though they were children at the time. We washed out and reused plastic bread bags and pieces of *Saran Wrap*. Our food scraps were composted and put into the vegetable garden. My mother canned vegetables from the garden and kept the *Mason* jars on shelves in the basement. We did not have a clothes dryer until I was in high school and we never had a dishwasher. We had a wringer washer and two large laundry tubs for rinse water in the basement. Wet clothes were carried upstairs and hung outside. In the winter they were hung on lines in the basement. Old dresses were saved for quilt pieces and other pieces of old clothing were torn into rags and crocheted into rag rugs. I still have some of those quilts and I can picture my mother's dresses in the patterns.

We did not get new clothes very often. We usually only got things for the start of the school year and the start of summer. I often wore my sister's hand-me-downs. Dad had exactly one suit and my mother only had cloth coats, nothing fancy or fur for her. When we bought a car, it was paid for in cash, and my folks did not have a 'credit rating' until they were in their 70s. Christmas wrapping paper was reused as were bows, and we made gift tags from the previous year's Christmas cards. My sister and I were expected to work when we were in high school and the money we earned went partially to a savings account and partially to meet our wants and needs.

My father did not trust banks because of the Depression and when he died we found $40,000 in small bills in a coffee can in the basement.

Lynn: Mom and Dad had different experiences growing up during the Great Depression, but they both emerged with a 'save now, for you never know what will happen' mindset.

Mom's dad, my grandpa Brown, was a foreman at an oil refinery and her mother was a stay-at-home mom. They were ensconced in the working class. Grandpa Brown never lost his job during the Depression, but his hours and pay were cut. Mom would tell stories of how Grandpa and Great Uncle Alf bought a pig that they slaughtered and cured, and then divided up the meat. Grandpa plowed up the family's small backyard and planted potatoes. For meals, Grandma would fry up slices of pork and then use the grease leavings in the pan to make a gravy, which they poured over boiled potatoes.

In contrast, Dad was raised in Beverly Hills, California, attending the same school as kids like Mickey Rooney. Grandpa Lewis owned a jewelry store and it seemed that he always was teetering on the edge of bankruptcy. From Dad's stories, Grandpa Lewis was a bit of a high roller so they lived in a fashion that didn't reflect too much of the hard times. Grandmother Lewis was a nurse and I think it may have been her paycheck and budgeting that kept them going.

By the time they were adults, both Mom and Dad had learned how to be frugal. From time to time, however, Dad could go a bit overboard when buying gifts. We'd always encourage him to go Christmas shopping with Mom. It seems Dad had a bit of his mother and a bit of his dad in him when it came to managing money.

Other than the occasional spending fling lapses, Dad let Mom manage the family budget. She was a strict manager. A portion of every paycheck went into a savings account as well as into a retirement account. Outside of a mortgage, they avoided debt like the plague.

Mom was ingenious about how to save money. For meals, we'd get a half of a juice glass full of orange juice which equaled about two ounces. It was years before I realized that a glass of juice could be more than just two swallows. Mom was masterful with what she could do with a half-pound of hamburger when cooking for our family of six.

My brother, Steve called her spaghetti meat sauce the "meatless wonder".

When they bought cars, the cars were new, but they were never the top of the line models like our neighbors' cars. And as for the houses, their rule of thumb was to own the smallest house on the block, because the larger houses would increase the value of the smaller houses.

As for clothing, Mom would haunt the discount stores. Name brands were considered frivolous. The only time I owned brand-named clothing was when I purchased it with my own money. When we lived outside of San Francisco, we'd travel the forty-five minutes to the clothing warehouse district. There we would comb through tables piled high with damaged clothing until we found something we liked that had only minor problems. At home, Mom would whip out her sewing machine and make the needed repairs.

Mom and Dad did pretty well for themselves for two kids raised during the Depression. We may have had one of the smaller houses in every neighborhood that we lived in, but there was a built-in swimming pool in the backyard. The cars may not have been the biggest and the finest, but we always had at least two. When it came time for retirement, they didn't owe a mortgage, didn't have car payments, and were able to pay cash for the many trips they took throughout the world. Even then we kids liked to have Dad go Christmas shopping with Mom, but she still made sure that everything was an off-brand.

Which type of 'clothes dryer' did you use?

Pressroom.padutchurbcountry.com

remodelista.com

Edenmakersblog.com

urbanclotheslines.com

Twowomenonalittlefarm.blogspot.com

You're a Boomer if you know what these are:

Flickr David Ellis

Flickr David Ellis

Flickr Bryan Costin

Flickr Renee

answers at the end of the chapter

TexasA&M agrilife

From garden...

... to fruit cellar

alsis 35

---

* *mechanical banks, pressure cooker gauge, rag balls for making rag rugs*

Turning Points

Television brought the brutality of war into the comfort of the living room. Vietnam was lost in the living rooms of America – not on the battlefields of Vietnam.
Marshall McLuhan

We shall live in peace, we shall live in peace. We shall live in peace, some day.
Pete Seeger, et al

wikipedia

The three women are carpooling to their book club where *The Help* will be discussed. At the last moment Terry goes back in to the house for her records...just in case.

Sara: I enjoyed the book. But I was pretty young in 1962, which was the beginning of the book, but I do have memories of those times.

Wikipedia

Lynn: Lots of things were happening in 1962. I started looking some stuff up while reading the book. Rosa Parks protested in 1955. Of course I've only read about that. You probably remember though, Terry.

Terry: Sure, Lynn, I think I was on her bus. I do remember my mom and dad talking about the *Woolworth* sit-in that occurred a few years later. Dad worked for *Woolworth's* and was concerned. They both grew up in a Southern culture so they saw things differently from how I later saw them.

Lynn: My family lived in California and I really didn't know any black people. There were a lot of Hispanic people but I just didn't have any exposure to them. I do remember walking across the street and a group of migrant workers was walking toward me, so I held my breath as I walked past. I just didn't know what else to do.
Sara: Did you think you were going to breathe their air?
Lynn: I think I thought they'd smell bad. Someone had told me that. They did have harsh working conditions and lots of people had misconceptions. I knew one little girl in my elementary who was Hispanic. We were pretty good friends. But I didn't have any black kids in my neighborhood.
Sara: I remember the images of those FBI agents walking little Ruby Bridges to school. There she was with these two huge men on either side of her and people who looked like my neighbors were screaming at her. I remember thinking, "Why do people hate this pretty little girl in her Sunday dress?"
Lynn: The nightly news showed people being fire hosed or having dogs snarling and barking at them.
Terry: Did you understand why this was happening?
Sara: No, I was just confused. I saw African American people in Madison but they didn't live in my neighborhood.

visitthecapital.org

It wasn't until I was in junior high in the mid 60s that I began to understand. That's when I went to Abraham

Lincoln Junior High which was the first intentionally integrated school in Madison. I was part of the first group of kids in Madison to be bussed as a result of integration. That's when I put together that the people I was seeing on TV were the same as my friends.

Lynn: Most of my memories of Civil Rights came from *LOOK, Saturday Evening Post* and from television. I couldn't fathom why people were being so mean to each other.

Terry: Because of my 'southern' background, I was told that black people were different. They didn't come into my grandmother's restaurant or go to the movie theater in Murphysboro. But my family all joked around with the maid and cook at the courthouse and hugged them when they left. That was very confusing. That's when I started questioning the separation I was seeing.

Sara: My friend Ivan told me about the time when he was a boy when he traveled to Tennessee and saw a bubbler....

Terry: It's a drinking fountain there.

Sara: Anyway, the drinking fountain had a sign over it that said, 'Colored'. So Ivan turned it on because he thought the water would be red or blue.

civilrights.uga.edu

Lynn: I think I would have done the same. We just didn't have signs like that.

Terry: One time, I was walking down the railroad tracks in Southern Illinois. Who would do that now? And some black girls started calling me names and throwing tomatoes at me. That one confused me too. I didn't know what I had done to them to make them mad at me. Now I understand.

Sara: By experiencing this when we were so young we were directly affected. We questioned what we were taught and decided to think differently. Look at each of our families. I don't think my mom ever expected she'd have a great granddaughter who is African American and a great grandson who is Hispanic.

Terry: And my daughter is Korean. Even more than that, Chad is from Mankato!

Lynn: My nephew is Black and Native American.

Sara: Here we are, raised with racism, changed by the Civil Rights movement, with children and grandchildren for whom race isn't even an issue. That's what we hoped for in the 1960s. I certainly never thought back then that we'd have a black president!

Lynn: So much was going on then that changed us. The 60s were a time of change and upheaval. It's mind boggling to think of all the things that happened back then and in a relatively short period of time.

Terry: Yes! Marilyn Monroe died in 1962. I remember that.

Sara: Yes, Terry, but before that big event, we had Sputnik. President Kennedy announced the Space Race in 1961, so we sent Ham, the Chimp, up followed by Alan Shepherd.

Terry: Was he a chimp too?

Lynn: No, he was the first dog. You know, shepherd.

airspacemag.com

Terry: Oh, yes. Alan the shepherd. Sara, why do you remember this so well?

Sara: My Uncle was Deke Slayton who was one of the original seven astronauts. You know, my uncle from Leon, Wisconsin?

Terry: Was that in 1969?

Sara: No, it was much earlier. By 1969 we had landed on the moon.

Deke Slayton-NASA

Lynn: We had that constant tension going on between Russia and the US.

Terry: Like the rumble from West Side Story!

Sara: Then, of course, there was President Kennedy's assassination. I was in 5th grade when that happened. The principal came on the intercom and called all the teachers to the office, which had never happened before. When they came back they were visibly upset. They told us what had happened and then they sent us all home early.

Terry: I'm older than you, although this is the only time I'll admit that, so I was in high school. We had just finished gym class when they told us what had happened. But they didn't send us home. My next class was math. We had the cutest teacher; he looked like Dr. Kildare from TV. Anyway, that day he had his head on his desk and he didn't lift it or say a word the whole hour.

Lynn: I was in the fifth grade too, Sara. We were at recess. This know-it-all girl, built like a brick with pigtails, told us Kennedy had been shot, and I didn't believe her, until we went back into class. Our teacher, Mr. Barrett was devastated but he was such a good teacher he drew out the similarities between the Kennedy and Lincoln

assassinations. Then they sent us home and for the next three days we just gathered around our TVs.
Terry: The assassination was the only thing on TV; there weren't even any commercials. Over and over again we watched the terrible events. And then there was the funeral with the riderless horse and that little boy saluting.
Sara: John-John. He's gone now too. I think it was the first time television brought the entire nation together like that. I'm not sure we ever were quite the same.
Lynn: We started seeing real life happenings after that, right on our TVs.
Terry: Television in the 60s brought war into our living rooms. Before then, people learned things after the fact through newspapers and radio.
Lynn: Now the images of the war and tragedies were everywhere. For the first time we watched events as they happened. We saw Lee Harvey Oswald being shot by Jack Ruby as it happened.
Sara: When Martin Luther King was assassinated in 1969, we saw the hotel, the shot, and people pointing, all on TV.
Terry: But a few months after the King assasination we saw Bobby Kennedy die in the kitchen hallway of that hotel. The Democratic Convention in Chicago was that summer. It brought politics and racial tension together. After the riots my dad took me to the neighborhoods that had been destroyed. He saw it as the fault of the Blacks. I saw it as hopeless people looking for change.
Sara: Just think. We were living under a threat of war from the time we were born. The Korean War, the Suez

Crisis, the Bay of Pigs, the Cuban Missile Crisis, and through all of this the Cold War. Plus we had the Civil Rights Movement and all these tragedies. And it was all on television.

Lynn: In the midst of all this, the Women's Movement really became strong. Women were now seeing other changes in the US and started pushing for equal rights too. What those women did in the 60s certainly affected what the three of us are doing now.

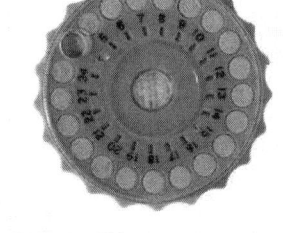

Terry: Well, the Pill had a part in that too. It gave women the freedom to choose the size of their families or even whether to have a family or not.

everydayhealth.com

Sara: Family changed too. Not only what a family looks like but the values too. We went from Ward, June, and the Beav' to Archie Bunker and now Honey Boo Boo. All this changed us. Television changed us.

Terry: I think our music changed us too. I think we were probably the first generation to own so many records. I had a box of 45s that I took with me everywhere.

Sara: We did own a lot more music than our folks. My parents had three albums and two of them were Christmas songs. I think the third one was Eddy Arnold.

Lynn: The music change was hard on my parents and probably everyone else's.

Sara: I agree. When I was little my mom would sing all her favorite songs from the forties and before. As she cleaned, our house was filled with songs like *Mares Eat Oats*, and *The Bugle Boy from Company B*.

Terry: I loved my mom's songs. I think my favorites were *Chattanooga Choo Choo* and *I'll Be Seeing You*.
Lynn: My mom played all those on the piano. Things like *The Way You Look Tonight* and anything by Bing Crosby or Frank Sinatra. Those were the songs they loved and danced to so when rock and roll with Elvis Presley, Chubby Checker, and Buddy Holly came along, I don't think they were ready.

Sara: Most of them never adjusted to the new music. Plus I'm not sure my parents liked that we listened to music constantly on our transistor radios which were such new technology. And we'd play them on hi-fis with the spindles and the arm that went over.

Community-bar.com

Terry: The 45s had that long thing you put on the spindle or those little plastic discs that you'd snap in the middle of the record. If they came off the record would wobble.
Sara: The first two albums I ever bought were the Beatles and the Supremes.
Lynn: Mine was the *Sound of Music*. I was a real rebel.
Terry: Gene Pitney for me. "What a town without pity can do!" Hey, I brought a bunch of albums along today to share with the book group - just for fun.
Sara: I think all my old albums are in my mom's basement. Where do you keep these? And why? What can you play them on?
Lynn: She probably has them next to her bed and they just play in her head.

Terry: Some are mine and some are my brother's so they are older. (she passes some up to the front seat for Lynn)
Lynn: Oh, look! Chuck Berry, Fats Domino, Little Richard. Can you remember any of their songs?
Sara: I do! *Ain't That a Shame* and *Blueberry Hill*!
Lynn: Here's Johnny Mathis. I listened to him. Any songs come to mind?
Terry: *Misty!* My mom named her dog after that song. How about Brenda Lee and Connie Francis?
Sara: I loved *Who's Sorry Now*.
Terry: I liked *I'm Leaving It All Up to You*.
Sara: That was Connie Stevens.
Terry: Well, I had the first name right.
Lynn: Here's Neil Sadaka; that's a name I haven't heard in a long time.
Terry: Really? I love his books, especially *Me Talk Pretty Some Day*.
Sara: It's *One* Day and David Sedaris wrote it. But that name reminds me of Ricky Nelson, actor and singer. He was Ozzie and Harriet's son but I loved his music. Can either of you name one of his songs?
Terry: There was one about a party in a garden.
Lynn: It's *Garden Party* and he also sang *Hello Mary Lou* and *Be-Bop Baby*. He was so cute!
Terry: My favorite group from my brother's albums was the *Kingston Trio*. We sang their songs at parties in college.
Sara: That was the beginning of all the folk singers like Pete Seeger, Peter, Paul and Mary, Joan Baez, and, of course, the great Bob Dylan.
Terry: And Allan Sherman!

All: *Hello Mudda, hello Fadda,*
Here I am at Camp Granada.
Camp is very entertaining
and they say that we'll have fun if it stops raining.
Lynn: I went to camp and I forgot my toothbrush and I came home with green teeth.
Sara: I went to Girl Scout camp. The lake had leeches and there was a raccoon in the pit of the outhouse. Fun times!
Terry: When we were first married, Ken and I ran a camp. We had raccoons in the garbage pit and Ken told a scary story about 'Coon Man'. Scared the pants off all the campers but it kept them in their cabins at night.
Lynn: Back to the albums. (she picks one out of her stack) Dionne Warwick!
 Boop, boop, boop….
All: *Do you know the way to San Jose?*
I'm going back to find some piece of mind in San Jose.
Sara: *Wishin' and hopin' and wishin' and hopin' and wishin' and…planning, and dreamin,….*
Terry: Is that the one where she's cooking the eggs in the morning? *One less egg to fry…One less bell to answer, one less egg to fry. One less man to pick up after.*
Lynn: Yeah, like that's going to happen.
Terry: I wonder how many men she'd had though. If it's one less now how many was she picking up after?
Lynn: (rolling her eyes at Terry) She probably ran a boarding house.
Terry: You know the song *Jimmy Crack Corn and I Don't Care*? If you don't care why'd you write a song about it then?

Lynn: (laughing and then suddenly stopping) Oh, you're serious...
Sara: And what's cracking corn anyway? But, look. Here's a Nat King Cole album.
Lynn: Ramblin' Rose
Terry: (coughs)
Lynn: What was that all about?
Terry: He died of lung cancer
Lynn: Ohhh
Sara: You are so cruel.
Terry: He had a 15 minute TV show, short and sweet!
Lynn: You've got a Cinderella album

45cat.com

in here with all the folk singers and rock and roll guys.
Terry: We were kinda' raised on Walt Disney, too.
All: *Cindrelly, Cinderelly, all I hear is Cinderelly.*
Bippity boppity boo,
Put 'em together and what have you got?
Bippity, boppity, Bippity, boppity, Bippity, boppity boo.
Sara: Dean Martin had a television show too.
Lynn: I loved his show. He would jump up on the piano and he'd say, "My leg, my leg! Oh, there it is."
All: *When the moon hits your eye like a big pizza pie, that's amore.*
Sara: Then there is the other 'Dean', Jan and Dean which was surfer music.
Terry: *The Little Old Lady from Pasadena*
All: *Go Granny, go Granny, go Granny, go*
Terry: (looking at the Jan and Dean album) He's cute.
Lynn: He is kind of cute.

Terry: But I don't remember if that's Jan or Dean. What was the other one about the car?
Sara: Little Deuce Coupe? But that was the Beach Boys.
Terry: No, the one that went *Beep, beep, beep. His horn went beep, beep, beep.* And then he couldn't get it out of second gear. I think the car was a Nash Rambler.
Sara: And the group was a one hit wonder but I'm not sure it was a real hit.
Lynn: My favorite 'wonders' had many more than one hit. The *Beatles*! Did you watch them when they appeared on *Ed Sullivan?* I did and then at school during recess, we pretended we were doing the show. I was Ed Sullivan by the way and I was quite good.
Sara: I was at my cousin Jim's house and we kids were just screaming. Our parents thought we'd lost our minds and they certainly didn't like the long hair!
Lynn: My brother, Mr. Crewcut, laughed at them and said they looked like girls. Not five years later his hair was much longer than theirs.
Terry: Did you know I saw the *Beatles* live in Chicago? They were appearing at the Stock Yards and the best seats cost $5.35. But I think everyone paid that price because we were way back and the place was huge. You couldn't hear anything because of the screaming. The warm up band was the *Righteous Brothers* and I couldn't hear them at all. I'm not sure I think it was worth my five dollars and thirty-five cents.
Sara: To see the *Beatles* and the *Righteous Brothers*? I think it was a deal! Our music formed us. That was the beginning of the British Invasion which shaped just about all our fads of the 60s.

Lynn: Plus there was a burst of TV shows that were centered on the new music. We went from *American Bandstand* to the *Monkees*.
Sara: I loved those idiots. Not too long ago I was thinking about them. You know those were the first music videos we ever saw. They really were ahead of their time.
Terry: There were lots of shows that had popular bands - like the ones in the Revolutionary war outfits. *Paul Revere & the Raiders.*
Lynn and Sara: Oh, Mark Lyndsay.
Terry: And *The Dave Clark Five.* That's when I practiced all the new dances. You could practice alone in the living room because you didn't need a partner anymore.
Lynn: The *Swim*
Sara: Well, we were land-locked, so we did the *Jerk*.
Terry: The *Watusi*! But wasn't that just the *Twist* updated?
Lynn: And then the music just changed--turned political— it seems like just within a few months.
Terry: We had political songs n the early 60s though, like *They're Rioting in Africa*.
Sara: Oh yeah, the folksingers.
Terry: They're still rioting in Africa. But we also had *Where Did those Flowers Go?, Give Peas a Chance,* and that really uplifting one, *The Eve of Construction.*
Lynn: When we moved to San Francisco I remember driving down to Haight Asbury. It was a tourist destination

tucec9.tumblr.com

with tour buses and cameras. But it was different than we thought it'd be. It wasn't romantic, with guitar-playing and dancing. The people looked worn, dirty, tired.
Sara: I saw a documentary about how that's where all the kids migrated to and they couldn't get jobs and there was no place for them to live. It was the Summer of Love and there were some really wonderful moments, but there was an edge to all of it. Even sitcoms had a new edge to them. They confronted social issues. The *Dick Van Dyke* show took on the issue of race when Rob accidentally dyed his hands black just before the NAACP dinner and he had to wear Laura's prom gloves.
Terry: *The Smother Brothers* were cancelled because of their political satire, right?
Sara: Yes, their views on Viet Nam.
Lynn: You know at the time, I didn't realize what the war was about. My parents accepted the rhetoric of the domino effect of communism, so I did. It wasn't until later, when I began realizing that everything is not as it's packaged and presented.
Sara: That's probably an important lesson. I figured it out a few years before you but that was because I lived in Madison. Demonstrations, protests, hippies, it was all in Madison and I was caught up in it. I wanted to be part of all the protests until the bombing at the university.
Lynn: That's when a line was drawn by the politicians, when they decided to change the age of when we became adults. We were in the first group of 18-year-olds to be considered adults. One day I was 18 and a kid, the next day I was 18 and an adult.
Terry: Letting us vote was to justify sending kids to war.
Sara: I thought it was about drinking beer.
Terry: I always think everything is about drinking beer.

Kitchen Café

an original story by Terry

I'm sure you have a favorite restaurant. My family likes a local Chinese place and my friend Bobbi *loves Happy Joe's Pizza*. But me? My favorite restaurant was a little place in Southern Illinois called the Kitchen Café. It was probably most famous for its pies but I thought everything about that place was just about perfect. Even if you weren't a local it wasn't hard to find. It was one block off the main street, which was Walnut Street, in Murphysboro on Locus Street. It was situated between two taverns so the smell of fried food and stale beer kind of drew you down the street.

The sign on the screen door said 'air conditioned' inside (remember when they used to advertise that?) so winter and summer you had to open the big wooden door. And inside? Well, it wasn't fancy. There was a long counter with stools bolted to the floor. They had red vinyl tops that spun around. There were twenty to twenty-five tables, wooden, no table cloths, not even any placemats. The tables were surrounded by wooden chairs with the curved backs with slats. And that air conditioner? It was inside and huge. It reached almost up to the ceiling, was about six feet long and two feet deep. But it kept that room cool and also provided the ice for the sweet tea. Don't even ask for unsweetened tea, they wouldn't have had any. But they did have pie. Oh, the usual fruit pies, apple, cherry, and peach in the summer time. But the ones everyone asked for were the meringue pies. The meringue on those pies was at least four inches high and if you were late for dinner, which was at noon, well there wouldn't be any left for you. I chose my pie first thing in the morning. I wasn't allowed to eat at dinnertime, which was for paying customers, but if I waited they would be all gone so, as soon as they were cooled and cut and brought out into the dining room, I'd make my choice. Sometimes I'd pick cherry but most often it would be one of those meringue pies, lemon or chocolate. I'd make my choice and then hide it away until it was time to eat it and then I'd be off for the streets of Murphysboro.

First I'd head off to the *Woolworth* store where my great Aunt Cat worked behind the candy counter. I'd talk to Cat for a while and then head up Walnut to my Aunt Imy's beauty shop. There I'd help out by sweeping up hair or cleaning the combs. I was always the guinea pig for Sharon the apprentice. I was the only eight year old with plucked eyebrows and a twice weekly manicure.
After I'd read *True Confessions* magazine for a while, I'd head down Walnut Street to the court house where my Uncle Gov was the sheriff. I'd take the elevator to the third floor where he and Aunt Imy lived and where the jail was, where the prisoners were housed. I'd talk to the maid and the cook there for a while and then I'd start to get hungry and I'd head back to the Kitchen Café and sit at that lone table in the kitchen and watch the action there.

Hazel was usually at the big black stove frying up something. She was a large woman, her brown hair tied up in a bun. She didn't talk much but boy, could that woman sweat. And then there was Lou. I loved Lou. She was tall and skinny and talked all the time—about her kids and her grandkids, her garden and putting picklelilly up the night before. I loved to listen to Lou talk; not so much for what she had to say but for the click. Lou had false teeth that didn't fit right and every second or third sentence they would fall and you could hear them click. Or sometimes she'd raise up her arms. Armpit hair! Lou was the only woman I knew who didn't shave under her arms and for some reason the sight of that hair could just make my day.

And then there was my grandmother, my pretty little grandmother, standing over the steam table dishing up the plates and the platters. She'd always come to work all dressed up: good dress, earrings, necklace, sometimes a broach. She had that blue gray hair that older women often had in those days—got it done once a week at Aunt Imy's. And no matter how hot it got in that kitchen, standing over that steam table, it never flopped or frizzed or frazzled. And she hardly ever went into the air conditioned dining room to cool off like I always did. No, she was always there, like the queen, with her crown of blue curls and her big silver spoon.

Everyone always said my grandmother was a good cook but you couldn't tell by me. I never ate an entire meal my grandmother made. When I was in Southern Illinois we always ate every meal, Monday through Saturday, at the Kitchen Café. On Sundays, when it was closed, we went to wherever Aunt Imy and Uncle Gov were and ate with them, or sometimes, every so often, we'd go to the barbeque place and get real Southern barbecue, pork shoulder cooked over an open pit in a vinegar base with a real bite to it.

The barbeque place was owned by a colored man, down in the colored part of town. That's what we said then, colored, unless we said something stronger. The colored part of town was down by the bottoms of the Big Muddy River. All the houses were wooden shacks until a tornado came through and knocked most of them down. The government came in and put up flat roofed, cinder block buildings. I didn't think they looked much like houses but I always felt sorry for anyone whose house hadn't blown down and didn't get one.

The barbeque place was just like those wooden shacks only two or three times bigger. I suppose you could have eaten inside but we never did. I'd wait in the car while MawMaw went to the window to order. Then she'd come back and sit with me, air conditioner on, until the owner came out with containers of barbecue and then we'd take them to wherever Gov and Imy were.

One time while we were sitting there I asked my grandmother if the colored folks ever came to the Kitchen Café to eat. I'd seen them at the back door selling produce and such but I'd never seen any in the dining room. She turned to me and said, "Why you hush now, Terry Lynn. You know they know their place." I didn't really know what she meant by that but I knew I shouldn't ask any further. We knew lots of colored folks. There was the lady that cleaned for my grandmother and the maid and cook at the court house. Everyone was always joking and laughing with them. So the only thing I could figure that she meant was that they LIKED their place, the barbecue place, like I liked the Kitchen Café and I left it at that.

And then one day, I was sitting at that lone table in the kitchen waiting my turn to eat when Uncle Gov walked in. He hardly ever ate at the Kitchen Café; he always ate at the court house after helping to serve the prisoners. He sat down at the table and then MawMaw left the steam table, in the middle of the noon hour, and sat down with him. Then they told me to move away. I went a little ways away and they didn't seem to notice. I was insulted. I was always allowed to listen to the grown-ups talk; I liked listening to the grown-ups talk. Especially Uncle Gov. I'd learned most of my colorful language from him like "Well, I'll be a suck-egged mule", whatever that means, and "You little peckerwood", I know what that means, and other phrases my mom didn't like. He was always joking and laughing and talking politics. John Kennedy had taken a nap on Aunt Imy's couch in the court house when he was running for president. My dad had voted for Nixon but I wanted Kennedy because Gov did.

But this day he wasn't joking or talking politics. It was something about the colored podiatrist in town. He was coming to the Kitchen Café to 'test' something out. I didn't understand what but I could tell that it had them worried, concerned, maybe even scared. I'd seen that podiatrist lots of times. He had a little office on the side street across from the *Woolworths*. If he was standing outside when I walked by he'd say, "Morning, Missy". Boy, I'd judged that man wrong. I decided right then that the next time I saw him, I'd cross to the other side of the street.

About a week later, a Wednesday, I was sitting in the dining room trying to cool off. It was right at noon time and I knew I wouldn't be able to stay there much longer. The place was really filling up; it was noisy with talking and laughter, mostly men. I was sitting at one of only three empty stools at the counter. At the tables there were the men from the electric company and the telephone company, men in suits from the businesses on Walnut and from the court house. And of course there were the county road workers. They were there all the time. They'd come in the morning for breakfast, and then back at ten for doughnuts and coffee. They'd be back again at noon for dinner.

Then the door opened and Uncle Gov walked in but he sat at a table with some other men so I knew not to disturb. The door opened again and in walked the colored podiatrist and that whole noisy room got completely quiet as everyone watched him walk across that dining room and sit at the empty stool next to me. I looked at Uncle Gov. He was scowling; I'd never seen that look on his face before. He jerked his head to tell me to get out of there but it was like I was frozen to the stool. Then two of the county road workers got up from their table. They hadn't finished their dinner yet; they hadn't even ordered pie. And they didn't walk to the cash register to pay; they walked toward me. I saw Gov stand up and then, from the corner of my eye, I saw the swinging door from the kitchen open up and out walked my grandmother, in the middle of the noon hour! She walked toward me too. I thought "Oh,oh, what did I do now?" But when she got to me, she turned her back to me, crossed her arms over her chest, and looked out at that dining room right at those two big burly county road workers. They stood there staring at each other for I don't know how long, a moment, a minute. And then finally one of the road workers put his eyes down and walked back to his table and after a bit the other did the same.

My grandmother stood there the entire time the podiatrist ordered, ate his chicken and dumplings, went to the cash register to pay and then went out the door. Gov got up and stood in front of the door. That room continued to stay quiet for a moment, a minute and then it exploded in loud, angry voices.

I think of that day often. I quickly figured out that the podiatrist wasn't a bad man and that my Uncle Gov would uphold the law no matter how he'd been raised. But mostly when I think of that day, I think of my grandmother, my pretty little grandmother, standing there in that room full of angry men ready to take on anyone who would mess with her Kitchen Café.

Madison Girl
an original story by Sara

I remember the day I had my senior picture taken. I was wearing this schizophrenic outfit...from the waist up I looked what my mother called "presentable". In other words, modest and in keeping with what was expected of good girls. You know, a little sweater with a pearl necklace, button earrings, my hair was set and I was wearing a touch of make-up. I would look like all the other good girls in my yearbook....exactly like all the other good girls. But, from the waist down, I was dressed the way I wanted to be. The clothes that made my mother shake her head and say, "You're not going out dressed like that."

I had on my favorite pair of jeans, bell bottoms I had made by sewing a wedge of reversed denim into the leg seams. They were ripped out at the knee and had a flag patch on the back pocket. I was wearing leather sandals and a toe ring. As soon as my photo session was over I went into the bathroom for the full transformation. Off came the 'stupid' sweater and the restricting, anti-feminist bra, which were replaced by an embroidered peasant blouse. I combed out my hair, braided it and put on a leather headband. Then the peace earrings, a bit of pale pink lipstick, and I was out the door, free at last. I stepped out into the summer sun and put on my granny glasses. I was no longer the little conformer. Now I looked like the other hippie girls on the street...exactly like all the other hippie girls on the street.
The photographer's studio was on State Street in Madison, Wisconsin. State Street is and always has been,

the main thoroughfare between the University of Wisconsin campus and the State Capitol building. In my day it was 'the place to be'. It was a microcosm of the world I was inheriting, a world that was trying to strike a new balance between the conservative 1950s and the burgeoning liberalism of the 1960s. Like a teeter totter, the weight of power kept changing and those caught in mid-air, on the high seat, felt groundless and fearful. It was a tension that was both intimidating and exhilarating.

In the 60s State Street was always full of students. Street musicians, handsome young boys with newly grown long hair, sang about social justice and the war, while they collected spare change in their guitar cases. Young girls wearing mini dresses or long flowing skirts traveled in bright groups swaying to the music as they walked, becoming comfortable with their new sexual freedom. The smell of pot and patchouli hung in the air. It all seemed very innocent and appealing to me.

But a closer look easily revealed the underlying tilt of this scene. The teeter totter jolted regularly between symbols and reality. These peaceful youths, sitting and singing in the street, did so in front of stores whose windows were covered with plywood. Store owners had seen what happened when the peaceful rallied and grew restless and they were tired of paying for new plate glass windows.

Inadvertently, this had put a favorite character from State Street out of work. We all just knew him as 'Snowball'. He was an old black man with salt and pepper hair who wore a white jump suit and carried a bucket of cleaning tools. He made his living cleaning windows for the merchants, but had now been reduced to panhandling. He was a casualty of the war at home.

At the fountain by *Memorial Union* students gathered to protest the war. Sitting there, listening to their heated rhetoric, was as intoxicating as the loose joints being passed through the crowd. I didn't know the intricacies of the political arguments but I had seen the 1968 Democratic Convention and I watched Walter Cronkite's death count from Viet Nam every night. I just knew I preferred peace; it was pretty simple for me. So, when the leaders linked arms and started to walk toward State Street, I was swept up in the excitement, but I was also afraid. I knew that from this point forward things would get intense. I had seen boys who burned their draft cards and protesters who refused to move from doorways being taken away physically by the cops. I followed, but at a distance that might keep me from being mistaken as one of them if things got bad.

By the time we reached Lake Street we were met by the police. I had been taught as a little girl reading *Dick and Jane* that 'policemen are your friends' but these guys didn't look very friendly. They wore helmets with dark face guards, gloves, chest pads, and they carried clubs, tear gas, and guns. They called it riot gear. The students looked so vulnerable in their blue jeans and T-shirts and it made me wonder who was inciting whom. The policemen formed a double deep line, faced the students and walked backward toward the Capitol Square in front of them.

All along State Street more people joined in the march. Or those who didn't join in cheered from second story windows where they had hung bed sheet banners condemning the Viet Nam war. By the time we reached the Capitol Square the crowd had doubled in size and passion. The protestors' chants had turned to rants and the wall of authority the police had raised seemed to beg to be battered.

In those days the National Guard kept a permanent presence around the Capitol building. In my childhood the Guard had been used mainly in times of emergency, to protect and serve fellow Americans. I wondered what was the emergency here. Who needed protection from what? It seemed the Guard provided a shield between the people and their right to assemble, the people and their right to free speech, between the people and their elected officials. These armed and stoic young men stood at full attention as the marchers began to occupy the Capitol lawn. The Guardsmen seldom moved or made eye contact even when they were taunted. I had seen protestors spit at them and yell in their faces. I had seen girls lay flowers at their feet and give them the peace sign. Sometimes I admired the Guardsmen for their restraint, but mostly they intimidated me. I always found it interesting that the Guards were the same age as the boys on State Street but their uniforms differed greatly. They were armed and, when given a direct order, they moved quickly, decisively, and without question, which made them dangerous.

The students eventually covered the lawn and the steps leading to the Capitol building. The marble steps were strategic because when the students controlled them, they controlled the traffic; no one could get in or out. The power visibly shifted. The students were grounded and the establishment felt itself on the high seat.

Now it became like the game we played on the teeter totter, "Farmer, farmer let me down. What will you give me if I do?" The students barked their demands through bull horns and called the politicians out to answer for what they had done.

It was at about this time that the local camera crews would show up. This made good nightly news and, if it turned into a physical struggle, it might get picked up by the networks. Madison made the national news more than once in that era. As a child I had never doubted the integrity of the media but, after watching their reports on these gatherings that I had attended, I learned that the same images could be used to support many different viewpoints.

In the end, the cops would tell the students to go home, that theirs was an unlawful assembly and that they must disperse immediately. The students would react to this by sitting down, holding on to their power by staying low. The patrol moved in closer, again the order to leave but now with the threat of arrest and forcible removal. I, along with several others, stepped back across the street, still cowed by the rules of our youth, but hundreds of students remained seated.

As soon as the police grabbed the first students and tried to drag them away, everything came undone. Boys and girls tried to liberate their leaders and were clubbed for their efforts. Others tried to block the path but the second wave, the Guard, let loose with canisters of tear gas. Immediately young people began to scream and run in all directions. Some of them held bandanas over their mouths and noses, while a few daring boys picked up the gas canisters and threw them back at the Guard. I ducked into the drugstore doorway and played innocent, all the while regretting my own lack of conviction. State Street began to fill up again, but this time with frantic kids on the run. I saw a young girl with puffy, watery eyes running past being dragged by her friend who could still see clearly. A trio of boys brushed me aside as they passed. One of them had a nose bleed and was leaving dark spots on the sidewalk. Still others paused during their retreat to turn back and yell obscenities at the cops. Their young faces twisted in rage and fear, veins standing out in their necks and on their foreheads.

I saw this scene played out time and time again during my high school years. And with that passage of time, the protests became more intense, more angry, more desperate. I was still intrigued by these brave, youthful leaders, but I remained fearful of authority.

On August 24, 1970 I was going camping with a group of friends. We were packing the cars at 4:00 that morning when we heard and felt an enormous explosion. Without a thought we all looked toward downtown. We knew where it had to come from. Later, on the news, we learned that Sterling Hall on the University campus had been bombed by four young men as a protest against the University's research connection with the US military during Viet Nam. The pivotal piece of news for me was that the bombing resulted in the death of Robert Fassnacht, a 31 year old graduate student with three young children.

When I heard this, it was as if I was on the high end of the teeter totter and my partner simply stepped off. I hit the ground so hard it took my breath away. I stood up, dusted off the flag patch of my bruised sensitivities and walked away from the movement. The anti-war movement in Madison changed after that day. It drew only those who were willing to take the radical, truly revolutionary steps. Finally I drew a clear line for myself. It was pretty simple for me. I preferred peace but I was not willing to sacrifice others in its pursuit.

Guest Essay
Sam's Story
an original story by Sam Hurne

Sara, your Madison story was so parallel with my experiences during those times that I can't help but comment. I was one of those college student protesters you found so intriguing, except that I was at the University of Buffalo campus. Your descriptions of the strained balance between peace and anger, love and rage, expression and destruction were like pages ripped from the personal journal I never wrote.

It was a period of involuntary enlightenment for me, and it shaped my view of the world for the rest of my life. I got my initial wake- up call when the Buffalo cops invaded the UB campus. They tore through the student union, arbitrarily billy-clubbing students, some of whom had no idea what was going on, in an over-reaction to a protest against the University's allegedly prejudiced basketball recruitment program. A window in the university president's office got smashed, the cops were called, and all hell broke loose. That was when I first recognized that the tensions about Viet Nam and the Civil Rights Movement had morphed our 'Big Buick America' into kerosene vapor, and the slightest spark could ignite a profoundly disproportionate explosion.

I was already dodging the draft with a 2S deferment for what seemed to be the practical purpose of getting a college education. Then one of my roommates burst into our apartment one night like he had just escaped the

Holocaust. He told us to turn on the TV to see what was happening back at the campus he had just fled from and my serious questioning of everything about the establishment began in earnest.

Back in my small home town of Hornell, NY, we had a cop named Officer Brewer. He struck us as an oddball at first. We had never seen anyone direct traffic with such...enthusiasm. His arm movements were like a mime performer on steroids. He was well built, with a naturally erect posture, and when Officer Brewer directed you, you knew exactly where to go. He earned a lot of giggles early on; but, over time, he earned a lot of respect. As far as I know, anyone who ever encountered Officer Brewer felt better for it. He took his job seriously, but he took each person seriously, too. He administered the law with care, as if results mattered.

There were no Officer Brewers to be found in Buffalo during the spring of 1970. They were a corrupt mob of self-infesting thugs. Whenever they arrived on a scene, the scene got ugly. I had hair in those days and wore it long. Generally, I also wore a tie-dyed tank top, a necklace, a leather pouch hanging from my belt, deliberately bleach-spotted bell bottom jeans, and pair of *Frye* boots or sandals. That was enough to make me stand out one night as I walked out of a bar, hopped in my car, and pulled away from the curb. A patrol car pulled me over almost immediately. When their breath meter could barely register a trace no matter how hard they made me blow, they trumped up some charges and sent me home. It took about two months of my part-time gas station attendant wages to pay a lawyer who finally got the charges dropped. On the plus side, the lawyer and I became bar buddies.

On another and more relevant occasion, I was taking part in an anti-Viet Nam demonstration on campus that continued past dark. I don't remember what happened, if anything in particular, to bring on the Buffalo PD that night, but, all of a sudden, a fleet of cop cars stormed the campus. Somehow, I got separated from the other marchers and found myself the object of one patrol car's attention. It was coming directly at me, but I was finally able to jump over a guard rail when it got to within about six feet of me and had to stop. Fortunately, the cops didn't get out to chase me.

There was an incident, though, when they did impress me. We had a particularly large and loud demonstration going on. It was broad daylight at the time. A whole string of cop cars pulled up, one behind the other, in front of the student union. Just their presence agitated us protestors and the chants got stronger, angrier and more vulgar. This was our campus and they were invading again. Hadn't they beaten enough students? After a while, chants and vulgarity weren't enough for some of the crowd. I saw a puddle form under the cars, then somebody threw a *Molotov Cocktail* into the puddle and it turned into a broad blanket of flames. There was no sign of panic from the cops, and they didn't come out shooting at anyone. I almost couldn't have blamed them if they had. As the flaming puddle burned itself out, a little teeter crept into my totter.

Kent State happened that spring, and in the wake of it, two of my roommates, Bob Mellas and Tommy Lux, and I rode down to Washington DC in Tommy's *VW Bug.* Bob was the guy who witnessed and escaped the cops beating students during their first invasion of UB. Tommy was a lady-killer who just happened to be a great guy. It was a pretty spontaneous trip and I don't remember how I got out of work. We weren't particularly prepared, but we had plenty of weed and music. When we got to within about 50 miles of DC, fellow protesters were already becoming predominate in the surrounding traffic. This rally was going to be huge. Tommy, Bob, and I had just pleasantly refreshed our buzz when we became aware of our extremely awkward predicament. Somehow in the arbitrarily shifting lanes of traffic, we found ourselves immediately behind an opened-back Army green truck full of National Guardsmen. Two rows of soldiers faced each other under the canvas covered truck bed and the two furthest back were no more than six feet from our windshield. The three of us didn't say a word to each other. We didn't want to make eye contact with them. We were of one mind about this issue; none of us blamed the individual Guardsmen who shot those Kent State students. We knew it was only our flimsy 2S status that kept us from wearing uniforms and carrying guns. A few minutes ago, we were singing badly and laughing easily; but, now we just wanted to hide. Finally, one of the two Guardsmen just above our bumper flashed us a peace sign. The three of us immediately erupted in two-handed peace signs and smiles and thumbs up and palpable relief.

That whole rally was one of the best experiences of my life. Lots of big name bands and musicians played, the crowd was peace-seeking, sex was in the air, and the DC cops were everything the Buffalo cops should have been. There were Officer Brewers everywhere. They were helpful, respectful, and they radiated competence without ever threatening us. Over 100,000 protestors gathered there that weekend. The University of Maryland opened its doors to as many as they could handle. The student residents who were able to go to nearby homes offered their rooms for us to use. In spite of the recent invasion of Cambodia and the shooting of American students only a week before, that weekend made us feel like we were part of a movement that really could give peace a chance.

That following year wore away at those feelings. I remember one particular march in downtown Buffalo, when I was yelling along with other protesters, "One, two, three, four, we don't want your f___ing war!" We got the usual treatment; the cops rushed at us with their cars and we ran away and aside as fast as we could to escape them, then we'd gather and yell again. Somewhere along that march, I noticed some people carrying signs saying something about grape workers. I didn't know anything about grape workers. I was out to protest against our actions in Viet Nam and to support civil rights. I saw a connection there, but I had no idea how I felt about grape workers. A little more teeter.

When I learned about that University of Wisconsin researcher who was killed, my totter finally hit ground. It didn't drop with one big plunk. It was a little more gradual than that. I'd bring up the subject of that tragedy when I was passing a joint among protestor comrades, and I didn't like what I heard, "That's just one life for the cause." For me, life was the cause, especially innocent life. If a cop had been injured or even killed as a result of beating protestors, I could have reconciled that. This was hugely different for me. Protests were beginning to collect so much opportunistic clutter and leave so much collateral damage, they were starting to resemble the war I was against.

Well, if you've read this far and you resent the time it's taken, I really think you share the blame. Your stories definitely get the memory juices flowing. I have a few regrets from those fledgling adult years (and most of the years since); but, overall, I'm glad I took an active part in the anti-war and pro-civil rights movements.

Thanks for reminding me.

Sam and family including his new granddaughter

Broad Chatter
The Lottery
Terry remembers

As a college student in the late 60s, I was against the war, had marched in a couple of protests, and listened to speeches by a beloved professor who was the organizer of the campus *Students for a Democratic Society.* But the war really didn't affect me. La Crosse wasn't Madison. We went to class, didn't watch much TV, and for the most part continued our college life as we always had.

I was, of course, aware of the draft, but no one really close to me had been called up. I knew that some of my high school classmates were in Vietnam and the husband of one of my college classmates was on a helicopter there. She was my closest link to the war. Before class she would sometimes read us parts of his letters and would express her worry. But to me it was almost not real. Then one day she was gone. Word on campus was that her husband's helicopter had been shot down and he was missing. I never saw her again. And, while that was real, it still didn't affect me. She was a classmate not a friend, so she and her husband were easy to forget. The war wasn't real to me.

The draft and the war got closer after I was married in the spring of my junior year. As a professional for the YMCA, Ken had been given a deferment for a year but one man on the draft board said, "We'll get you next year. Be ready." Now things were getting real. Ken went to Minneapolis for a physical, which he passed, and we waited and hoped for anything that would change that man's threat.

Then it came, the draft lottery. Birthdates would be chosen at random. We knew those whose dates were picked first would definitely be drafted. Those at the end of the list would never go. The list would be in the morning paper. We got up early, bought the *Milwaukee Sentinel*, and started scanning for Ken's birth date, June 14. When we got to the 250th date, we figured we'd missed Ken's birthday, so we started at the top again. Down and down. It wasn't there. So we kept scanning and then, almost at the end, there is was--June 14 was number 356! That is a number we will never forget. He was safe and we were elated. I think that is the first time I really did the Happy Dance!

Now to share the great news with our friends! We headed to the student union where everyone hung out at the huge round tables. We had big smiles on our faces and that wonderful number in our heads--Yippee skippee—356! But as we walked in, we saw the faces of the guys at the TKE table. Our hearts sank as we listened to their numbers---fourteen, twenty-six, thirty-eight and so on. We knew anyone whose number was under one hundred would go. These were our closest friends, guys that we'd laughed with, partied with, studied with. On that day, the war became real.

Do you remember?

Lost45.com

im1004.tumblr.com

En.wikipedia.org

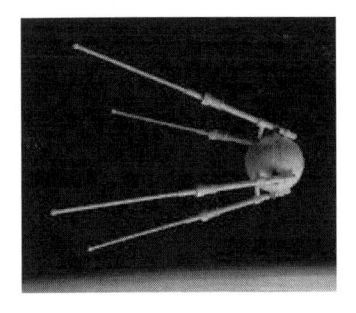

quizmodo.com

Flickr pds209

Flickr James Vaughan

> Record adapter or 'spider; 1969 Woodstock; 1965 Volkswagon bus; Sputnik 1, Nikita Kruschev, Walter Cronkite

281

Do you know these dates?
Match the event with the date.
*Answers at the bottom

(a) February 1, 1960
(b) April 2, 1960
(c) November 8, 1960
(d) May 3, 1961
(e) August 13, 1961
(f) April 12, 1962
(g) October 14-28, 1962
(h) August 28, 1963
(i) November 22, 1963
(j) February 9, 1964
(k) March 1, 1964
(l) August 5, 1964
(m) March 7, 1965
(n) September 28, 1966
(o) March 1, 1967
(p) January 31, 1968
(q) April 4, 1968
(r) June 5, 1968
(s) August 26-29, 1968
(t) July 20, 1969
(u) August 15, 1969
(v) May 4, 1970
(w) August 24, 1970

1. Afro hairdo introduced
2. Beetles appear on Sullivan
3. Berlin Wall is erected
4. Bloody Sunday
5. Bobby Kennedy assassinated
6. Bombing at Sterling Hall
7. Cuban Missile Crisis
8. Democratic Convention
9. First Heart Transplant
10. First Sit-In
11. Freedom Riders
12. J. F. K. Assassinated
13. J. F. Kennedy Elected
14. Marilyn Monroe Dies
15. Kent State Shootings
16. M. L. King Assassinated
17. MLK's Dream Speech
18. Moon Landing
19. Ban on Cigarette Packs
20. Tet Offensive
21. Twiggy Fashions Introduced
22. The Twist Introduced
23. Woodstock

a10, b22, c13, d11, e3, f1, g7, h17, i12, j2, k19, l14, m4, n21, o9, p20, q16, r5, s8, t18, u23, v15, w6

The Boomers Grow Up

The voices in my head may not be real, but they have some good ideas.
Thomas Ryan Stone

Sometimes I can look at my watch three consecutive times and still not know what time it is.
Moment of Truth Mike

Old age—you don't get to practice. This is the first time I've ever been this old. It just crept up on me.

Lynn, Sara and Terry

The women are in Lynn's back yard having just returned from a middle school basketball game. Lynn's granddaughter was a cheerleader.

Lynn: Hey, Sara you were a cheerleader, right? Do you think you could still do a cheer for us?
Sara: Of course. V-I-C.... Oh, my, I think I pulled something. I guess I gotta' work on that.
Lynn: You okay? This aging thing is not for wimps.
Sara: Like the first time the bag boy called me 'Ma'am.' I'm not a ma'am; that's my mom. But my feet, and elbows, and knees, they make noise: they pop, they creak, they snap.

Sara bottom row middle

Lynn: And that's what happened to our moms and to our grandmothers.
Terry: But they did not tell us that stuff. My mom never told me my toenails would get thick!
Sara: At the same time your hair got thin.
Lynn: Do you visualize yourself a certain way?
Sara and Terry: Oh yeah!
Lynn: Then I see a candid picture of myself and it doesn't quite match.
Sara: My ninety year old mother looked into the mirror one day and gasped. I asked, "Are you okay?" and she said, "Yeah, I just don't know how I got so old." I think about how gravity has worked against me too. I went on vacation with my sister in Jamaica and we were doing that thing where you pull the skin on your legs up and say, "20" and you let it go and you say, "50."
Terry: The secret to aging gracefully is having everything sag at the same time.
Lynn: It all about gravity and it's happening to…
Sara: Us!
Terry: Ken says the most popular bra size in the nursing home is 38 long.
Lynn: You already told us that one, don't you remember?
Sara: (sneezes) Oh! Excuse me, I've got to go to the bathroom. When did sneezing and peeing start happening at the same time? (Sara leaves the room)
Lynn: Have you seen my glasses?
Terry: Did you look everywhere?
Lynn: Yes, I can't find them anywhere. I looked in the kitchen, bathroom, on this table. Where did I put them?
Terry: I think you missed a place. (Terry points to her head. Lynn looks at Terry's head, then realizes her glasses are on her own head)

Lynn: Thanks. I hate losing them because then I can't see to find them.
Terry: Did you know the best birth control for people over 50 is nudity?
Lynn: Maybe I don't want to find my glasses.
(Terry crosses to get herself more coffee but can't find the pot and looks around for it. Sara comes back from the bathroom)

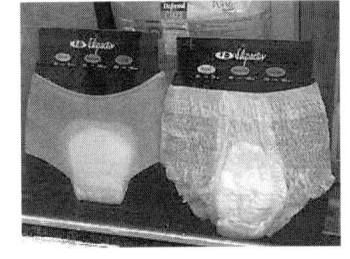

wikipedia

Sara: I hate this peeing thing. It happens more and more when I laugh or sneeze.
Terry: I guess it just 'depends'.
Sara: Very funny. My aunt was just this petite, dear, sweet woman, but when she was in her 80's, she'd walk across the room and she'd just putt-putt-putt. She'd never apologize or anything. This is why they didn't tell us about growing old.
Lynn: Would we have believed them?
Sara: Probably not. They were the old ones, not us.
(Terry finds the coffee pot in an odd place)
Terry: Who put the coffee pot in here?
Sara: I didn't, did I?
Terry: Dementia is another thing my mom didn't tell me about.
Lynn: They used to call it senility. I think we'll watch you more carefully from now on. But I think you'd better keep an eye on me, too.
Sara: Better watch me, too. The other day I was trying to remember the name of my favorite movie. I'd just talked about it to Paul the day before and then...bam, it was gone.

Terry: Me too. I've been trying to remember the name of the movie where the guy was from Africa…or was it South America?
Lynn: The movie with the boat?
Sara: Which one?
Lynn: The one in Africa.
Terry: He was in that other movie at the bar with the piano.
Lynn: But he didn't marry that one, he married the other one.
Terry: The one who was in that first movie with him?
Lynn: No, the one with the long blond hair. You know, where he whistled. Yeah…Humphrey, Humphrey…
Terry: Hubert Humphrey! That was such a good movie.
Sara: What are you two talking about?
Lynn: Our favorite movie. Didn't you see it? Hey, we know the guy but not the name of the movie. It was…….
Sara: (completely baffled) I'm getting a pop. Then I can pee again.
Terry: It's called a soda.
Sara: Pop
Lynn: Coke
Terry: Let's just settle on beer.

When the Clouds Gather
an original story by Lynn

Warren was a handsome man. He had thick dark hair, beautiful clear hazel eyes, and a smile that oozed charm. Part of that charm was his enthusiasm. Warren was passionate about so many parts of his life.

He adored his wife, Betty, and always seemed delighted with his two sons and two daughters. He was passionate about his work, which always seemed a little strange to me because Warren was an entomologist; this guy was really into insects. I'm not sure where this passion came from, but it was genuine. I'd be out playing in the neighborhood and Warren would be working in his yard and he'd call out, "Hey, Lynnie. Come over here for a minute."

I'd always run over because, after all, it was Warren who was calling me. When I'd reach him, he'd hold out his hand and there, on the palm of his hand, would be the most hideous miniature monster with huge horns rotating at the top of its head and saliva dripping from its mouth. Warren would say, "See the way he's moving his antennae? He's checking out this strange environment that he's in. And see how his wings are stacked one on top of another? That's because..."

As Warren would talk, gently pointing his finger at the frightened creature, that terrifying alien would transform into a magical little being. Warren once gave me a framed, 8x10, black and white blown-up photo of a housefly, with its hundreds of eyes glaring out through the frame's glass.

I was quite proud of that picture. I insisted that it be hung in a place of honor directly over the head of my bed against the blue and pink ballerina wallpaper.

I grew older, as kids tend to do, and I left for college. Warren retired, and he and Betty sold their house and moved to the Rocky Mountains in Utah where they built their dream house. Over the years, we stayed in touch with one another. Once I had to write a paper about insects for a biology course. Of course, I thought of Warren. So I wrote him a letter, something we did back then, asking if he had any information for me to use in the paper. About a week letter, I received a huge packet crammed full of articles, notes, and Xeroxes of labeled pictures of insects. I got a 100% on that project.

After I married, my husband Brent and I moved to a home about an hour from where Warren and Betty lived. That's when we discovered that they had taken up the game of golf. Warren played golf with the same enthusiasm he'd lived his life. He owned every golf video and golf magazine, took lessons, and had all the latest clubs and paraphernalia. He was constantly changing his swing. As a result he was never a consistent golfer.

Brent liked golf too, so we'd go out on foursomes with Warren and Betty. It'd be time for Warren to tee up, and he'd carefully wrap his hands around the club's handle with whatever the grip of the week was. He would stick the tip of his tongue out of the corner of his mouth as he did whenever he was fully concentrating on something. He'd shuffle and rearrange his hands and his feet. Then he'd take several practice swings until he'd pull the club back and up, as if to fully swing at the ball, but instead he'd bring the club back down and restart the shuffle and rearrangement of his grip and stance. I'd watch him repeat this over and over, and I'd think, "Hit the ball. Just hit it." I think Warren got more swings out of one hole of golf than most people get in the first nine holes.

For about a decade, retirement was good for Warren and Betty. Then things began to change. Betty had a heart condition and suffered a stroke during one of her surgeries. Warren's changes were more subtle. He began to forget things. He'd get lost going to places he'd been to hundreds of times before. And his beautiful hazel eyes became cloudy. He'd squint as if he were peering through thick clouds while looking right me. I wasn't always sure he was seeing me. His charming smile became tight, uncertain. His once straight, strong posture became stooped, like a question mark.

But the two of them kept each other going. Betty used to say in her thin, hollow voice, "I'm the brains and Warren is the brawn." With the help of friends and family they were able to keep their fragile lives going on that mountain side. Until the day when Warren accidently set their house on fire.

Warren had decided to charge the batteries of both their vehicles at the same time inside the garage. He had a portable charger that was plugged into the wall which he connected to the first car, then he daisy-chained the charger to the battery of his four wheel drive vehicle. He had both vehicles' hoods up and the engines running when Betty called that lunch was ready. So Warren closed the garage door and went upstairs, completely forgetting about the two vehicles that were still running in the garage.

The fire marshal's report surmised that there must have been a build-up of carbon gases that ignited when there was a spark. Betty heard the explosion. She said it sounded like a loud pop. When Warren went downstairs to check on the noise he opened the door to the garage to find black, thick smoke which billowed into the house.

"The house is on fire!" he yelled. Without pause Warren hit the electric garage door opener on the wall and ran between the two flaming cars singeing off both of his eyebrows. He ran through the open garage door to a nearby garden hose, turned on the water and began to spray the water on the cars that were now engulfed in flames.

Warren was so focused on getting to water that he forgot to close the door leading into the house and the black smoke streamed up the stairway to where Betty was.

Betty later told us that, "I leaped up, and ran to the front door". This was hard to image since the stroke had left her entire left side paralyzed and she could do little more than shuffle with a cane. But Betty did make it to the front door, punched the fire alarm, and went out to the front porch.

Their house sat on a steep wooded lot, so the only way for them to get in and out of the house was by stairs, a fact their children had brought up to them many times. Betty navigated herself to the first landing when the fire erupted directly in front of her. She couldn't go forward, nor could she go back up to the house with smoke seeping out of every crevice. So she did the only thing she could think of doing. In her stroke-thinned voice she cried for help.

This is where the miracle came in. Two men working on a house above them, heard the explosion and saw the smoke rising above the trees. One of the workmen actually heard Betty's weak cry. Charging down through the steep woods, the man ran to Betty, threw her over his shoulder, and carried her down to the street where he deposited her on the front lawn of the house across the street. The entire time Betty was yelling, "My husband Warren, you've got to get him. Get Warren!"

The workmen ran up the driveway, and found Warren, still with the garden hose spraying water on the garage which was consumed by the fire. They tried to get him to put down the hose and go with them, but Warren was focused on putting out the fire and fought them off. Betty sat on the lawn across the street, yelling "Knock him out! Take him out!" Finally, the two men dragged Warren down the driveway away from the fire.

Warren and Betty lost nearly everything. Their youngest daughter, who was the first person the neighbors had called, took them home with her while they figured out what to do. Losing their home and independence proved to be too much for Betty. Physically she withered, and within three months she fell sick with pneumonia and died. Warren spiraled into his dementia.

He kept trying to get back to his wife and was frustrated that his children wouldn't let him go to his house in the woods and help her. "Betty needs me," he'd tell them. "She'll be worried."

Watching Warren was a 24/7 duty. Someone always had to be with him during the day so he wouldn't wander off. At night, Warren would "sundown", a common symptom of Alzheimer's when the patient wanders aimlessly about the house. Before the family would go to bed, they'd disconnect the stove, unplug the phone so he wouldn't try to call Betty on their old number, hide the cooking knives, the iron, and anything else that could be dangerous. They kept their bedroom door open and their children's doors closed, and would lie in their bed at night listening to Warren wander about the house, making sure that he didn't go outside and get lost.

Warren was confused and afraid. His children knew he was unhappy and consulted with one another trying to come up with a solution that would give him some independence and peace of mind. They concluded that perhaps their father would be happier if they moved him to his own apartment at an assisted care facility. This would give him a place of his own with someone on hand to help. After some searching, they located a new, luxurious, one bedroom unit in an assisted care place The children bought new furniture similar to that which was destroyed in the fire, and hung family pictures throughout the apartment before moving Warren in.

Brent and I lived close to the facility, so I told the family that I'd go over and check on him. The next morning I knocked on Warren's apartment door. When he opened the door, his face lit up. "Lynnie! How in the hell did you find me? You're something, you really are. Come on in."

I followed him into the living room. "You know it's the damndest thing. Last night I guess I must have gotten a hair up my butt. I jumped into the car and headed north. Didn't even tell Betty I was going. I drove for quite a while and got tired. That's when I saw this hotel, went into the front desk and asked how much for a room. The clerk told me, two bits, and I said, At that price, I'll take it." I always knew Warren was a tightwad.

"This is a nice place," he continued, "but there's no phone in the room. And I've got to let Betty know where I am, she'll be worried."

I looked around the room filled with his furniture, and said, "This isn't a hotel room; this is your apartment. Look." I pointed at a wall with a montage of photos. "There are pictures of your family on the wall." He smiled. "I told you this was a nice place."

Warren only lasted two weeks at the assisted care facility. He kept trying to leave and they wouldn't let him. He got frustrated and would run out to the parking lot, yelling that someone had taken his car. He'd sneak outside and begin hiking home until they'd find him and take him back. His anger at the staff holding him hostage escalated until he threatened a nurse with a pair of scissors. The facility's director called the daughter and informed her that it was too dangerous for Warren to stay there. They weren't equipped to keep him from wandering off or attacking someone. However, he informed her that there was an opening at a superb secured facility that only cared for residents with dementia.

The daughter visited the secured facility and consulted with her siblings. They solemnly determined that perhaps this was the best place for their father. So Warren was moved to the *Garden Terrace Alzheimer's Center of Excellence*. A committee had to have come up with that name. The family gave away most of the new furniture and moved what furniture would fit into the available room along with the family pictures.

All the wings at the *Garden Terrace* were named after flowers. Warren moved into the *Morning Glory Wing* which was where the most 'functional residents' lived. Once he was settled in, he seemed to relax. He even seemed happy. He gained weight, he participated in all of the activities, he even flirted with the female residents. Here was a man who was the model of fidelity for over 50 years of marriage, but it seems that before he married, Warren was a bit of a lady's man.

He'd shuffle down the hall until he'd pass a group of women sitting in the hall staring straight ahead. His shuffle would take on a swagger with some 'attitude' and he'd give the ladies his most charming smile saying, "Hi there. You're sure looking fine today." Sometimes when I'd visit him, we'd walk down a hall together and pass a twenty-something nurse who would say, "Hi, Warren." He'd give her his best smile, then gesturing at her he'd whisper to me, "She likes me."

But as happy as he seemed, he kept trying to leave. And he was successful. At least, he was successful getting out of the *Morning Glory Wing*. They'd find him in the main hallway setting off the center's alarm by opening a side door to the outside. They'd find him in the parking lot, his feet sticking out from under a car that he was convinced was his, looking for the magnetic box in the wheel-well where he had kept a spare key. Or they'd find him in the laundry room asking when the next bus was leaving.

One evening during dinner he had enough of a moment of clarity to slip a butter knife into his pocket and then he headed for his room. By the time an aide found him he'd removed the small screws that kept the window from opening more than a couple of inches. Once he had the window fully opened, it was simply a case of popping the screen out of the frame. There was only one floor so there wasn't much of a drop.

It was reported that Warren had one leg swung over the window's ledge and was trying to get his other leg to follow when an aide came in to check on him. She must have seemed rather distraught as she yelled, "No, Warren!"

She said that Warren stopped, said, "Oh." He allowed her to help him bring his leg back over the sill and into room. Then he gallantly offered his hand to help her out the window, saying, "Ladies first." Another aide came in and between the two of them they were able to distract Warren with brushing his teeth.

After the 'butter knife incident', the *Garden Terrace* called the daughter to say they were moving Warren to a more secure wing, called the *Violet Wing*. No matter from which direction the *Violet Wing* was approached, a person had to go through a minimum of three sets of secured metal doors before entering. *Violet* was the smallest wing in the center and had the most staff per resident. It wasn't for the most functional residents or for the least functional, it had the residents with the most character.

One resident pushed a laundry cart up and down the hallway asking for the way to the clubhouse. Another sat in his room all day yelling, "Call the police, an s.o.b.'s in here." Warren seemed to fit right in.

I visited Warren a few times a week, and every time I'd visit I'd hang up my reality at the shiny front doors and walk through the three secured sets of doors into whatever reality Warren was in at that moment. Usually we were in the army. He couldn't figure out why he'd been drafted, but he'd say, "That's the government for you. Can you believe it? Here I am, 50 years old and they draft me." By that time Warren was 80. Sometimes we were 'on the job', but I never could figured out what 'the job' was. One day, Warren was on a cruise when I visited him. I liked that day.

When the weather was nice, we'd go for walks. There was a park bench that we'd sit on at the top of a hillside, and down below we could watch softball games. Sometimes we'd look up and watch the clouds drift past the mountains as Warren told stories about when he was a radio operator in the U.S. Air Corps, or about when he had a pilot's license and flew a cub two-seater. He would take me though a specific flight, then he'd stop, loop back to the beginning of the story, and word for word would re-tell the story to the same point before stopping and looping back again.

I'd take him places. We'd go out to lunch or sometimes shopping. We also went to the golf course. Warren couldn't play a game, but I'd take him to the driving range. I'd carry a wood and an iron and buy a small bucket of balls as he'd shuffle beside me. His steps grew lighter, and his face lit up as he'd recognize the surroundings.

I'd tee up his ball and he'd square himself up, his hands naturally falling into one of his many grips on the club. He'd swing only once and hit the ball, then watch the ball arch away from us, drop, and roll to a stop. He'd turn to me and give me his smile. I'd smile back and point to the new ball I'd just teed up. He'd look down at it, surprised, saying, "Oh!"

He'd swing, hit the ball and watch arch away from us. Then he'd turn to me and smile, and I'd smile and point to the new ball on the tee, and he'd look surprised. "Oh!" He was always surprised that there was a ball there. We went to the driving range until the day came when Warren couldn't remember how to swing a club.

Warren lived at the *Garden Terrace* for about a year and a half when a hairdresser noticed a large sore on the back of his head. His daughter was called and she took him to a dermatologist who performed a biopsy. Warren was diagnosed with an aggressive melanoma. His children consulted with each other and decided not to fight the cancer, but to do everything that could be done to keep their father comfortable.

Two weeks before Warren died, Brent and I were visiting on a Sunday evening. Warren was lying on his bed, his legs crossed, his hands clasped behind his head. I was sitting on one side of his bed, Brent was on the other. For just a moment the clouds in Warren's eyes parted and he looked at me with clear hazel eyes and said, "I don't think I have much time left. I'm afraid I'm checking out."

I said, "When you do, I'll be right here with you."

Warren smiled. "Ah, Lynnie, I can always count on you."

And for the last time the clouds in my dad's eyes drew back together.

Time it Was
an original story by Sara

...and what a time it was,
it was a time of innocence,
a time of confidences.
Long ago, it must be,
I have a photograph.
Preserve your memories,
they're all that's left you.
Simon & Garfunkle, 1968

In the 1960s science fiction plots often included time machines and time travel. Although we never attained this mechanically, it seems that time travel happens anyway. Time is so fluid, so magical, stretching out in front of and behind me and then snapping like a rubber band into the present. The present that seems unreal, "How can I be this old?" The present that steals my facade, "How can I look this old?" The present that disappears in holiday celebrations, pivotal birthdays, and bed time.

STRETCH AND SNAP...It's 1961 and I am celebrating my golden birthday, turning eight years old on October 8th. Seven little girls from school are at the party wearing their pretty dresses and patent leather shoes. My mother has made golden decorations from foil and glitter. We play *Pin the Tail on the Donkey* and eat ice cream cake roll, my favorite dessert. I get a paint by number set, a jump rope, a purple headband, and a white stuffed dog. I have no concept of the passage of time. I just recently figured out I would be 46 in the year 2000, the millennium. I only know this because it was a math problem at school. My life stretches out in front of me in endless summer days. I hope that when I grow up I will be a cowgirl. I already have the boots, which I wear everywhere.

STRETCH AND SNAP...It's 1969 and I'm 16 and taking my behind the wheel driver's test. At school today we had 50s day and I am dressed in my sister's old circle skirt, crinoline, Peter Pan blouse and saddle shoes I screw up a little on my parallel parking, but I pass anyway. I think the tester guy feels sorry for me, surely I must be a nerd to be dressed this way in 1969! Tonight I pick up my best friend and we drive around the *Madison Square* in my dad's *Plymouth Fury*. I vaguely realize this is the beginning of freedom.

STRETCH AND SNAP...It's 1971 and I turn 18 years old. This birthday I have been aware of for months. I go to the bar for the first time; well, the first time legally. They have a bed check at the dormitory. They only do this in the girls' dorms, and I am not there when they check my room. They call my mother around 1:00 a.m. to tell on me. She simply says, "It's her 18th birthday. She's probably at the bar." Now that's a mother who knows her child. As a result of my infraction I get put on 'social probation' for two weeks. This also only happens to the girls. I have to spend every night from 7 p.m. until 7 a.m. in my room. But I do have bathroom privileges, so I spend hours in there visiting with my friends.

STRETCH AND SNAP...All of a sudden it's 1983 and I'm pushing 30. For the first time I don't feel my age. Thirty year olds are supposed to be grown-up, aren't they? But I still feel like a child. I still want my mom and dad to make the tough decisions in my life, although I have stopped asking them for money. I wonder when I will feel like a real grown-up. When I will understand how the world works? What makes someone an adult?

STRETCH AND SNAP...It's 1993 and I'm barreling toward 40. Now this is getting serious. What has happened? Time is warping and slipping into the future without my awareness. I'm married with two children. I am a professional in my field and I am in charge of other people. How can that be? I don't even know what I'm doing. I realize that grown-ups never did understand it all. They were just making it up as they went along, the way I am doing. I begin to realize that a moment can have the power of years, and years can pass in a moment.

STRETCH AND SNAP...It's 1995 and I'm holding my grandson in my arms. He is perfect and I am perfectly stupefied to be a grandma. I am only 41, but I realize that he will always see me as old. He will live his life thinking I have been an old woman for a long time. And when my grandson turns 41, he might do the math and be amazed at how young I was when he was born.

STRETCH AND SNAP...It's 2001 and I have pancreatic cancer. This could be the end of my time. I ask myself the burning question, what have I done with my time? I fear I might have wasted it. I fear that there is not enough time left. If so, do I have regrets? Things I wish I would have done differently or things I wish I had done at all? That's when my husband comes into the bedroom with a bunch of old photo albums. As I look at all the pictures I realize I have had a good life and if it ended now I could be satisfied.

STRETCH AND SNAP...It's 2008. In the 1960s we used to say, "Never trust anyone over 30." Now that includes both of my sons. I swear they aged five years for every one I recall passing. In my mind's eye I should be their age and they should be my grandson's age. Somehow my children have become my peers. So why then when I look at them do I still see the two little faces, fresh from the bath, dressed in their footie pajamas? Why do I feel as if I have lost something?

STRETCH AND SNAP...It's 2013 and my youngest son is the same age my mother was when she had me. So watching him with his baby, I see myself as the grandmother, the mother, but also as the baby. I'm on the down side of 59 getting ready for a head-on collision with 60! That's the age of old people; gray- haired, slow moving, nap taking, wrinkly people. And I think to myself, "Well, if the shoe fits, Sara..."

I have never really understood time. How yesterday becomes last month, then last winter, then last year, then two and five and ten years ago. Then one day I have to stop and think before I can say how long ago it was. I catch myself recalling some event and saying, "Oh, that must have been at least 15 years ago." And then I realize it was 35 years ago.

I recall the soap opera opening, "Like sand through the hourglass, so are the days of our lives". But time doesn't fall away so neatly or so predictably. It twirls like the sands of the desert, blowing us backward and forward until our memories are as close and present as today. The sand swirls constantly, and continuously changes the landscape of who we are.

I guess John Lennon was right when he said, "Life is what happens to you when you're busy making other plans".

Broad Chatter
It's Not So Bad
Thoughts on Aging:
three views

Terry: I have trouble with my age….or at least telling it. This is not a new phenomenon. I've had trouble with this since I turned 29. Because I am quite short, I always assumed I was the youngest in the room and I liked that. Then, at 29, I realized I wasn't the youngest teacher in my school or the youngest person in belly dancing class, or even the youngest of my friends. This was quite a shock. I started comparing myself to actors on TV, especially in commercials, to see if I looked 'old'. At first it was: "She's much older than I am" and "I'm about his age". This didn't last long as I soon realized I was older than the commercial people! That's when I started not revealing my age to anyone, even at the doctor's office. In 'those days', they didn't ask your birth date; they'd ask how old you were. Now my first reaction was to say, "Look at the chart and add one to last year's number; it's not that hard. You went to college." But, of course, I couldn't say that. I'd grit my teeth and say the dreaded age word. The year I turned forty, I couldn't even say forty, so when the nurse asked my age I said, "30-ten". She laughed and the doctor chuckled. The next year I said, "30-eleven" and they both smiled. When I said, "30-twelve", the doctor told me I needed new material. Spoil sport. Not telling my age has continued; I don't even celebrate birthdays outside of my home. My mom would call this 'cutting off your nose to spite your face'.

While I don't reveal my age (who am I kidding but myself?), if the truth be known, I really don't mind being…..this age. See, I didn't say the number! There are lots of things to love about this age such as:
I know how to get many stains out. I've been married to a wonderful and fun guy for… (oops, almost said the number). I've been to many amazing places and could afford the trips. I have friendships that have lasted 30, 40 and even 50 years. I am sometimes taken seriously although I'm not sure how much longer this will last. I appreciate history and learning about it. I've lived through some truly extraordinary times and events, and some bad ones too. I love the knowledge that I've gained although I'd still rather read a good murder novel than a non-fiction book. I have fewer frivolous worries, especially ones about what other people think of me. I wear what I want either to stay warm or cool or because I like it. I sometimes sound like my mother and I'm good with that.

But the best thing about being this age is that I'm still growing (okay, not taller, wider maybe but certainly not taller) and I didn't expect that. As a child I thought people got old, stopped working, and stayed home baking cookies and sitting in rocking chairs. But that hasn't happened. After a long and wonderful career teaching people shorter than me (I only taught third grade and younger), I've become a professional storyteller and a professional speaker giving workshops for storytellers, teachers, and even business people. My mom would be shocked. I now teach people taller than I am at a local university. And now, this, the *Three Boomer Broads*. Storytelling was one thing, but now writing, producing, and acting in a play… no four plays! This was never expected. Nor was writing this book. I wonder what will happen next.

Lynn: I hang out with more interesting people than I did when I was younger.

When I'm with younger people sometimes I manage to create an illusion of mystery, of having experienced something they may never encounter. Usually though they just treat me like I'm 'so cute'. It's okay to be eccentric, because, hey, I am cute.

When you're younger and nap during the day you're lazy, but now naps are encouraged.

I no longer feel a need to have the perfect body.

I don't have to worry about running through the pain to come in first in a race. I'm considered a winner for just plodding across the finish line.

I've given up doing speed work during workouts because I've already 'won'.

Sara: Although I have often bemoaned the changes that have occurred to me as I age, I am also aware, and grateful for the good things that have changed with the passage of time. These are the things that truly make my later years "golden".

> ...I am more gentle, sentimental, tender, and patient as I age.
>
> ...I am becoming an elder in my family and my community. My opinions are accepted and matter. I have fewer questions and there are fewer things that truly matter in the long run.
>
> ...I have developed long-term friendships that are priceless. I have people in my life who have known me for decades and have gone through many changes with me.

...I have lived to see my children become adults.
...I am living the dreams of my parents and grandparents. I have graduated from college with advanced degrees, I have traveled to the homelands of my family, and I have lived many of the dreams of my youth.
...I have read thousands of books and travelled thousands of miles.
...I am now free to do what I want, when I want.
...I know more about my limitations and accept them, but I have also learned more about my talents.
...I have fewer fears.
...I am better able to judge what's an inconvenience and what's a true problem.
...I have learned to listen.
...There are people in my life who I can trust in any situation, without question.
...I can recognize family traits that have been passed down through the generations.
...I have family stories to share.
...Things my parents said to me now make sense.

Change and Progress
thoughts from Sara

I think the world is just getting too complex for me.

I never did understand how a phone really works; how your voice was transmitted through a wire to another person. And that was before mobile phones on which I can send music, videos and pictures, and text everyone in the world. I am not ready to live like this!

It used to be that our phone conversations were private. Now I hear everyone's conversations everywhere. What I've noticed is that it's pretty banal, "Hi. Where are ya'? What ya' doing?" Did you really need to stop what you were doing for that? The other day I was waiting in line at the bank (I know I could do it on-line, but I like seeing the person with my money) and the guy behind me started talking. So I put on my polite smile and turned to face him before I realized he was on the phone with that clip-over-the-ear thingy. He looked at me as if I was interrupting something. I just turned away red-faced. And what's with famous men sticking their phone down their pants and taking pictures? I can't think of a single woman I know who wants to see that while she's walking around the mall.

We also used to know where the phone was, on the wall in the hall. Now I spend hours looking for it under the couch cushions, in dirty laundry baskets, or asking myself, "What coat was I last wearing?" I actually have the audacity to turn the phone off. In my day, if you left the house you didn't make a phone call or receive one unless you had a dime in your loafer for the pay phone. And then it better be a real emergency. People say that's why they get their kids cell phones – in case of emergency – but I have yet to see a 15 year old pull out his cell phone and yell, "Help!" into it.

I used a GPS on one vacation and I named the voice Sylvia. Although it looked pretty cool on my dashboard, I very quickly found Sylvia to be somewhat annoying and rude. Every few minutes she would sarcastically say, "Recalculating". You would think she could be nicer. It was like she could barely tolerate me. Sylvia would sigh and then tell me to make a U-turn, which was impossible on the freeway. So I made a right turn instead. Well, it was not a good relationship. When I get lost now I make my husband Paul look at the map and figure out where we are. He's starting to develop the same tone as Sylvia, but at least I know he still loves me.

I have owned the same music in at least four different formats over the years. First it was vinyl records that played at 45 or 33 rpm. Then it was cassette tapes, then CD and now MP3s or ITunes. We used to have cassette tape decks in our cars. We'd play our favorite music and then eject it when it was finished. That's when the tape would unravel and get stuck in the gears of the tape deck. It was not uncommon to have nests of little brown tape laying around in your car or to see them on the side of the road.

I reluctantly got a Facebook account which I rarely even look at. People I haven't heard about in 40 years now want to be my friend. Some of them were not even my friends back then. I think 'friend' has a whole new meaning these days. And once in a while a get a message out of the blue that says three people just 'unfriended' me. I'm left with ambiguous feelings of rejection. What am I supposed to do with that?

When I was a child I promised myself that I wasn't going to lay a bunch of crap on my kids about how much harder or better I had things when I was young. But I find myself doing just that when I really get frustrated with it all. For instance, when I almost collide with someone because they have their head down texting as they are walking. Or last night when I hit one of the 43 buttons on the TV remote and now I can no longer change channels. That means I will spend a good half hour today looking up some little code-thingy.

Paul says, "Just because we can do something doesn't mean we should." I think he's right. Change doesn't always mean progress. I am tired of trying to remember all my PIN numbers, my passwords, and my secret codes. I have no desire to watch an entire movie on a 4" screen and no time to view the 500+ pictures of my relatives online.

Don't get me wrong, there are lots of things I like about the new technology; I like being able to email people and get an answer quickly, I like writing on the computer and not having to use correction ribbons, *Wite-Out* or erasable typing paper, I like doing my work at the local coffee shop, I like being able to look things up and learn new things instantly. But it all still feels like magic to me! But when the magic is interrupted, there's no way I can get it back. I'm just no magician.

I'm tired of trying to keep up and not succeeding.

The 60s, it's not just a decade anymore.

How Did I Get Here?
thoughts from Terry

How did I get here? Not this place, this age. I knew people got older but I just didn't expect it to happen to me. It just creeps up on you. I'll never forget the day the clerk said, "Senior citizen's discount?" And I was torn. I wanted the discount but how did she know?

The 60's. That was my decade, a wild and crazy time. And now the 60's are back, but this time with hips and no huggers, grooves that aren't groovy, and hickey like things that appear without the assistance of any boyfriend. Now I am twice as old as the people I thought were old when I wasn't. And I don't trust me much now either.

See, I have always had trouble saying my age. I don't tell how old I am, how long I taught or how long I've been married. That way I could rationalize that I was 12½ forever. Then my age became obvious to everyone. It started with my hair, but I could rationalize this too. I just decided it was a free 1970's frosting and I didn't have to have someone use a crochet hook to pull small strands of hair through tiny holes in a plastic cap. But then the frosting got kind of heavy and I bowed to peer pressure and got it 'colored'. Notice, we don't say dyed anymore; a little too close to home? But after about a year of this, I realized that sitting still for two hours at the beauty shop (yes, I still say beauty shop) was just too much and I went back to my rationalized frosting.

At this same time my hair started to get thin. Now I could rationalize this with the fact that I had inherited this thin hair from my grandmother so it had nothing to do with age. But then the swirlies came in the back of my head. I'll comb my hair--looking good-- and then look at the back. A swirlie! The hair going around in a circle with a little island of skin in the middle. I'll put a bunch of goop on, do a Donald Trump come over and even spray it. But then, an hour later it's back. There's probably one back there right now.

I never thought very much about wrinkles. I thought I'd get the little crinkles at the sides of my eyes that show people what a great sense of humor I have. But no, I didn't get those; I got deep mouth grooves that make me look like *Mr. Magoo* or that sad dog, *Droopy*.

But the worse is still evolving, my neck or should I say waddle? In a few years I won't be able to go outside at Thanksgiving. That means no more plunging necklines. Well, I never really had those anyway; I didn't have the chest for them. Soon my closet will be filled with just turtlenecks and scarves. I'm convinced that we Boomers are the reason this scarf fad has lasted so long. Yep, turtlenecks and scarves. Oh, and I wonder if really good bathroom lighting would help. I've got to check on that.

The 60's, it's not just a decade anymore.

The Conspiracy
thoughts from Lynn

I need to warn you about a movement that is going on. It's a movement of body parts. Not everyone is aware of this sinister conspiracy because the people behind it move swiftly and with cunning accuracy.

I first became aware of it a few years ago when I was drying my hair and I noticed that the fleshy part of my underarms were flapping in the breeze of my blow dryer. I realized that someone had taken my taunt underarms and switched them out with these dangling, overfed wiener dogs.

But they didn't stop there. My hips? Gone. I can tell because mine were smooth and slender, while the hips they left me are lined with a lunar landscape. They also are broad enough to prop up a four door sedan.

The conspirators are even going after our minds. You know all those times when you go into a room to get something and you can't remember what you went into the room to get? How clever! They take our memories hoping we'll forget what our bodies are supposed to look like.

I've been watching for when the switches take place. My best guess is at night. But like I said they work fast. I haven't been able to catch them in the act even though I'm awake most of the night.

I'm also trying to figure out exactly who these conspirators are. One theory is that they're a secret society of medical professionals who are stripping out our premium parts and selling them to the highest bidders to pay off their student loans. But that just sounds crazy. I think it has something to do with body-parts-switching aliens.

Whoever 'they' are, they have discerning taste. A couple of months ago, I'm pretty sure I saw my behind on a young woman jogging past me. And I can tell you it looked *good* on her.

When my neck started its amazing disappearing act, I began doing some research. I went online and discovered that this is a national epidemic. So I contacted the F.B.I. I wasn't able to get any further than the Missing Persons Department. When I asked for the Missing Persons' Parts Department, they hung up on me. This just shows how high up this conspiracy goes.

But now that the word is getting out, we can all take precautions.

I recently read about a woman who woke up one morning to discover that her breasts were missing. Fortunately, when she stood up she found them under her armpits. Now she hides them in her waistband.

The 60's, it's not just a decade anymore.

Can You Match the Pictures to The Boomer Broads?

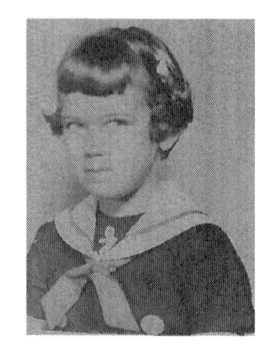

*answers below

*Terry Visger, Sara Slayton, Lynn Wing

Acknowledgements

Many people helped us in writing, producing, and performing the plays that made this book possible. The Boomers would like to thank Paul Heckman, our director, emcee, and critic, who is also Sara's husband. Without Paul's help, our performances would never have had the same level of quality that our audiences came to expect. We would also like to thank Ken Visger for being the ticket taker who got the audiences 'primed' for the shows and also for acting as substitute emcee on several occasions. Brent Wing gave us wonderful support and help as well.

We would especially like to thank Toni Asher, director of the Pump House Regional Arts Center in La Crosse, Wisconsin. Toni took a chance on three old broads by letting us perform at that beautiful facility. She made us look legit even before we earned it.

Our sound guy, Blais Portner, was wonderful. Blais understood all the technical stuff that we did not and which made our plays run so smoothly. Sam Hurne was the videographer on all of the shows and became a good friend.

Sue Hessel also deserves a thank you for being our sounding board for putting this book together.

We would also like to thank all the audience members who came to the shows and laughed, cried, and remembered with us. We were able to take our shows 'on the road' because of the people in Wisconsin who believed in us. We thank those supporters in Galesville, Coon Valley, Viroqua, Hillsboro, Adams, Horicon, and Lake Geneva (Northlands Storytelling Conference).

A big thank you also to all the storytellers who have influenced us either by sharing their stories with us or by listening to ours and helping us to grow in this old and interesting art.

*If you enjoyed this book
you will love seeing the live performances!*

*DVDs of each of the four shows
are available.*

*Contact:
sara.slayton@gmail.com
for further information*